YOSEMITE

IN PHOTOGRAPHS

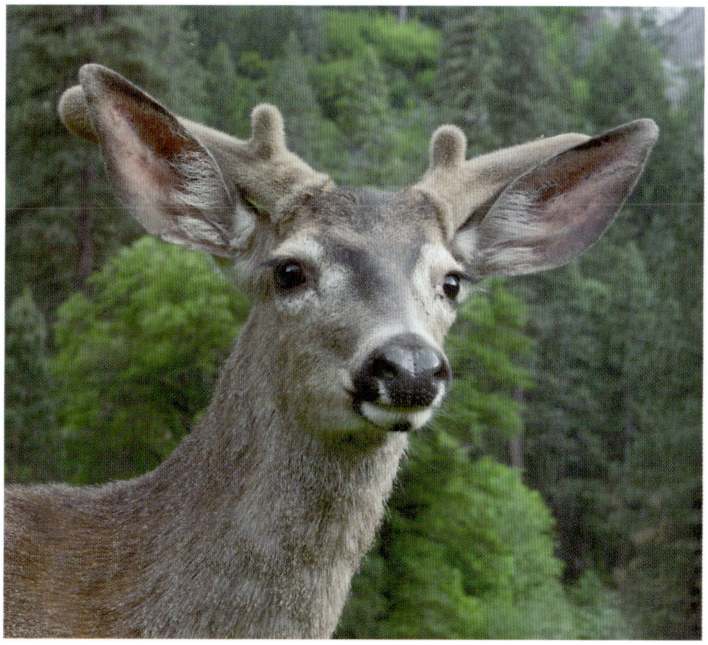

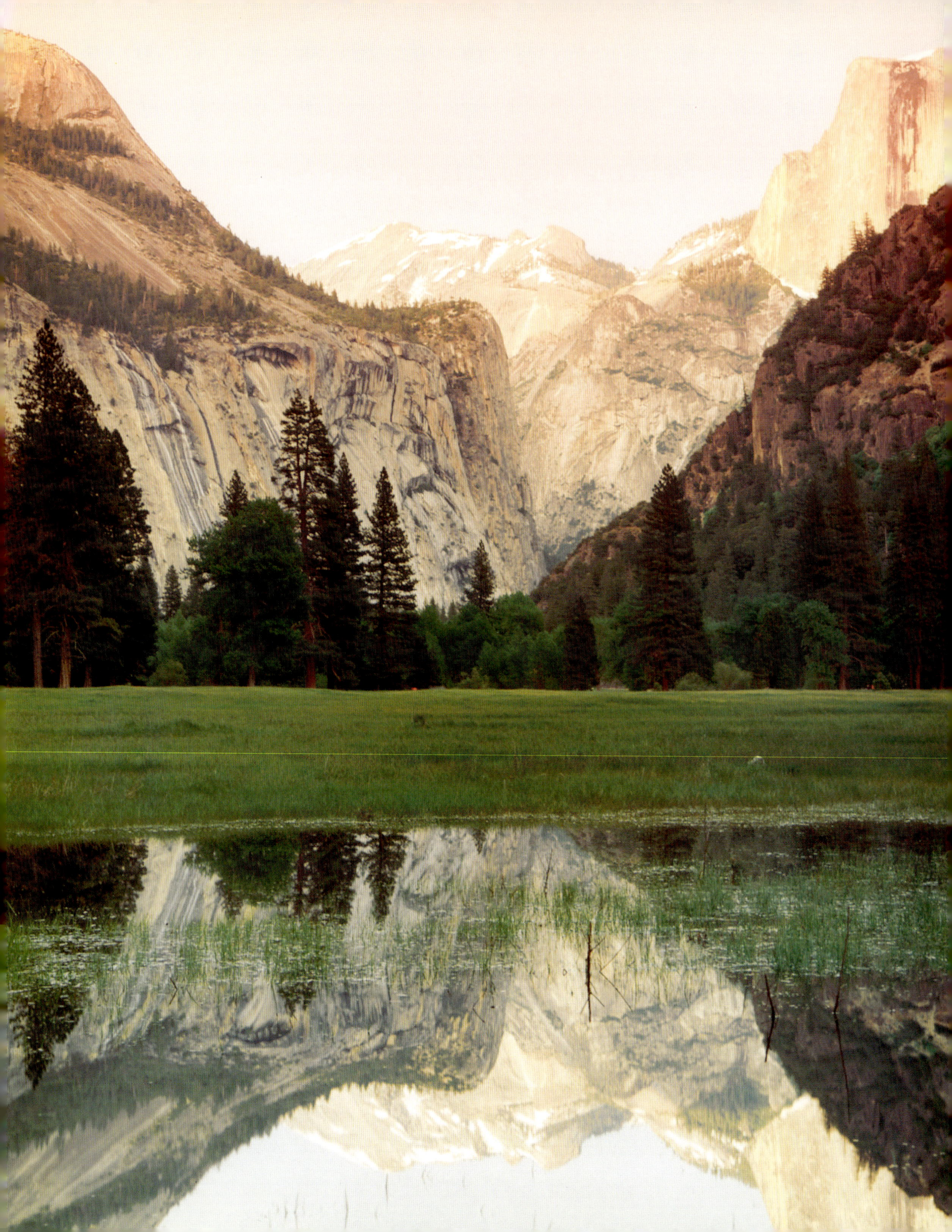

YOSEMITE

IN PHOTOGRAPHS

David M. Wyman

GRAMERCY BOOKS
New York

An imprint of Chrysalis Books Group plc

Published by Gramercy Books, an imprint of Random House Value Publishing,
a division of Random House, Inc.,
New York, by arrangement with Chrysalis Books, London.

Gramercy is a registered trademark and the colophon is a trademark of
Random House, Inc.

Random House
New York • Toronto • London • Sydney • Auckland
www.randomhouse.com

Printed and bound in China

A catalog record for this title is available from the Library of Congress.

ISBN 0-517-22708-8

10 9 8 7 6 5 4 3 2 1

Credits
Editor: Felicity Martin and Katherine Edelston
Designer: Helen Garvey
Picture Researcher: Carla Penagos
Production: Kate Rogers
Reproduction: Anorax Imaging Ltd

Additional captions
Page 1: A young Mule deer.
Page 2: North Dome and Half Dome.
Page 5: (Left) Not a common sight in Yosemite, parasitic fungi like this one near Bridalveil Fall can exhibit bright colors, typically orange, red, or yellow.
(Middle) Yellow-bellied marmots are denizens of the high country, making their homes near or above the treeline in rocky places, where they can protect themselves from hawks, bears, and coyotes.
(Right) Many wildflowers can be found in the park, especially in spring.

Picture Acknowledgements
T= Top B= Bottom C= Center R= Right L= Left

© **CORBIS**: © Galen Rowell/CORBIS Front Jacket, Back Jacket, 6, 16-17, 20, 44, 45, 53TR, 54, 55, 60, 63, 64, 66, 67, 72-73, 75, 77, 78, 85TR, 89. / © Marc Muench/CORBIS 2. / © David Muench/CORBIS 9. / © Ted Spiegel/ CORBIS 10. / © Lake County Museum/CORBIS 11. / © Joseph Sohm; ChromoSohm Inc/CORBIS 15. / © Judyth Platt; Ecoscene/ CORBIS 40. / © Darrell Gulin/CORBIS 41. / © Craig Lovell/CORBIS 65TR. / © Andrew Brown/ Ecoscene/CORBIS 68, 88. / © Phil Schermeister/CORBIS 74BL. / © Kennan Ward/ CORBIS 93T.
© **Frank Lane Picture Library**: / © Bruce Coleman Inc/ Phillip Colla - Visual & Written/FLPA 12-13, 23, 26, 35, 49, 51. / © Tim Fitzharris/ Minden Pictures/ FLPA 18-19, 32-33, 82-83. / © Foto Natura Stock/FLPA 22. / © Bruce Coleman Inc/ Mark Custance/ Peter Raven/ FLPA 34, 36, 37. / © Bruce Coleman Inc/ Lee Foster/FLPA 42-43, 52. / © Frans Lanting/Minden Pictures/ FLPA 48. / © Bruce Coleman Inc/ John Elk III/ FLPA 50, 86, 90. / © Bruce Coleman Inc/ Mark Taylor/ FLPA 62. / © Fritz Polking/FLPA 70. / © Bruce Coleman Inc/ FLPA 71. / © Bruce Coleman Inc/ Kerry T. Givens/FLPA 95T.
© **LIBRARY OF CONGRESS**: Prints and Photographs Division (LC-USZ62-52000) 8.
© **Tim May**: 84.
© **Photolibrary.com:** Jon Arnold Images 61.
© **George Wuerthner**: 58-59, 69, 76, 87.
© **David M. Wyman**: 1, 5BL, 5BC, 5BR, 7, 14, 21, 24, 25, 27, 28-29, 30, 31, 38, 39, 46, 47, 56-57, 79TR, 80, 81BR, 91, 92, 93BR, 94-95B, 94T.

CONTENTS

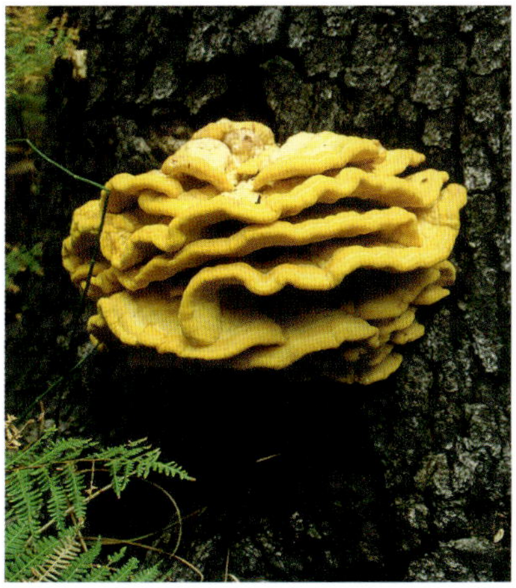

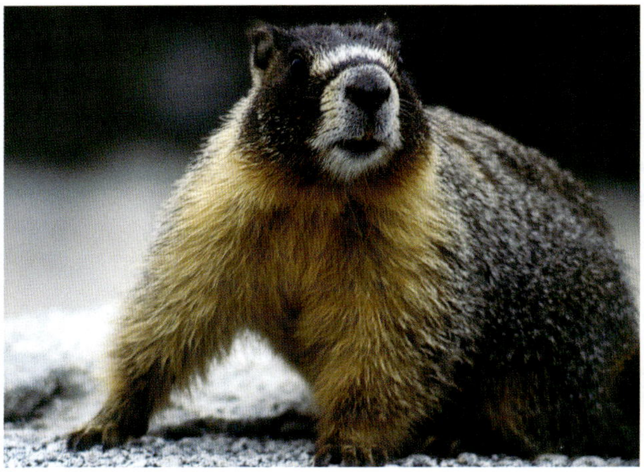

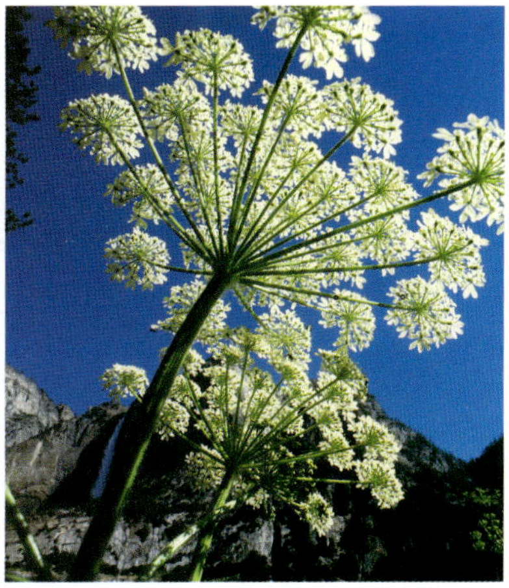

THE MAGIC OF YOSEMITE

It happens each year in the Sierra Nevada Mountains of California. It is as predictable as the snows that settle over the summits in the winter, as sure as the wildflowers that carpet the meadows in the summer, as inexorable as the spring runoff that spills over the stupendous granite cliffs to fill the waterfalls and rivers, and as certain as the maples and aspens turning colors in autumn. Each year more than four million visitors will explore the natural wonders of Yosemite National Park. The names of the places people will visit are iconographic: Yosemite Valley, El Capitan, Yosemite Falls, Half Dome, the Grizzly Giant, Clouds Rest, Tuolumne Meadows, Cathedral Peak. People will arrive by car and by bus and sometimes by bicycle. A few visitors will even walk into the park. They will want to view the steep cliffs, towering waterfalls, enormous rock domes, giant sequoia trees, alpine meadows, and jagged peaks. These visitors will bring their hiking boots, trail guides, maps, rucksacks, and, of course, their cameras.

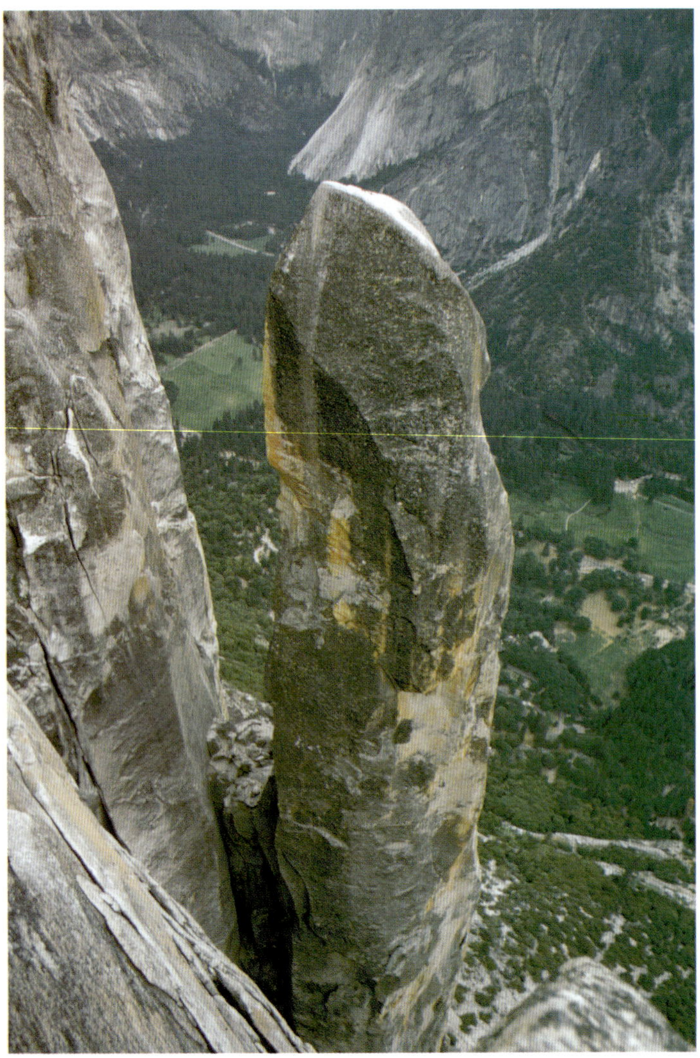

THE PARK

Most visitors to the park will travel to Yosemite Valley, the seven-miles-square centerpiece of the park. Ansel Adams, the photographer most associated with the park, wrote "Yosemite Valley, to me, is always a sunrise, a glitter of green and golden wonder in a vast edifice of stone and space."

In Yosemite Valley, hikers strain against gravity as they begin to zigzag up trails toward Glacier Point, Half Dome, and Vernal and Nevada Falls. Yosemite Valley is where cyclists pedal along 11 miles of bicycle trails. Rock climbers attempt to prove the shortest distance between two points is a straight line, ascending the granite walls that so precipitously enclose the valley.

The majority of accommodations in the park are located in Yosemite Valley, including four campgrounds, the tent cabins at Curry Village, Yosemite Lodge motel rooms, and the exclusive Ahwahnee Hotel.

Deer in Yosemite Valley graze in the meadows and coyotes sometimes stand next to the roads, waiting for a forbidden handout from tourists. Under cover of darkness, Black bears will readily sniff out parked vehicles and quickly break a window or rip open a trunk in search of illegally stored food that should be stashed in special "bear boxes" or motel rooms; these creatures

Left

The Lost Arrow spire offers one of the most exciting climbs in Yosemite. The spire, about 1,500 feet high, stands on the top of a remnant sheet of granite that did not completely peel off the face of Upper Yosemite Fall.

Right

The resplendent colors of a Sierra Nevada autumn are reflected in a quiet bend in the Merced River, near the Sentinal Beach picnic area.

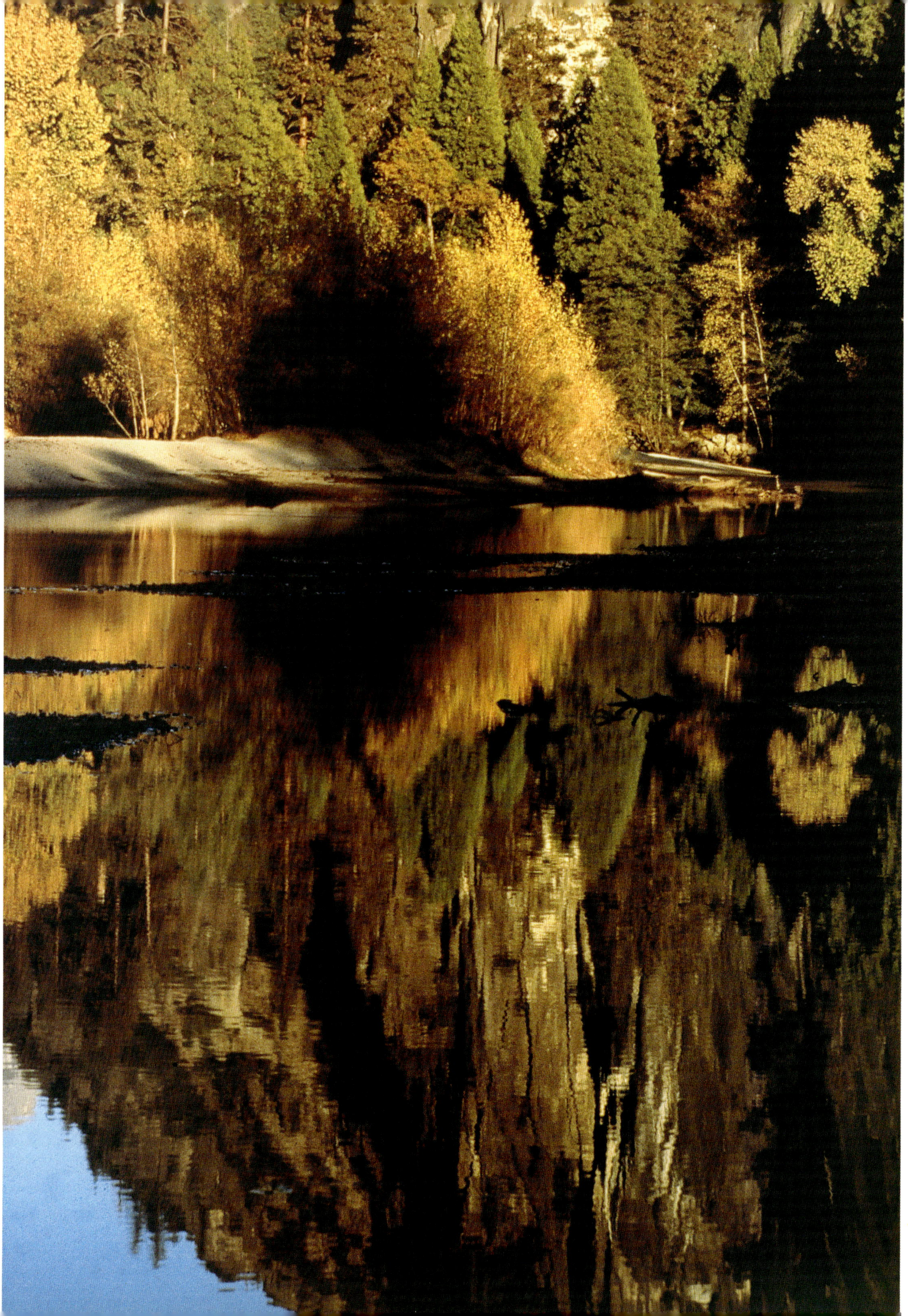

are otherwise ordinarily harmless and usually quite shy around humans, preferring to climb a tree rather than risk a confrontation.

Beyond its famous valley, Yosemite National Park includes about 1,180 square miles, most of it open only to those willing to travel on foot or by horseback. In the high country above Yosemite Valley, mountaineers clamber up granite domes and peaks, wield ice axes over the Mount Lyell Glacier, swim in alpine lakes, and watch the stars come out before snuggling deep into their frost-covered sleeping bags.

HOW WAS IT FORMED?

Most of the landscape appears much the way it did when the last significant glacier melted away, perhaps 10,000 years ago. Yosemite itself began to form about 10 million years ago, a mere blip on the geologic time scale. Mountain-sized formations of granite—a type of once-molten rock—began to lift and tilt westward, the result of titanic forces at work beneath the surface of the earth.

Beginning 1.5 million years ago, during the Great Ice Age, glaciers grew in the Yosemite high country. Gravity made them flow down the path of the Merced River, toward Yosemite Valley, straightening, deepening, and widening it, turning a river valley into a glacial valley.

The eventual retreat of the glaciers left the creeks, which once flowed directly from side canyons into the Merced River, high but not dry. These creeks became waterfalls that spilled and leapt out over the vertiginously imposing cliffs.

The last glacier put the major finishing touches on the valley, leaving in its wake Yosemite and Bridalveil Falls. The bottom of the valley filled in with sediment from the ancient Merced River, born when the Sierra Nevada Mountains began to rise.

Today, the granite cliffs, domes, and mountains of Yosemite continue to be shaped by the forces of weather erosion, including frequent freezing and thawing of granite that can break apart the natural fractures in the rocks. Occasinal earthquakes can also trigger rock falls, both large and small. Suprisingly, the great domes visible from Yosemite Valley, such as North Dome and Half Dome, and Fairview and Lembert Domes in the high country at Tuolulmne Meadows, were shaped almost completely by erosion from weathering and exfoliation, and not through the process of glacial erosion.

The person who first understood that glaciers had so profoundly sculpted Yosemite Valley was John Muir, the naturalist, explorer, and writer. Something of an eccentric, Muir had emigrated from Scotland with his parents to the United States as a child. In 1868, when he was 19, Muir found his way to the Sierra Nevada. Rather than ride in a bumpy stagecoach, Muir chose to make the 200-mile journey from San Francisco into Yosemite Valley on foot. He would write about his walk into the mountains: "Then it seemed to me the Sierra should be called not the Nevada, or Snowy Range, but the Range of Light...the most divinely beautiful of all the mountain chains I have ever seen." He founded the Sierra Club, a renowned environmental organization, and with his writings, Muir became a driving force that helped make Yosemite a national park in 1890.

In 1864 Congress and President Abraham Lincoln had granted Yosemite Valley and the Mariposa Grove of Giant Sequoias to the state of California to administer as a public trust. This was the first time in the history of the world that a federal government had set aside land in order to preserve it. Muir's subsequent efforts on behalf of Yosemite led to its designation as a national park, as well as to a substantial increase in size.

THE PEOPLE OF YOSEMITE

Archeological evidence of human occupation before 1400 BC in Yosemite is slim. After that date, various groups of Native Americans lived in and around Yosemite Valley. The last such group to live in relative freedom were known as the Yosemites, the name given to them by surrounding tribes of the Miwok people. The meaning of the word Yosemite has been translated as both "grizzly bear" and "the killers." The Yosemites, led by Tenaya, their chief, named the valley "Ahwahnee," their

Below

John Muir (1838–1914) is considered by some to be the father of America's national parks.

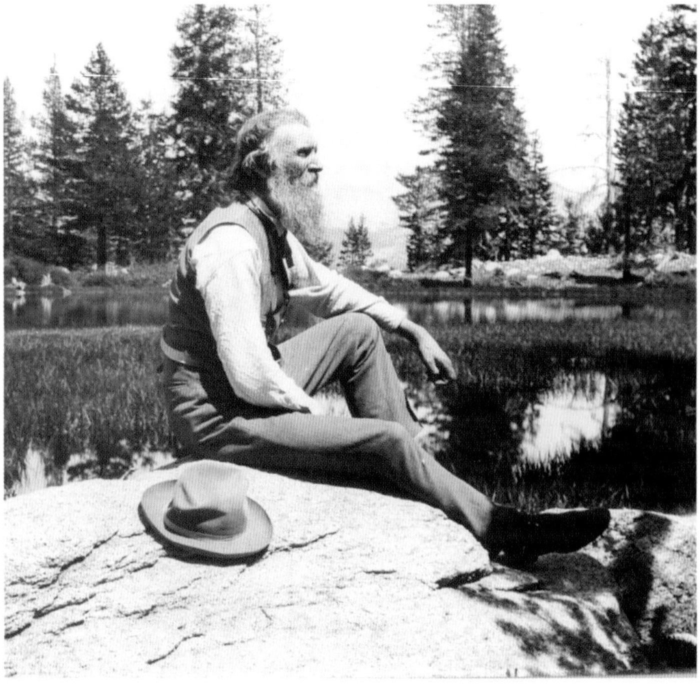

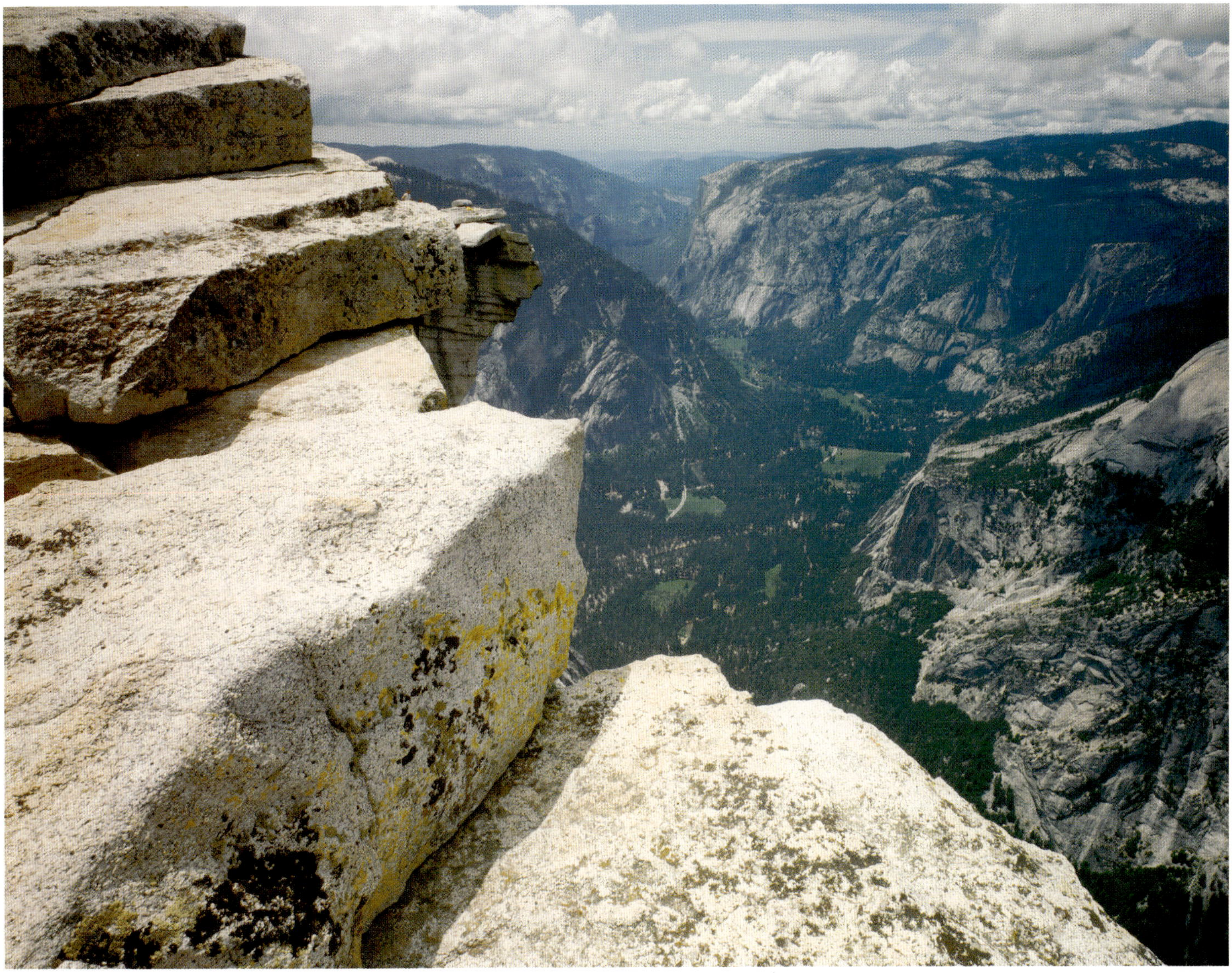

Above

Its high cliffs and waterfalls make Yosemite Valley a highlight of the park. Here it is seen from a rocky overhang on Half Dome, 4,000 feet above the floor of the valley.

word for an open mouth. Native Americans were a continuing and dominant human presence there until the middle of the nineteenth century.

The first white people to view Yosemite were members of the Joseph Reddefield Walker expedition. The Walker party, 70 strong, had been ordered by the U.S. government to spy on the Mexicans who ruled the state. In 1833, they found themselves on the northern rim of Yosemite Valley; the steep cliffs kept them from entering the valley itself. The Walker party also wandered through one of the groves of giant sequoias to the west of the valley.

The Ahwahneechee Indians, as the Yosemites called themselves, might have remained indefinitely in Yosemite, if not for the legendary California gold rush. Beginning in 1848, California experienced the greatest migration of human beings in history. Before the gold rush the total non-Native American population count was about 2,000. Most of these people lived in the southern half of the state. By 1853, there were more than 300,000 non-Native Americans.

Frequently displaced from their land and sometimes enslaved by miners and settlers, Native Americans occasionally—and futilely—fought back. In reaction to an attack by the Ahwahneechee, the aptly named John Savage, one of the more colorful characters to come out of the gold rush, was appointed to command the state-authorized militia known as the Mariposa Battalion. The Battalion first tracked Tenaya's band into Yosemite Valley on March 27, 1851, at the beginning of the "Mariposa Indian War."

Dr. Lafayette H. Bunnell, a private in the militia, was not aware of the name the Ahwahneechee had for the valley. He suggested "we give the valley the name of Yo-sem-i-ty, as it was suggestive, euphonious, and certainly American; that by so doing, the name of the tribe of Indians which we met leaving their homes in this valley, perhaps never to return, would be perpetuated." After their arrival in the mid-nineteenth century, white miners and settlers took up the name Yosemite too.

The "Mariposa Indian War" and a few subsequent skirmishes in Yosemite were over in a few months. The Ahwahneechee were relocated to flat reservation land in the San Joaquin Valley. Although Yosemite Valley lost its name and its people, the Ahwahneechee are still honored by the name given to the historic Ahwanhee Hotel.

Visitors began to arrive at the park as word of Yosemite's natural splendors spread. The first tourists either walked into Yosemite or rode on horses. Later visitors arrived in stagecoaches over private toll roads. The first car arrived in Yosemite in 1900, and more cars would follow, although they were banished in 1907, deemed incompatible with stagecoaches and wagons pulled by horses. That decision was reversed in 1913 and cars began to arrive over roads now maintained by the state and federal governments.

Below

Ansel Adams (1902–1984), inspired by a childhood trip to Yosemite, became the best-known photographer of the park.

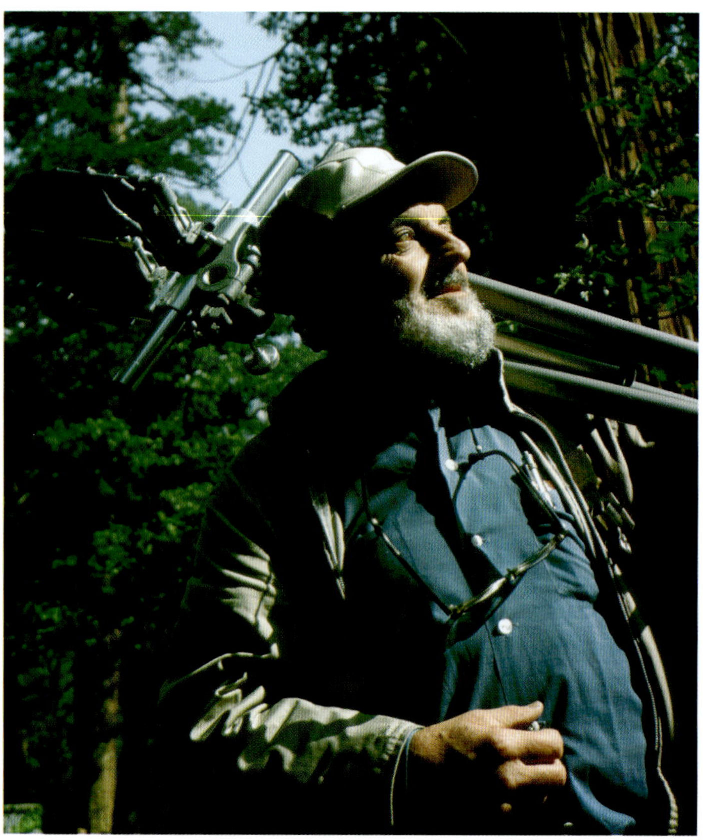

Visitors came from California and then from around the world. People have continued to visit Yosemite since, from anonymous campers to Queen Elizabeth of Great Britain. Some visitors decided to make their homes in Yosemite, including John Muir and Ansel Adams. Muir lived for a time in a treehouse before moving to a cabin near Yosemite Falls. Adams gave his name to the oldest family-run business in the U.S. national park system, the Ansel Adams Gallery.

GETTING AROUND

John Muir may have walked to Yosemite, but visitors today can make the same trip in a car or bus in just a few hours. From the west, there are three principal routes into the park, all of which lead into Yosemite Valley.

California State Highway 41 runs about 65 miles from the city of Fresno, in the San Joaquin Valley, to Yosemite. The community of Wawona is about five miles beyond the park entrance. Originally called Clark's Station, after Yosemite pioneer Galen Clark, Wawona was a stagecoach stop on the way to Yosemite Valley. Today, most people who enter Wawona on Highway 41 simply continue to the valley, still some 30 miles distant, even though Wawona has a significant number of attractions that make it a worthwhile destination in its own right, including the historic Wawona Hotel, the Yosemite Pioneer History Center, the Covered Bridge spanning the south fork of the Merced River, and impressive Chilnualna Falls.

About 30 miles past Wawona, Highway 41 drops into Yosemite Valley. Just before it does so, the road enters the nearly mile long Wawona Tunnel, which was blasted through the granite to provide a shorter, easier route than the original toll road that climbed above the tunnel. Wawona Tunnel Overlook, the classic viewpoint of Yosemite Valley, lies just beyond the far end of the tunnel. Colossal granite cliffs surround the valley floor. On the south side of the valley, Bridalveil Fall drops 620 feet. Half Dome and Clouds Rest Peak rise in the background while massive El Capitan, its vertical granite face a lodestone for mountaineers, rises on the north side of the Valley.

Most of these natural wonders can be viewed at reasonably close distance from the roads that loop around Yosemite Valley. Shuttle buses travel around much of the upper half of the valley, while paved and dirt trails lead walkers to the base of the Yosemite and Bridalveil Falls, along the Merced River and everywhere else.

State California Highway 140 travels from the San Joaquin Valley town of Merced, over the foothills of the Sierra Nevada and

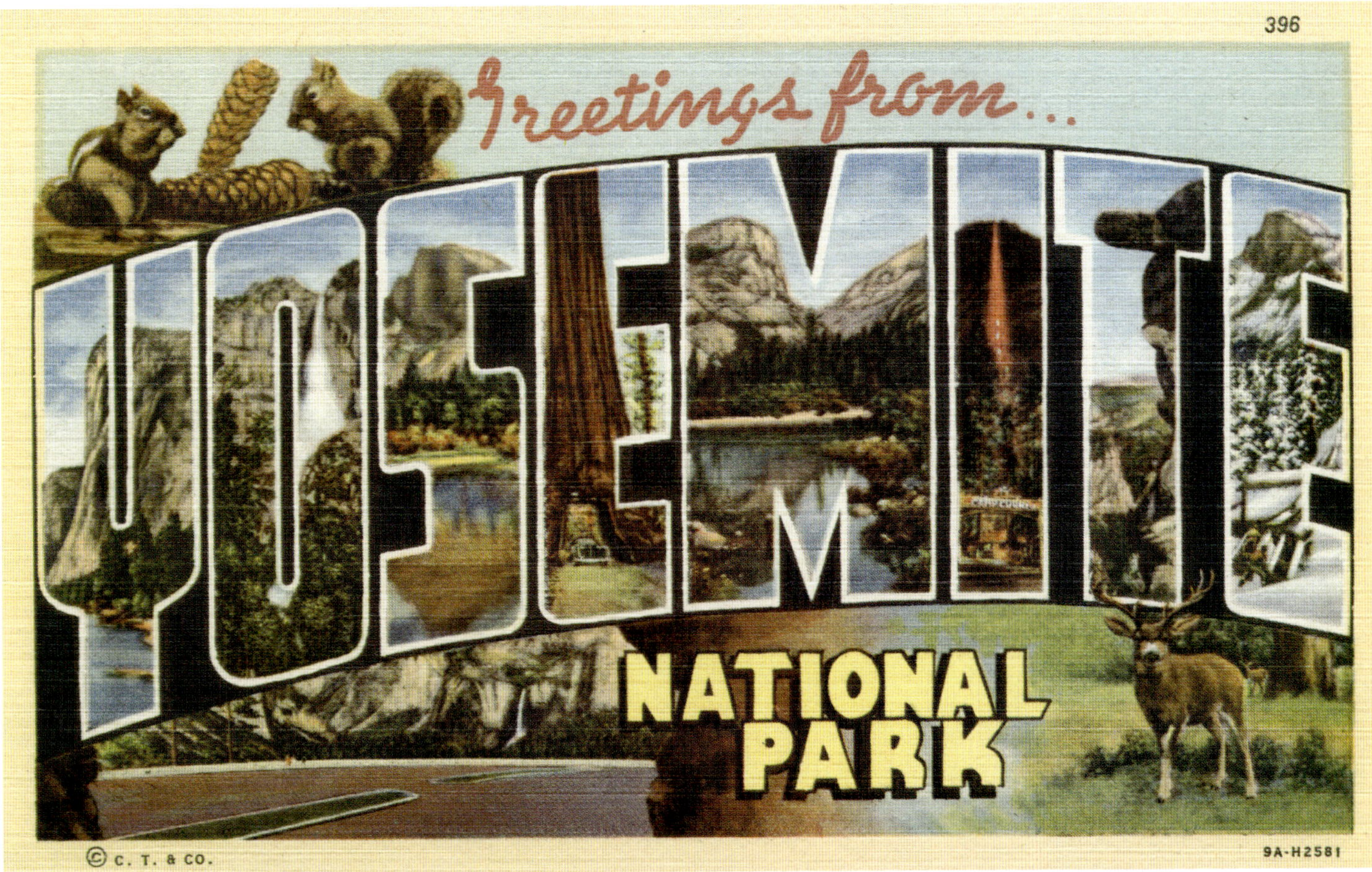

along the lower course of the Merced River. This is the lowest and therefore the most reliable road into Yosemite, as it is the last to close from winter snows. At the community of El Portal, the highway lurches suddenly up into the impressive Merced River Gorge, to travel one mile to the park entrance. Yosemite Valley lies six miles beyond.

Above
A postcard from around 1939: "Y = El Capitan; O = Yosemite Falls; S = Half Dome; E = "Wawona" Big Tree; M = Mirror Lake; I = Fire Fall; T = Overhanging Rock; E = Winter Sports."

California State Highway 120, north of Highway 140, is the consistently highest of the three western routes into Yosemite. Once in the park, it travels past the turn-off to Hetch Hetchy Valley, once considered a twin of Yosemite Valley. After a series of legal battles in the early twentieth century, Hetch Hetchy Valley was dammed to provide drinking water and power to the city of San Francisco.

Highway 120 turns east toward Tioga Pass, at Crane Flat. But an extension of the western portion highway beginning at the Crane Flat junction, called Big Oak Flat Road, continues 10 miles to Highway 140, just shy of Yosemite Valley. Along the way, Highway 120 passes the turn-off to the little residential community of Foresta, a private inholding of homes dating back to the earliest days of the park. The Foresta barns, in the adjacent Big Meadow, await the occasional visitor.

East of Crane Flat, Highway 120 is also known as the Tioga Pass Road. Snows close the highway each year, but from late spring until late autumn, the Tioga Pass Road grants access to the hiking trails, lakes and creeks, and campground in the Yosemite back country. Beginning not far from the Mono Lake, with its strange towers of calcium—known as tufa towers—that jut out of the water, Highway 120 rises in seven spectacular miles along the steep, northern side of Lee Vining Canyon, crossing into the park at Tioga Pass, the highest auto pass in California at 9,986 feet above sea level. The road continues to Tuolumne Meadows, where hiking trails lead into the back country. The meadows are surrounded by views of impressive domes and mountain summits.

Why travel to Yosemite, in person or through the pages of this book? John Muir articulated it this way:

"Thousands of tired, nerve-shaken, over-civilized people are beginning to find out that going to the mountain is going home; that wildness is necessity; that mountain parks and reservations are useful not only as fountains of timber and irrigating rivers, but as fountains of life."

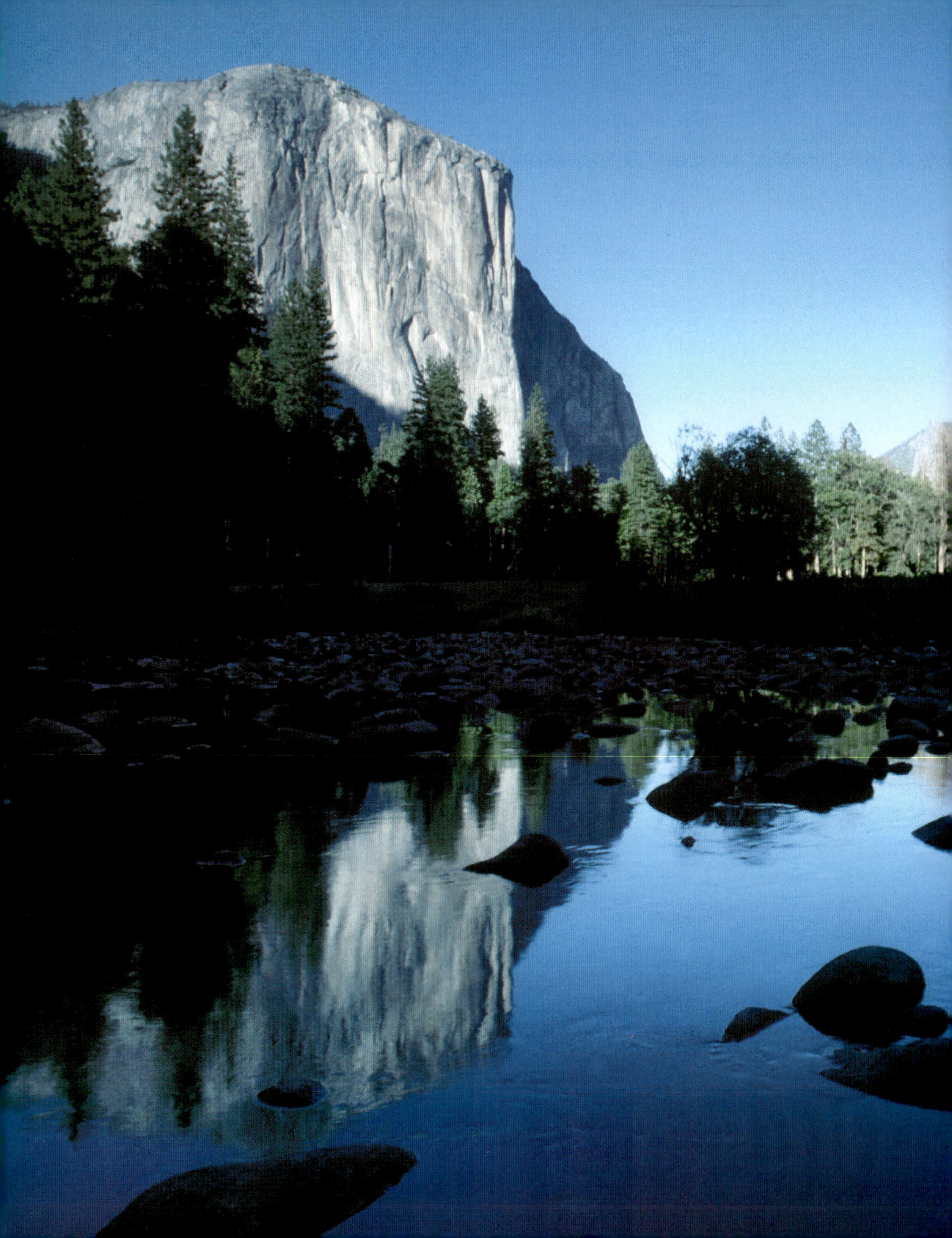

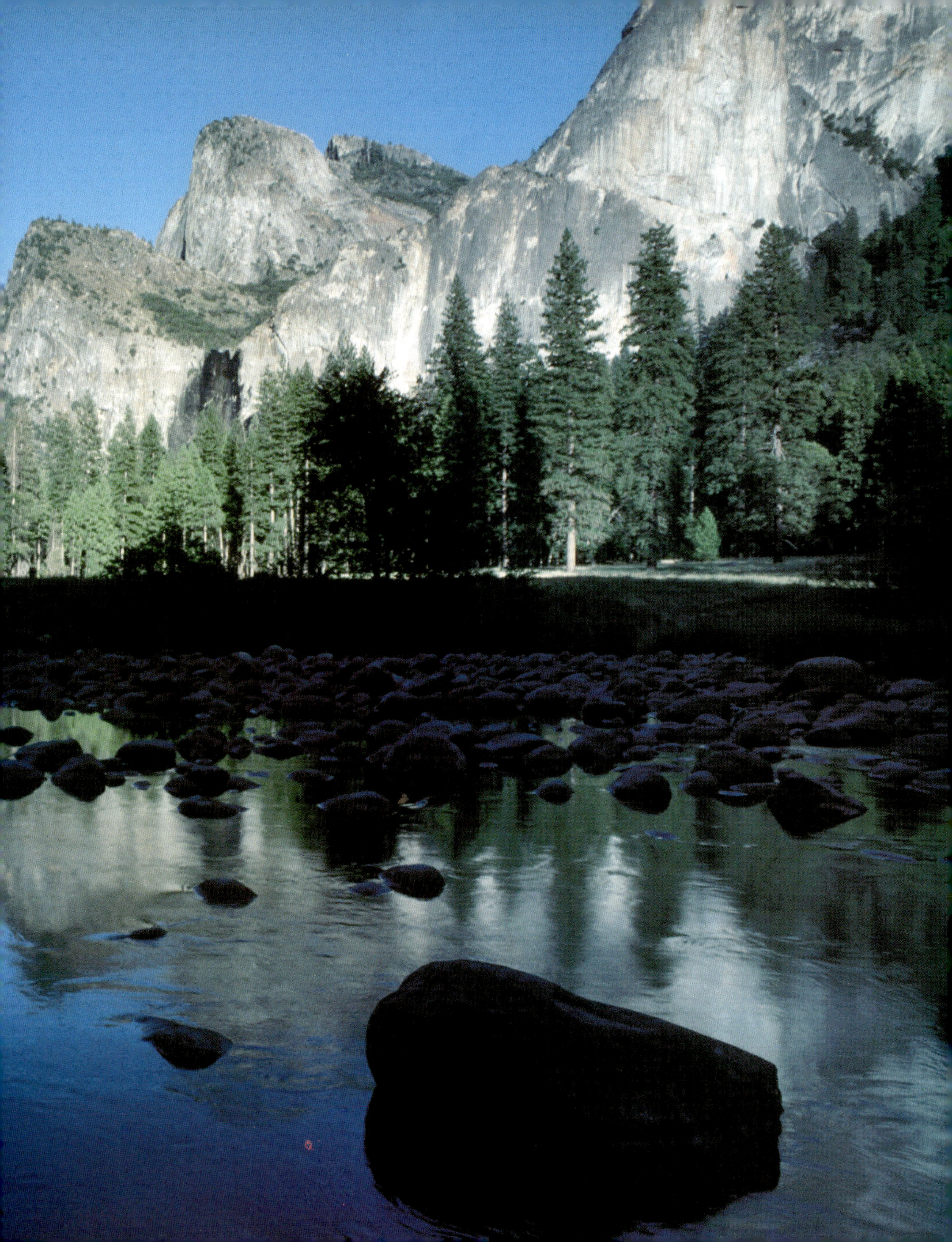

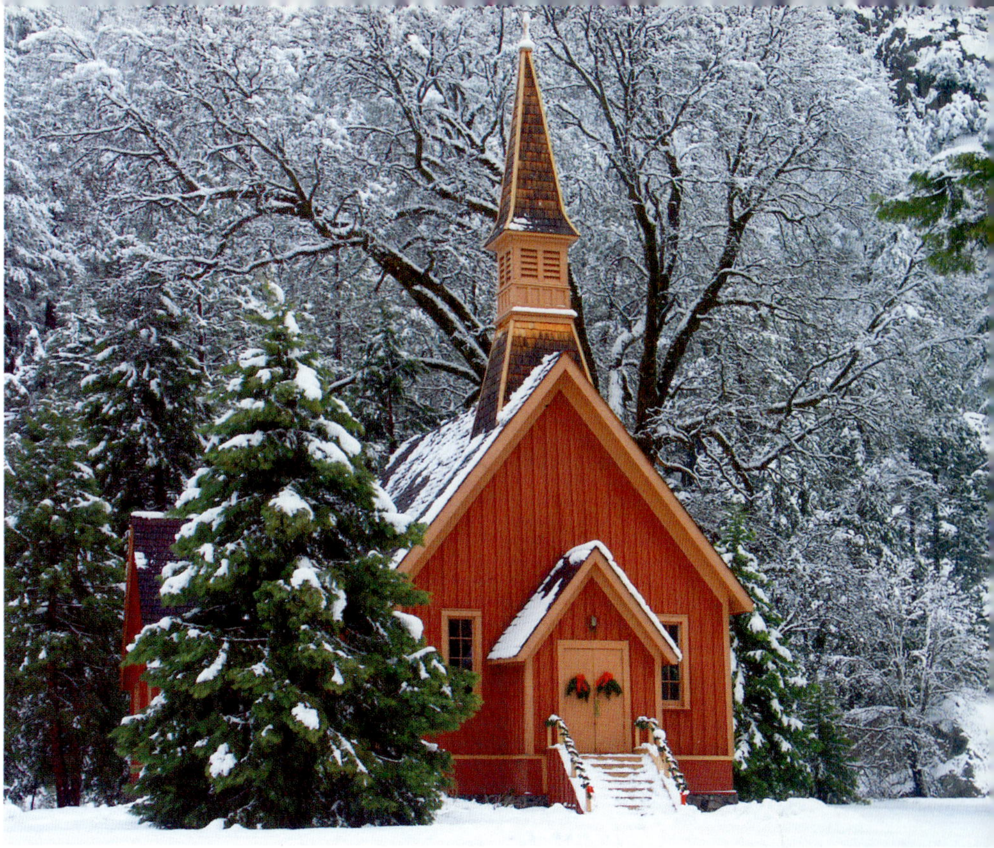

Previous page

GATES OF THE VALLEY

Along Northside Drive and the Merced River and near the mouth of Yosemite Valley, a turnout looks back at a panoramic view. Here, at Gates of the Valley, El Capitan is on the left, and Cathedral Rocks and Bridalveil Fall are on the right. The historic 1997 floodwaters rose more than six feet above the viewpoint's parking lot.

Above

YOSEMITE CHAPEL

The lovely Yosemite Chapel is near Sentinel Bridge, on the south side of the valley. Constructed in 1879, the chapel is the oldest building in continuous use in the valley. When the chapel first opened, naturalist John Muir joined a distinguished roster of ministers in addressing delegates of a national Sunday School convention. Popular with visitors, about 350 marriages are performed each year in the chapel.

Right

BRIDALVEIL FALL

Located near the mouth of Yosemite Valley, Bridalveil Fall is the first major waterfall most visitors see in the park. Bridalveil plunges more than 600 feet, and it is the only fall that flows over the lip of Yosemite Valley throughout the year. During autumn and winter, when the flow of water is low, the misty fall does look like the wispy veil of a bride. The Ahwahneechee had another name for the waterfall, Pohono, which may have meant "puffing wind."

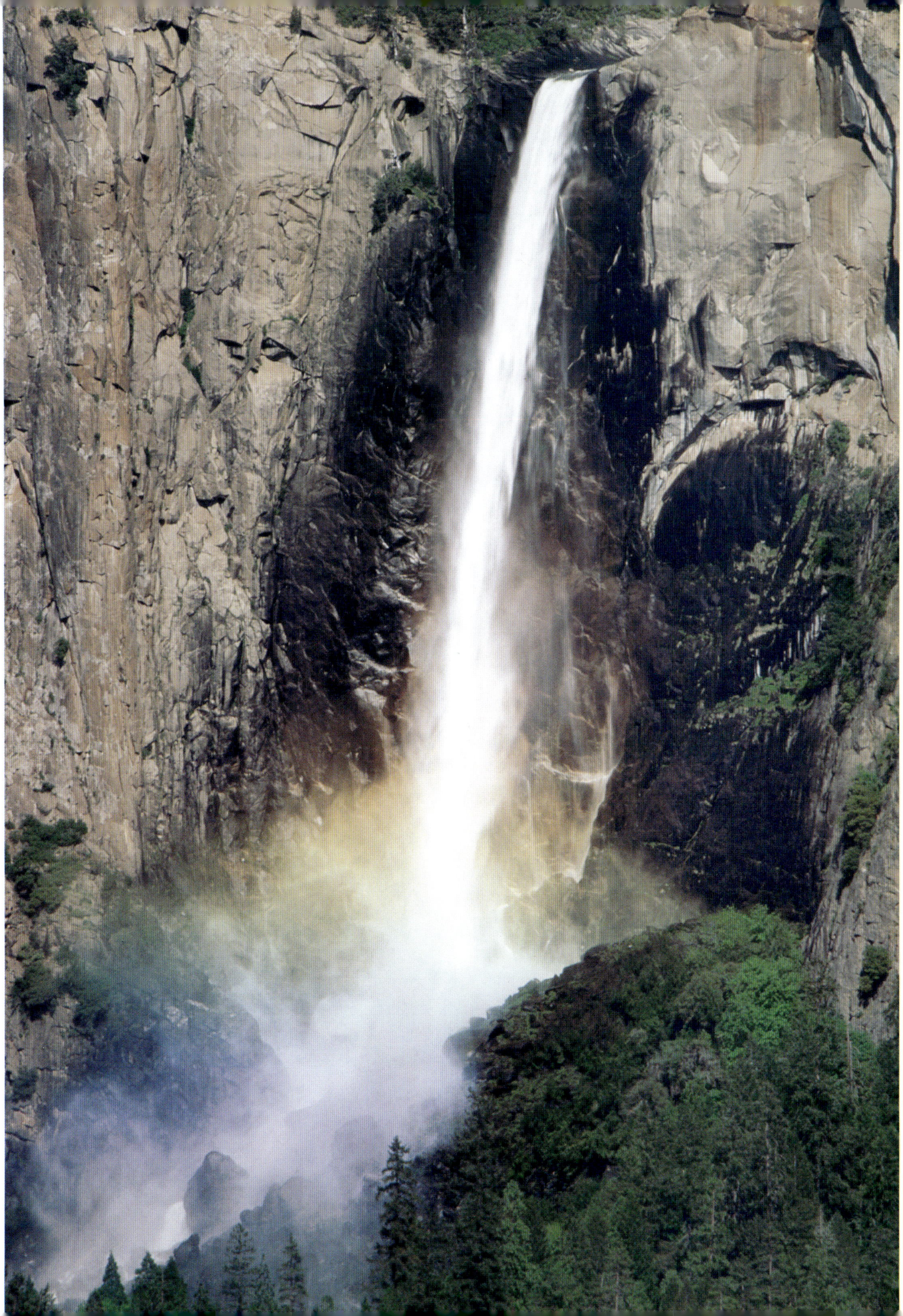

Right

CATHEDRAL SPIRES

Located on the south side of the valley, Cathedral Spires is part of a series of beautiful buttresses, cliffs, and pinnacles. James M. Hutching, a British expatriate and entrepreneur, brought the first tourists to Yosemite Valley in 1855. He named the Cathedral Spires in 1862. The adjacent cliffs were given the name Cathedral Rocks a year later, by the California Geological Survey.

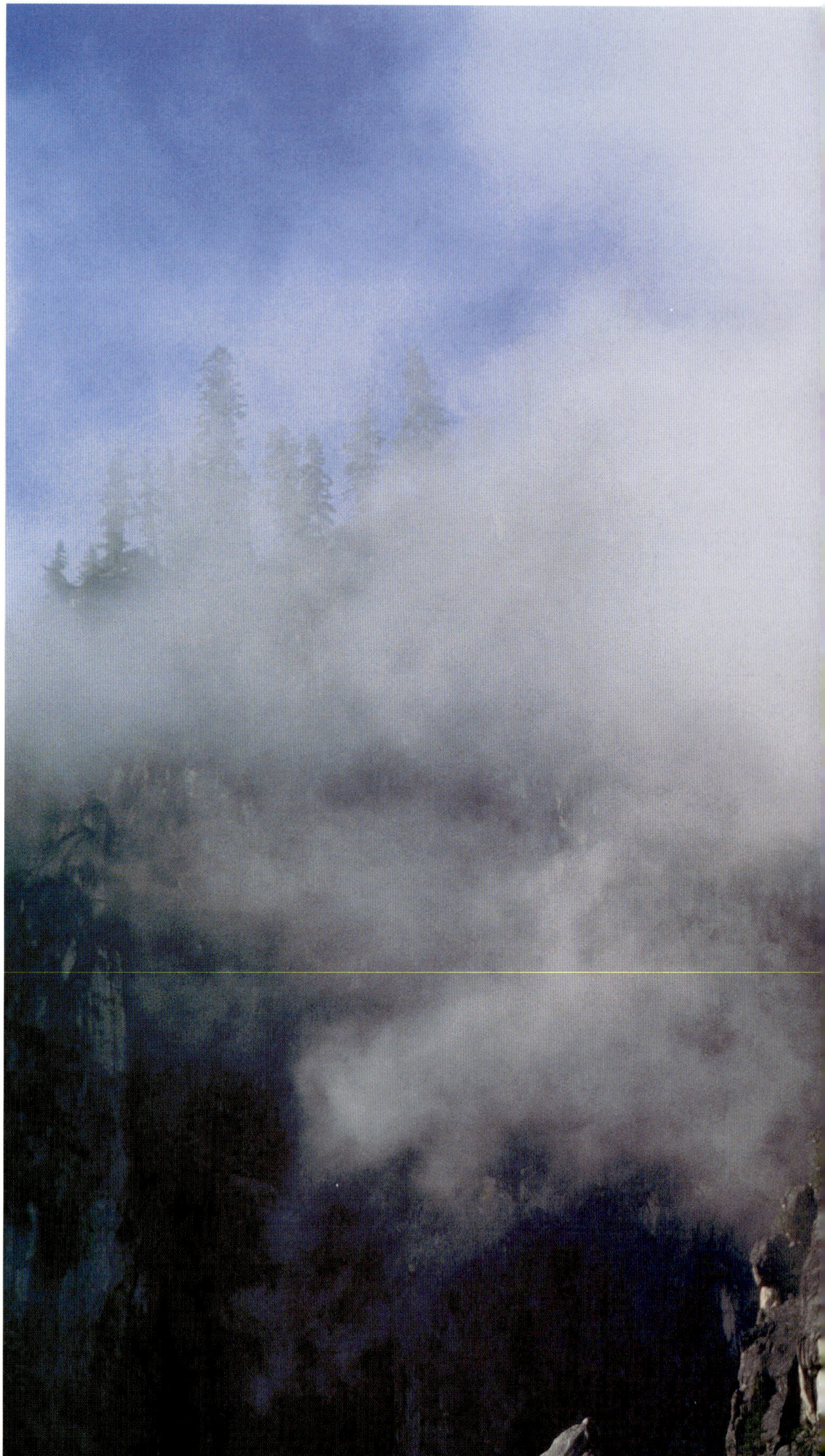

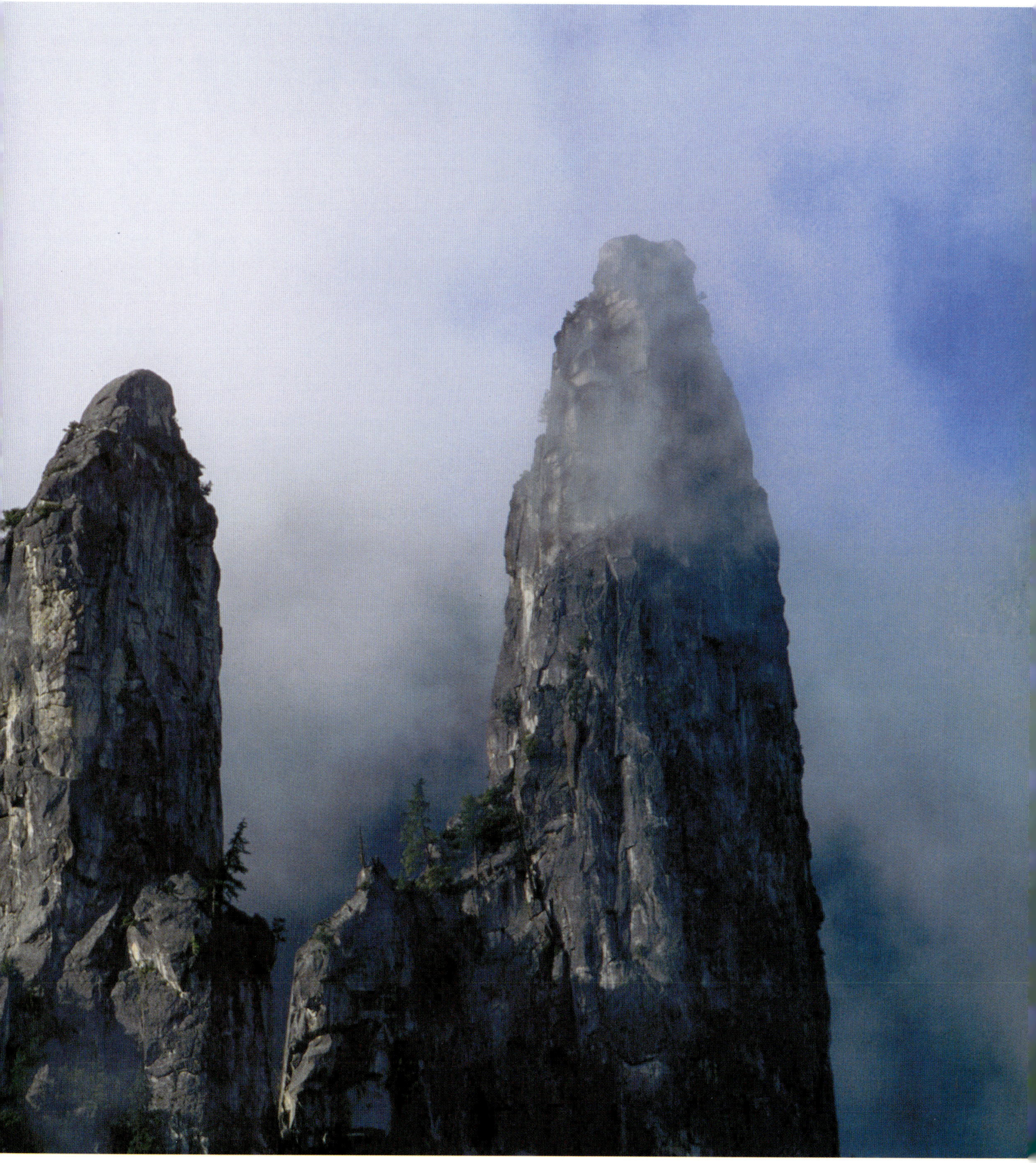

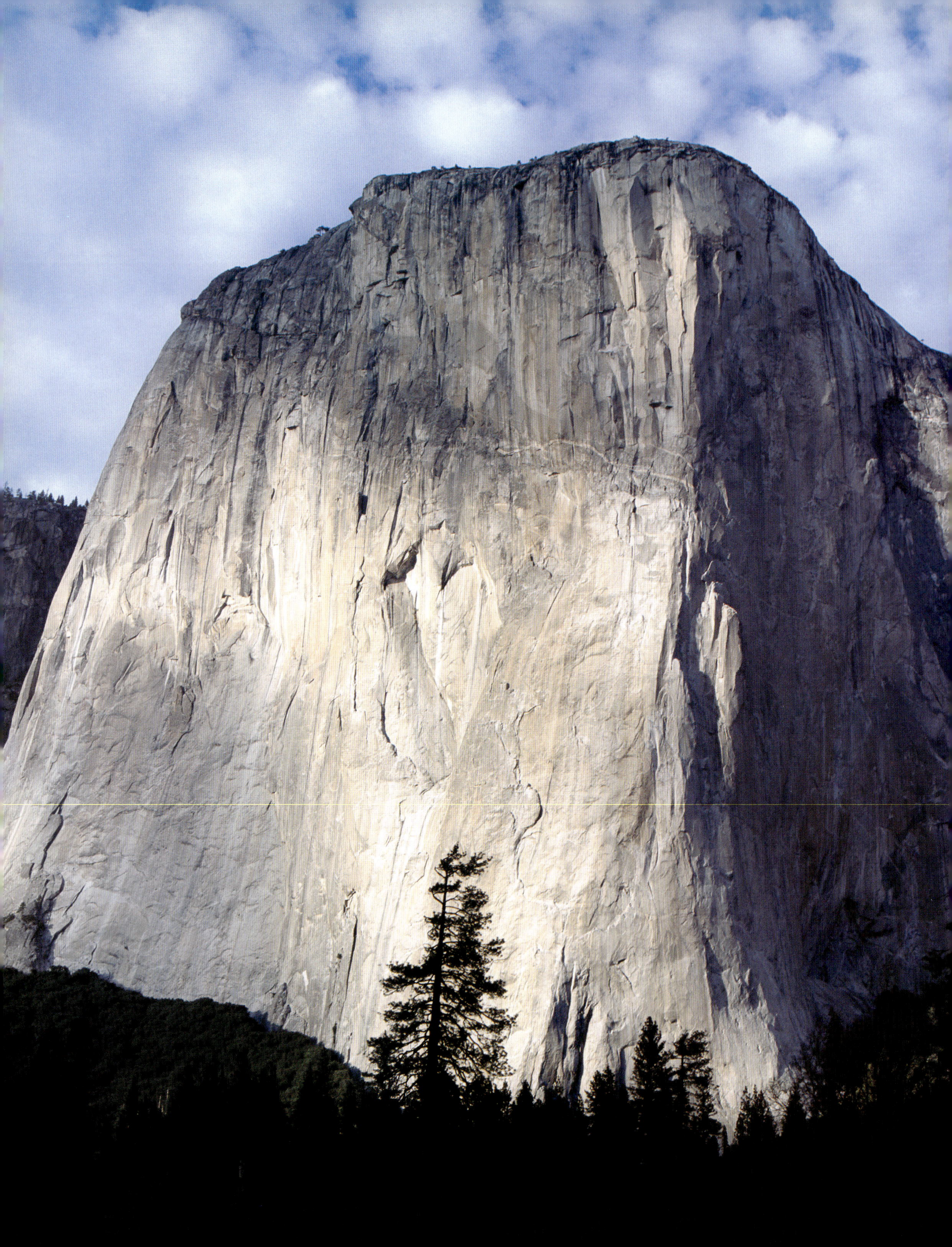

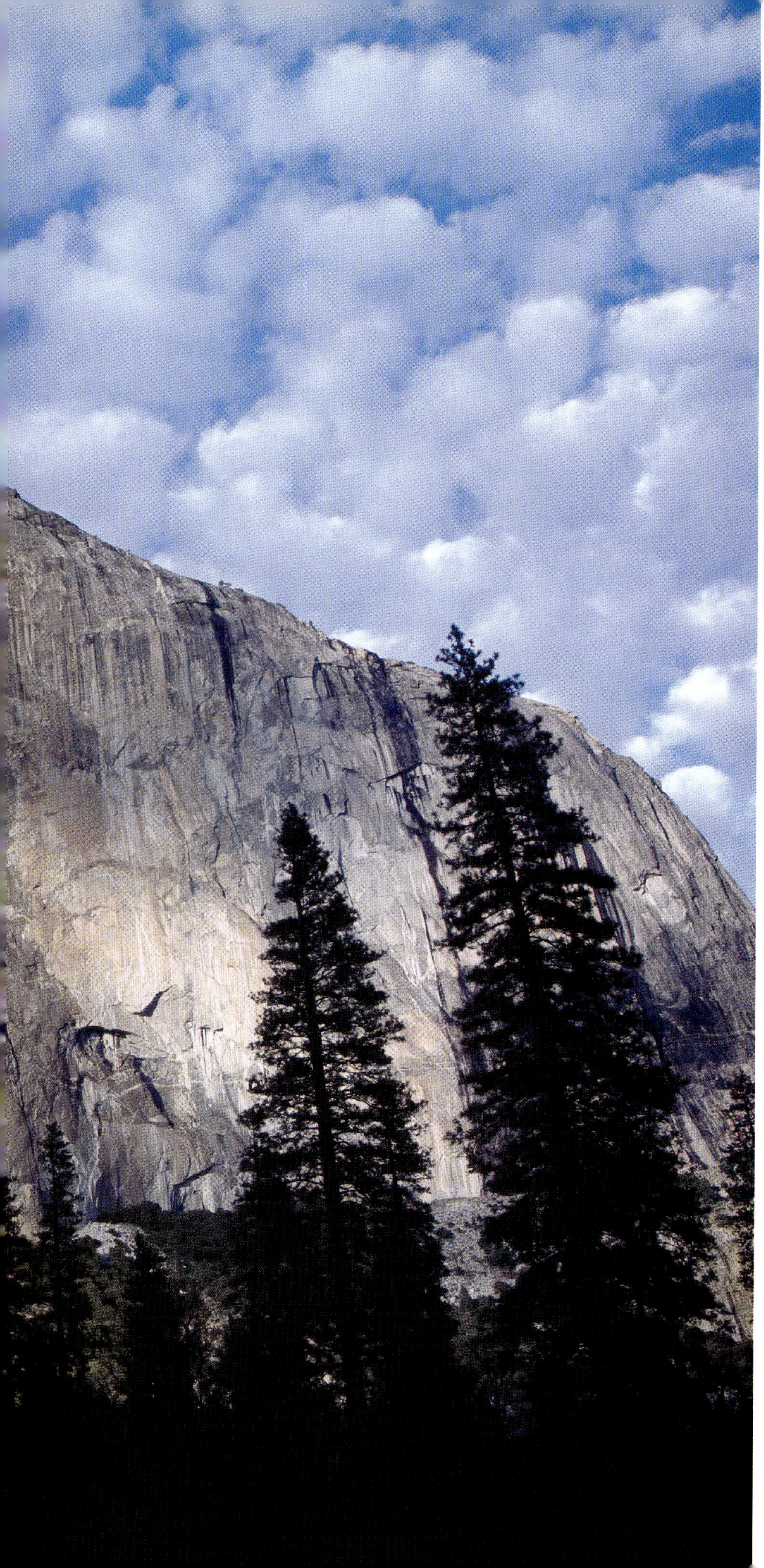

Left

EL CAPITAN

The massive granite face of El Capitan rises more than 3,500 feet from the floor of Yosemite Valley, topping out at 7,569 feet. The Mariposa Battalion named El Capitan in 1851, using the Spanish term for "The Chief." The Native American name, sometimes spelled as Tul-tok-a-nu-la may have had another meaning. One legend claims El Capitan was named for a lowly inchworm, which crawled up the cliff to rescue two bear cubs. Today, El Capitan is magnet for rock climbers from around the world.

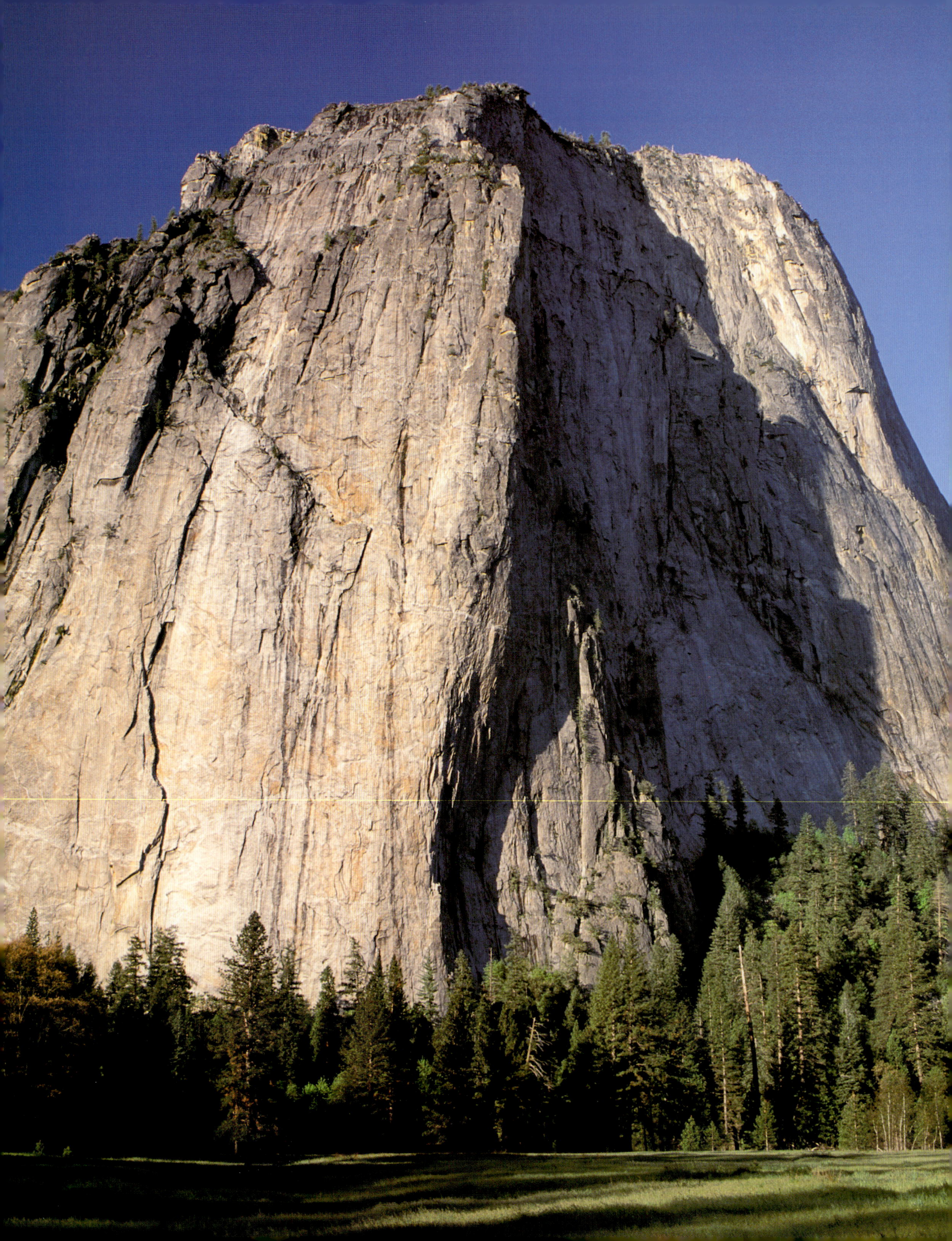

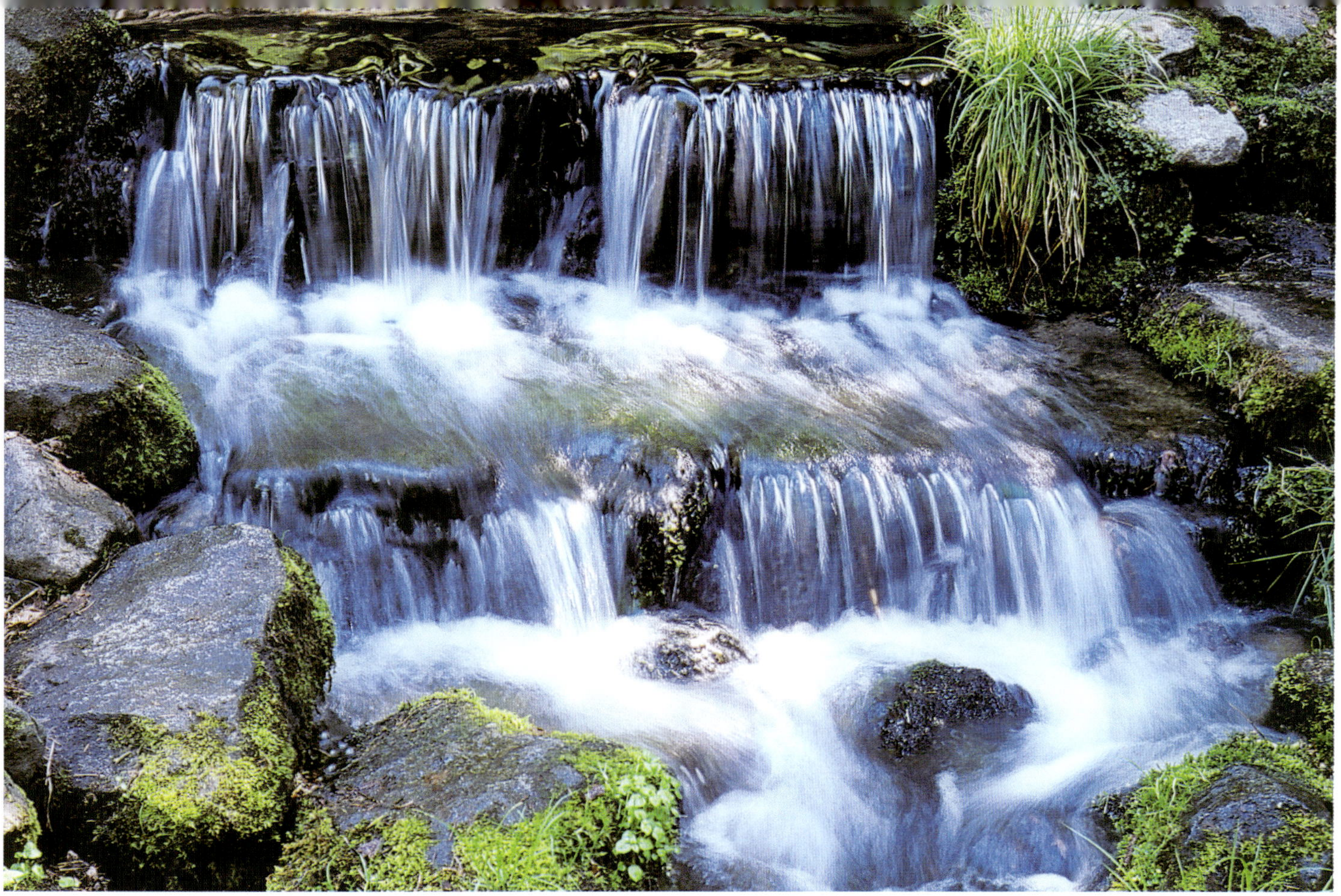

Above

FERN SPRING

No more than a few feet in height, Fern Spring is affectionately and humorously known as Yosemite's smallest waterfall. The spring is on the western edge of Yosemite Valley, just south of Pohono Bridge, on the right side of the one-way road.

Left

CATHEDRAL ROCKS

Morning light slants across the impressive face of Middle Cathedral Rock. The nearby Higher and Lower Cathedral Rocks, along with Middle Cathedral Rock, were once known as the Three Graces. Today the Cathedral Rocks are renowned for their challenging climbing routes, some of them with whimsical names such as "Ticket to Nowhere" and "Central Pillar of Frenzy."

Right

AHWAHNEE HOTEL

Opened in 1927, the massive, six-story Ahwahnee Hotel rises beneath towering cliffs of granite. The ground floor of the hotel features twenty-three-foot-high windows topped with stained glass, cathedral-like ceilings, and collections of Native American and Oriental rugs, Miwok Indian baskets, and historical photographs. While rooms are not inexpensive, both guests and visitors are free to enjoy the comforts of the Great Lounge in the hotel at no charge.

Below

YOSEMITE VALLEY

This is Yosemite Valley on a sunny afternoon in late winter. The imposing granite face of El Capitan is on the left, Half Dome and Cathedral Spires are in the background, while Cathedral Rocks and Bridalveil Fall are to the right.

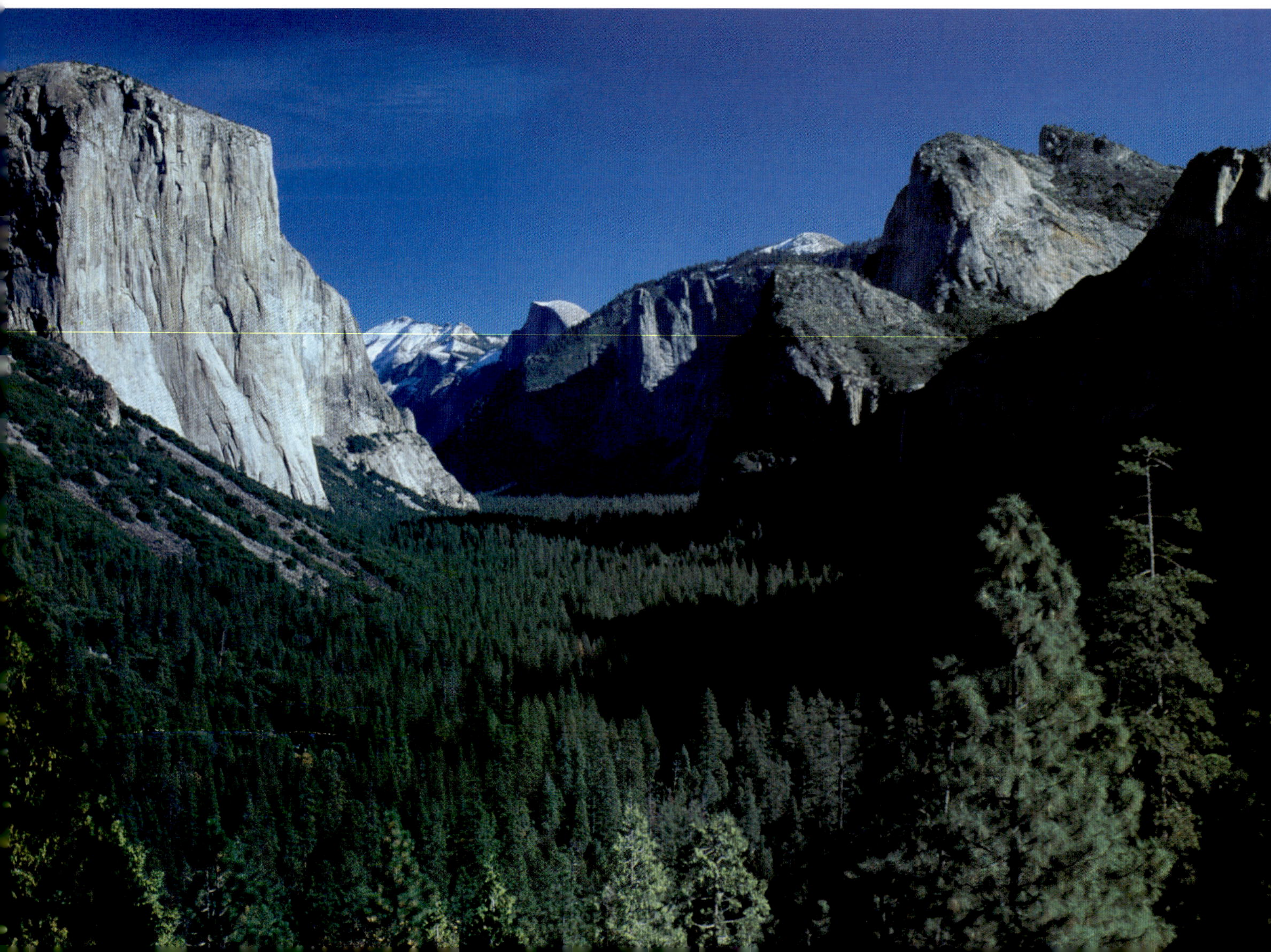

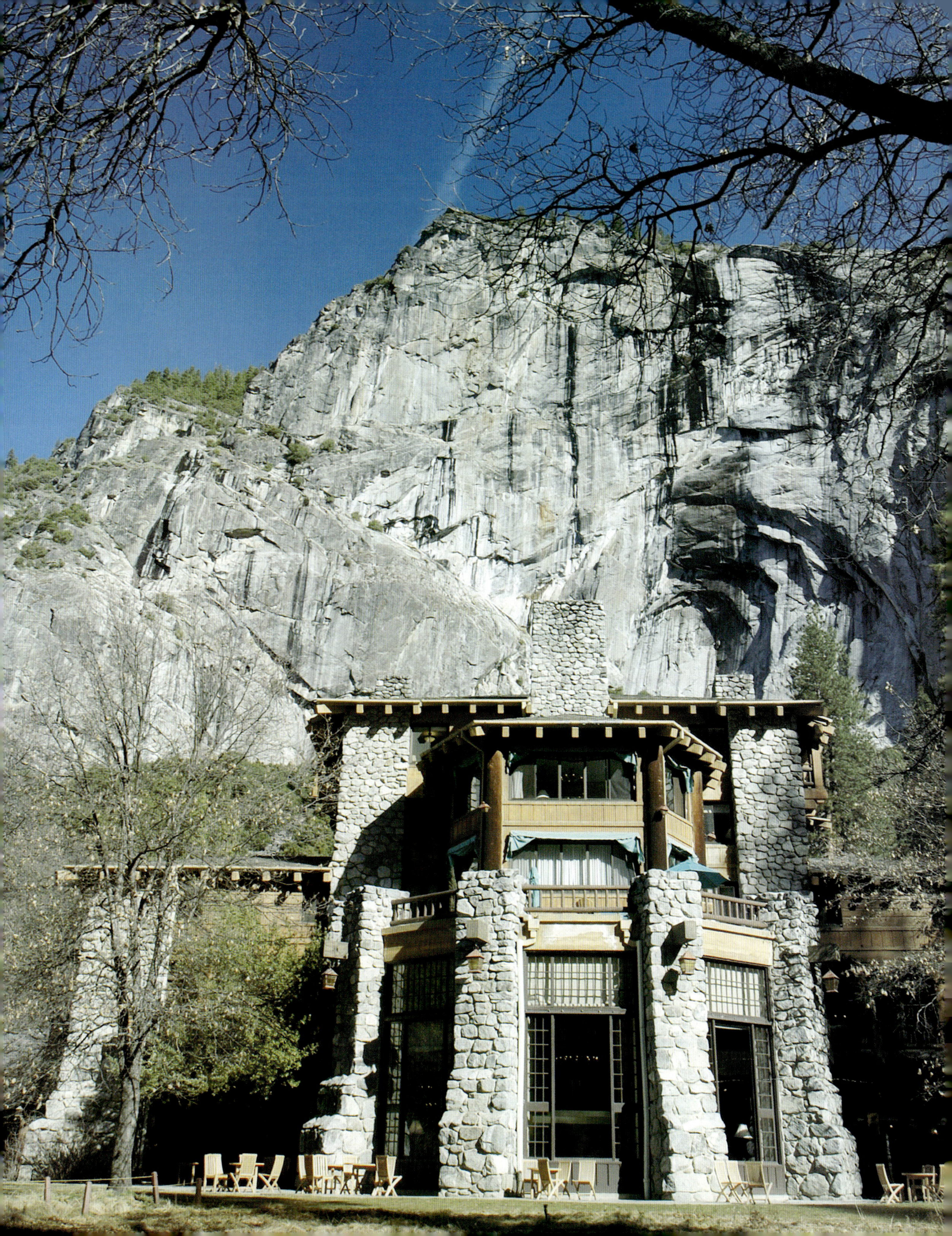

Below and Right

HALF DOME

Probably the most recognizable landmark in Yosemite, Half Dome dominates the eastern skyline of Yosemite Valley. Known for a short time as South Dome, because it sits across the valley from magnificent North Dome, it did not take long for "Half Dome" to appear on official maps. The view to the right is across the Merced River after an early winter snowfall. Glaciers moving beneath Half Dome may have undercut and weakened the northwest side of the dome, which then fell away due to weathering and exfoliation, leaving behind the Dome's distinctive sheer cliff.

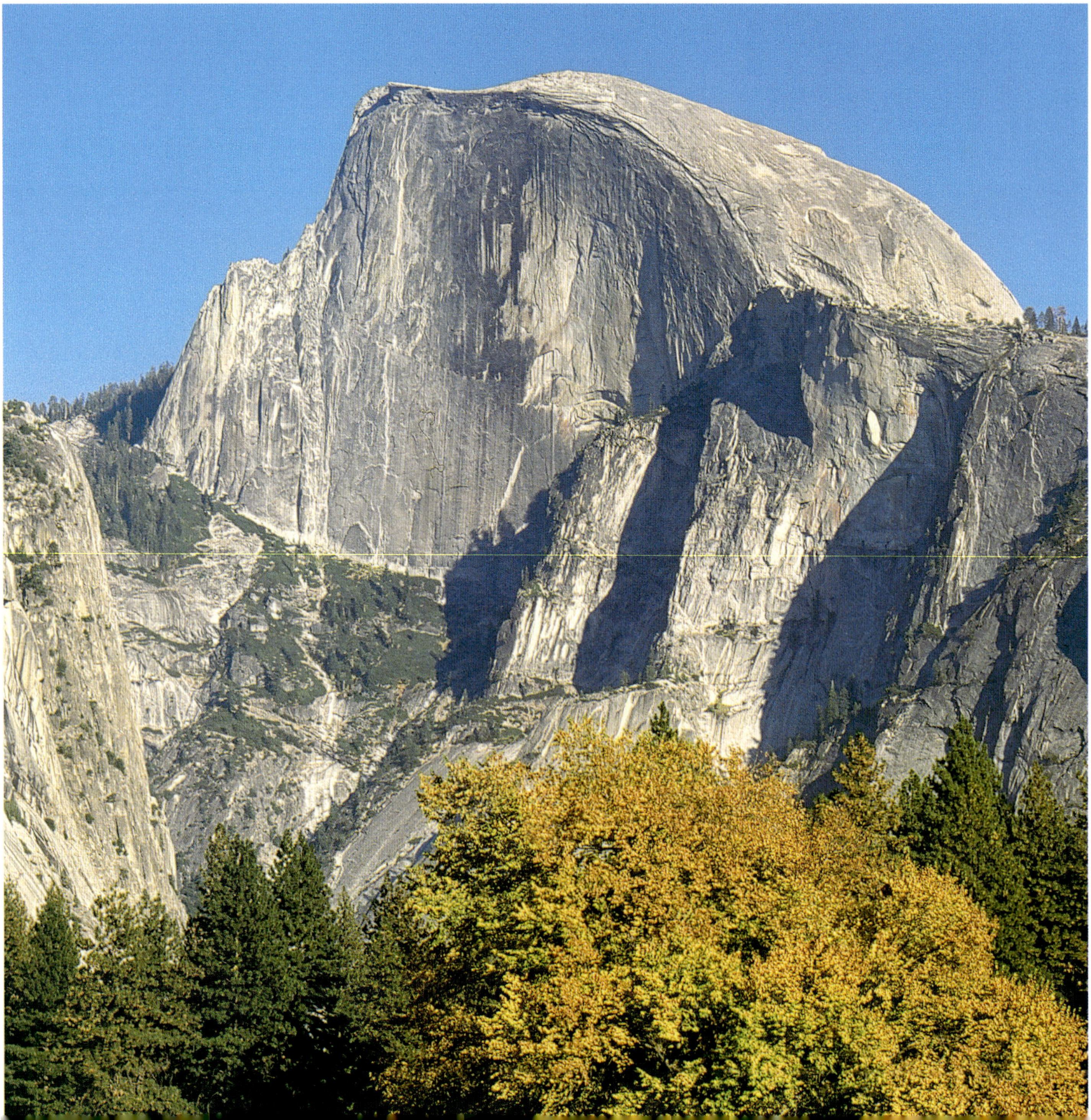

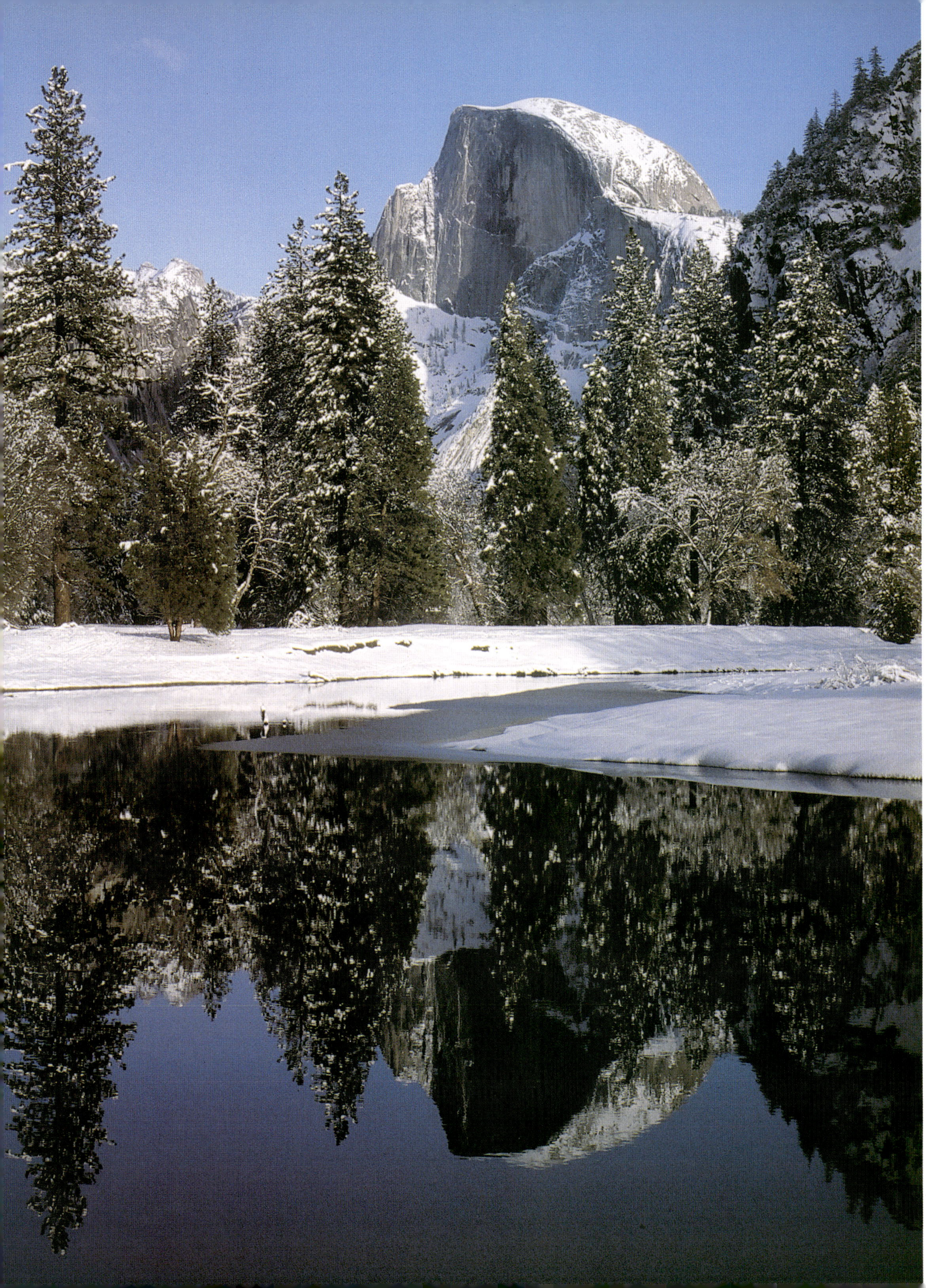

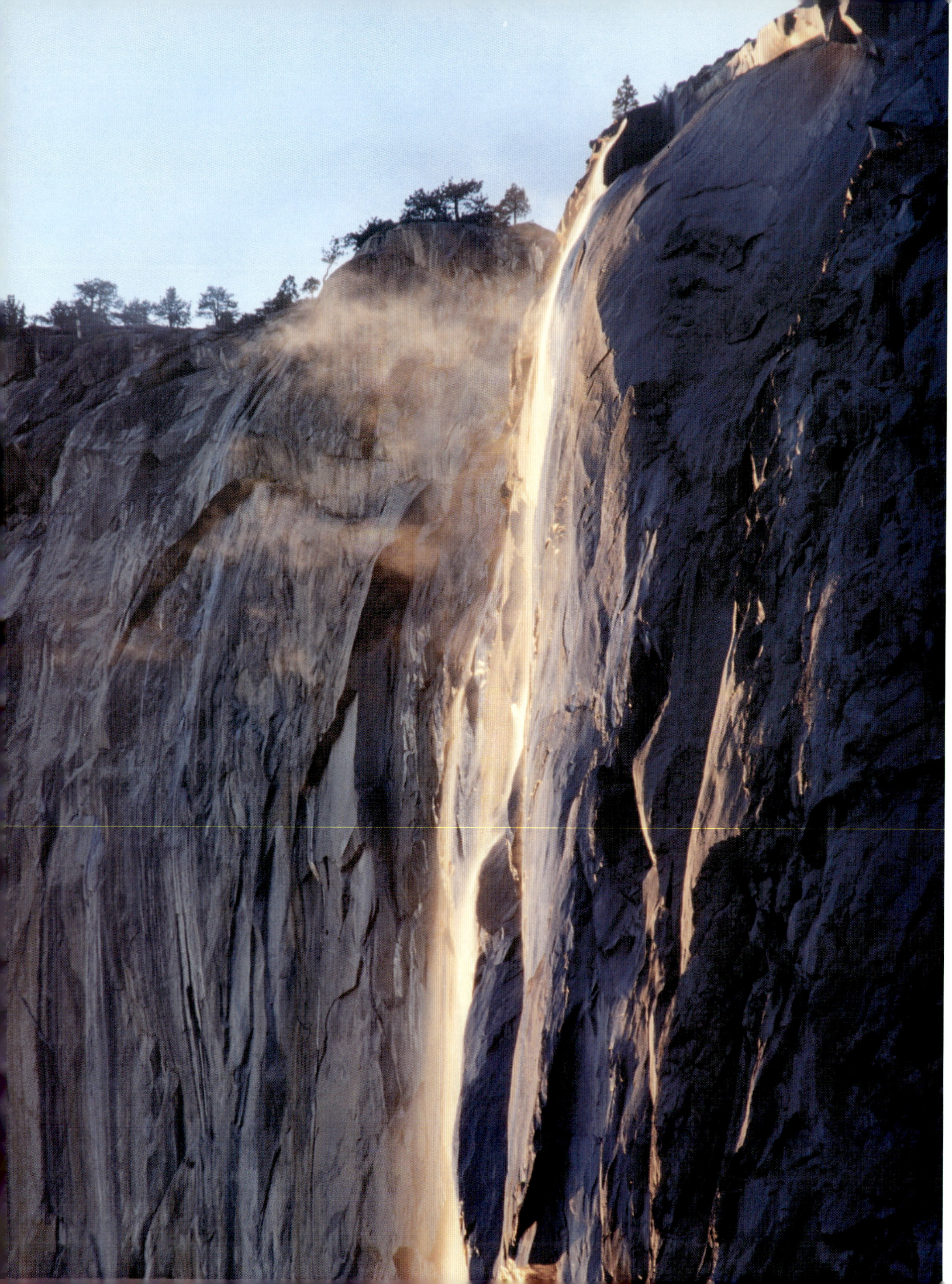

Left

HORSETAIL FALL

Many waterfalls in Yosemite are known as "ephemerals," usually disappearing by early summer. Horsetail Fall, on the eastern edge of El Capitan, is a beautiful example.

Below

LEIDIG MEADOW

This beautiful meadow, just to the west of Yosemite Lodge, was the site of a two-story hotel built in 1869. In 1987, almost a century after the old hotel was torn down, a massive rock fall bounced boulders over Northside Drive, across the Merced River, and into Leidig Meadow, part of which was cordoned off for several months for fear of more slides. Now visitors can walk safely into the meadow to enjoy panoramic views of the granite cliffs and waterfalls.

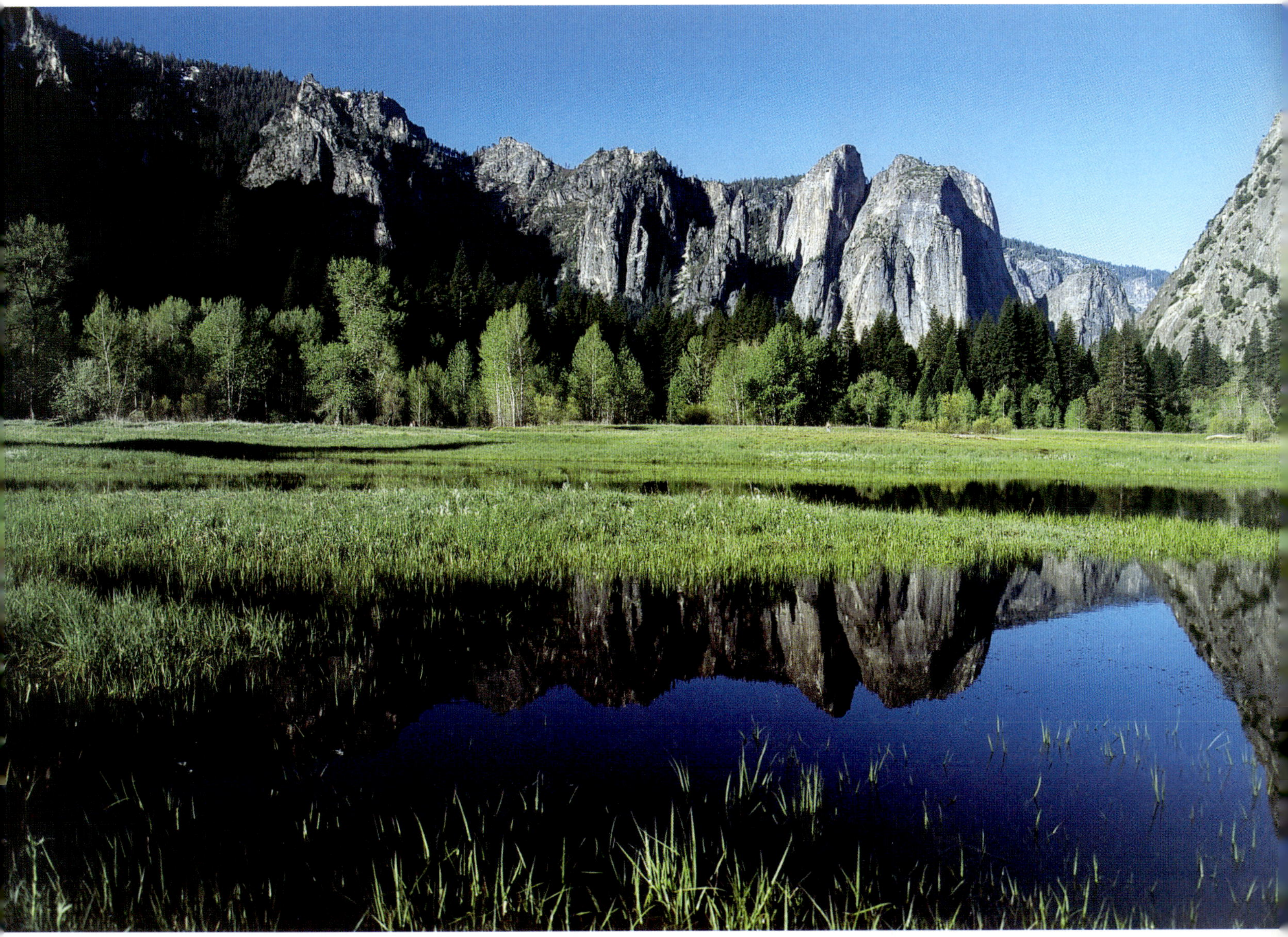

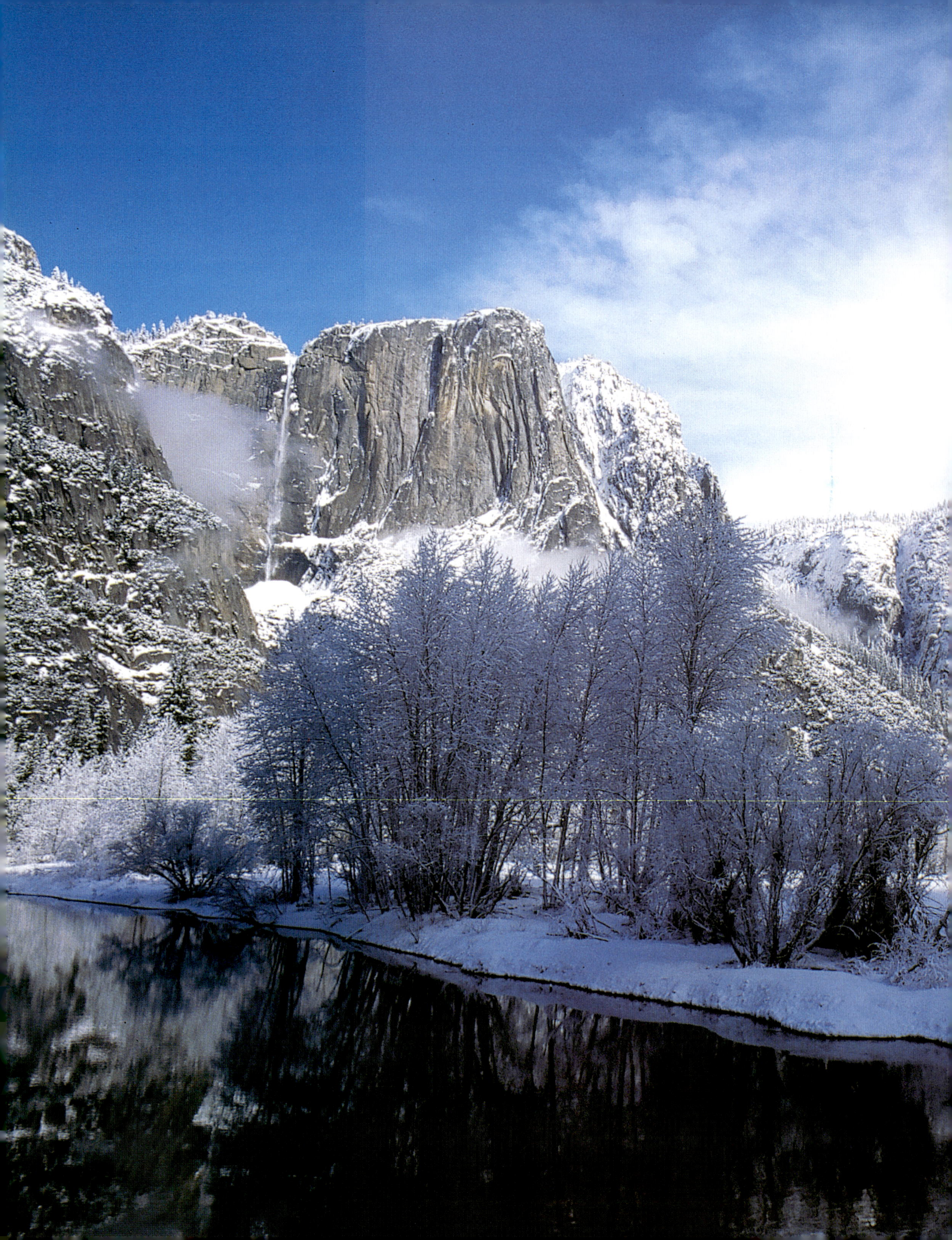

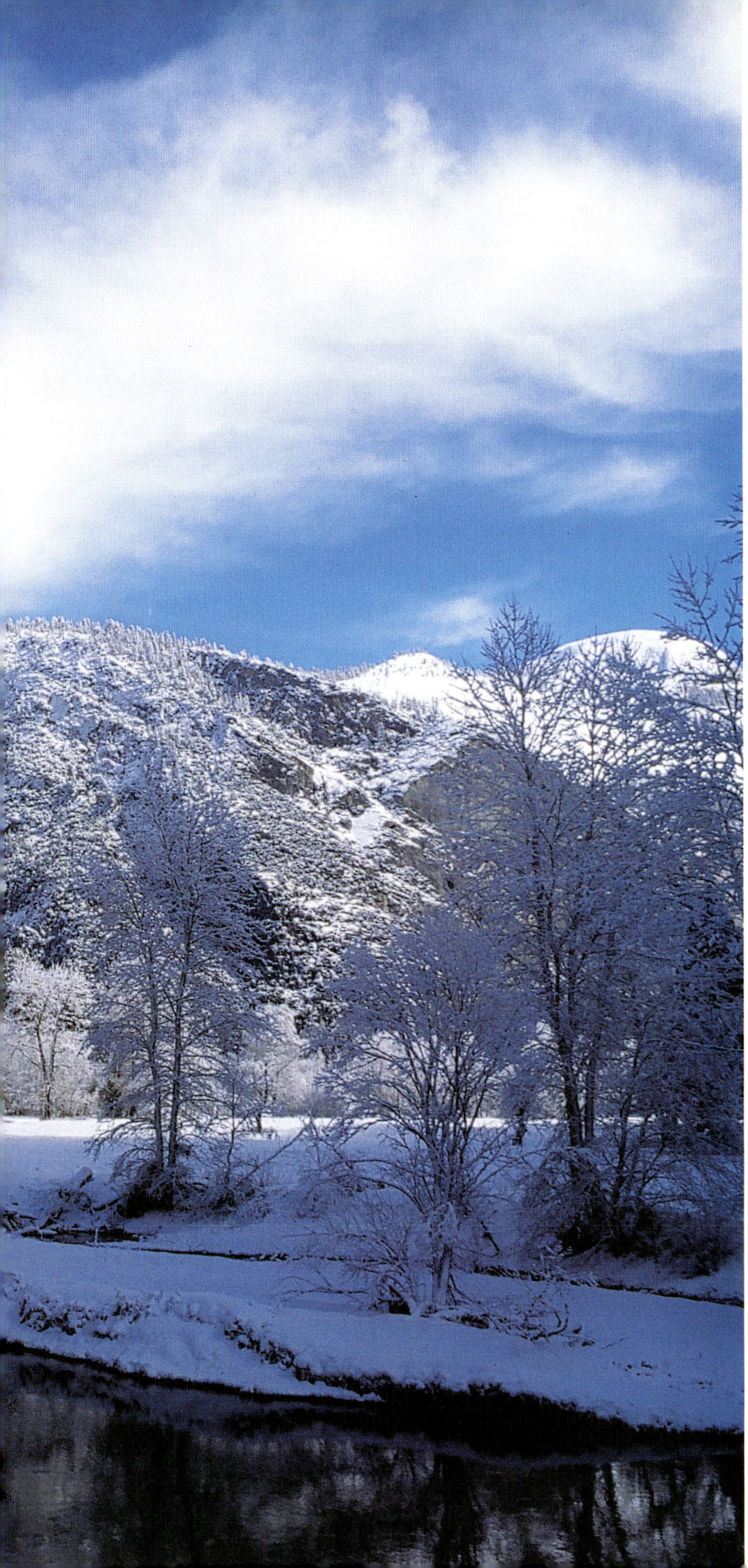

Left

MERCED RIVER

With Yosemite Falls in the background, the Merced River meanders beneath the granite cliffs of Yosemite Valley during the middle of winter. Usually placid, the river occasionally floods over its banks during spring, when heavy winter snows melt too quickly.

Below

MERCED RIVER

The river in spring, reflecting a grove of black cottonwoods.

Right

TREES AND SMOKE

Mist rises from the trunks of these pines in what was once Upper River Campground. During the first few days of January 1997, the "Flood of the Century" coursed through the Yosemite Valley. The park service decided to allow the damaged campground, and the adjacent Lower River Campground, to return to a natural setting. Now visitors are free to wander through a quiet stretch of forest that runs along a section of the Merced River.

Overleaf

MIRROR LAKE

Mirror Lake, near the upper end of Yosemite Valley, offers a beautiful reflection of Mount Watkins (named for early Yosemite photographer Carlton Watkins). The lake, created when a massive chunk of Half Dome slid into Tenaya Creek before recorded history, is slowly filling with sediments washed out of the surrounding mountains. By summer each year Mirror Lake is usually dry.

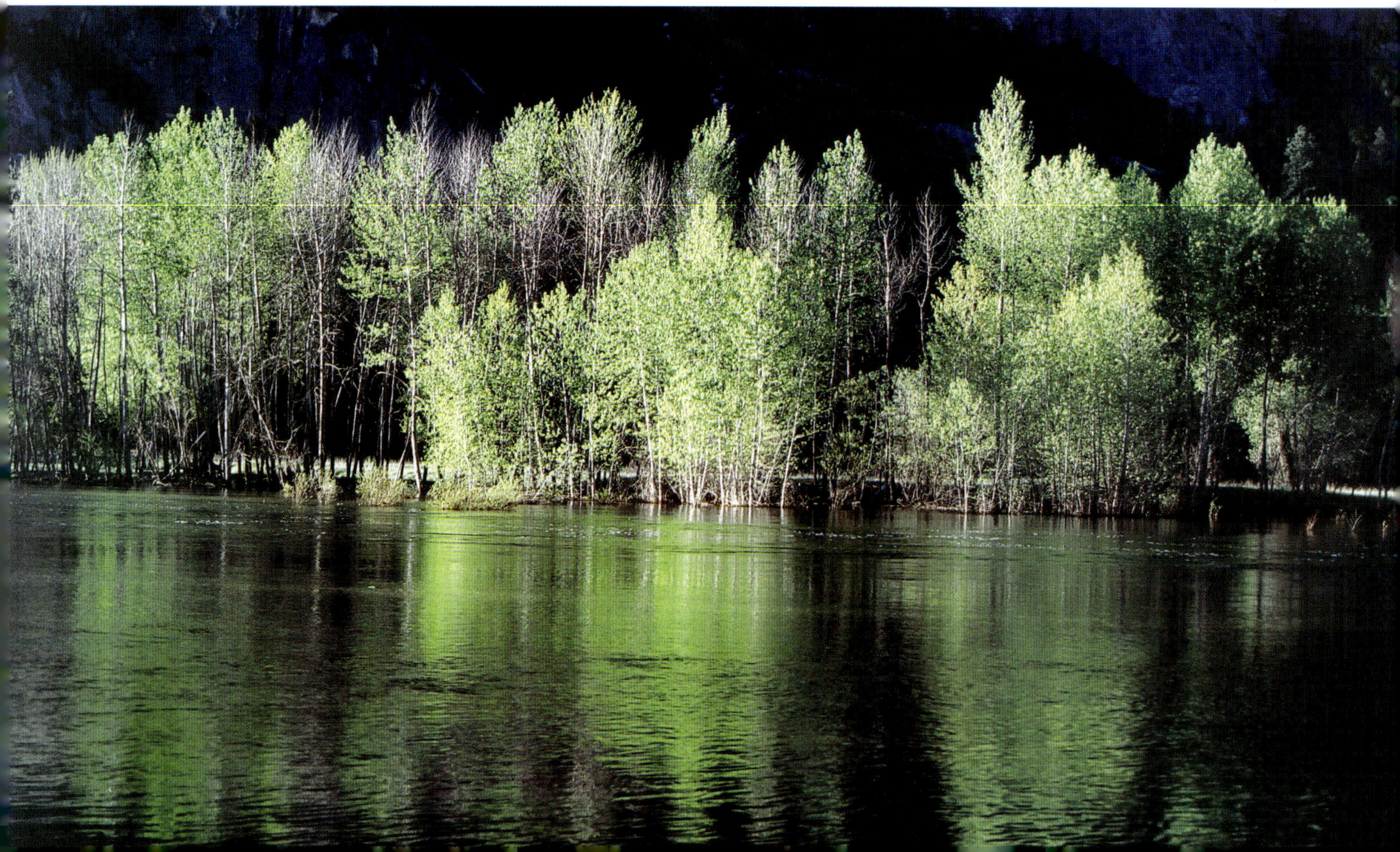

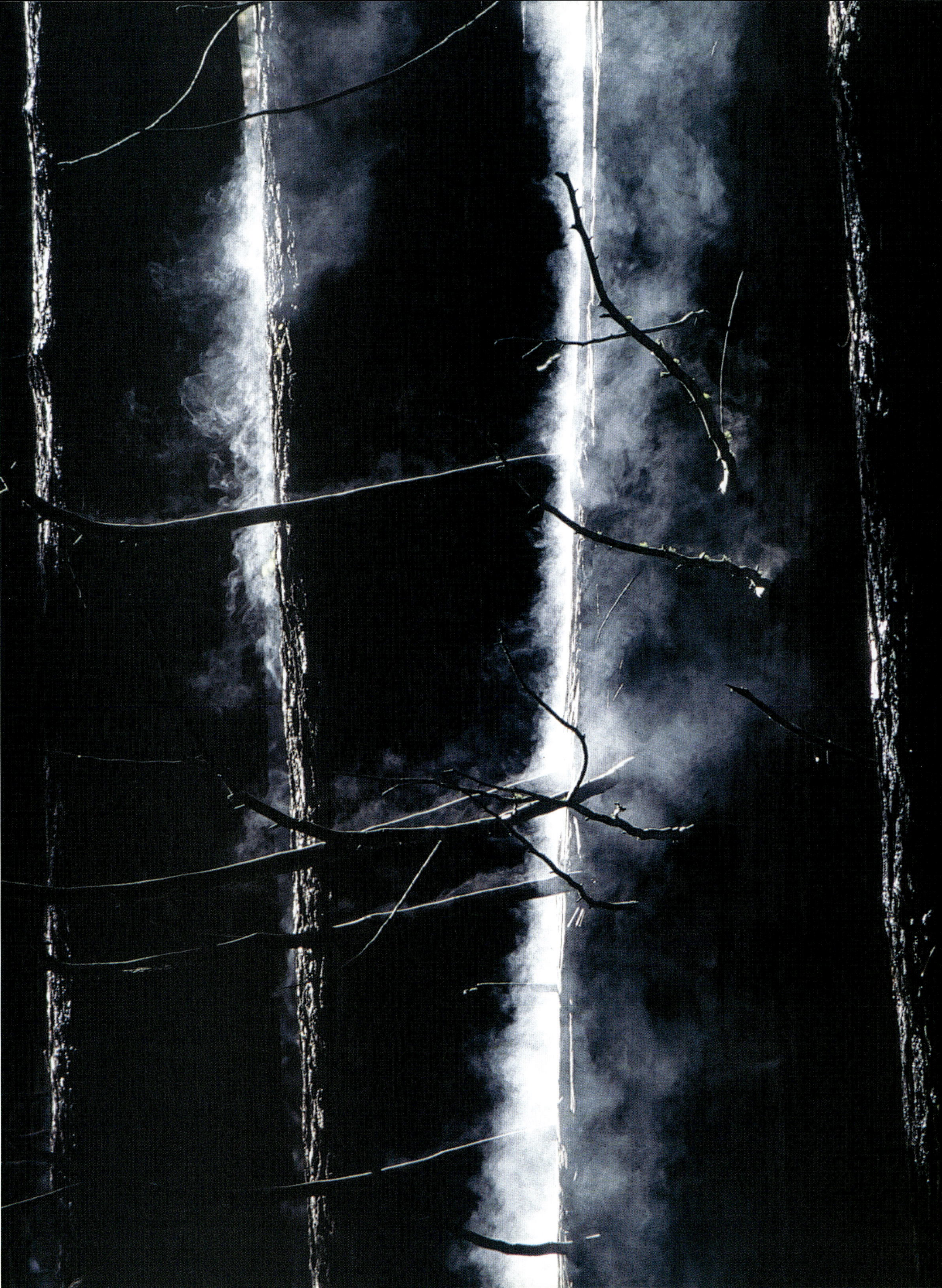

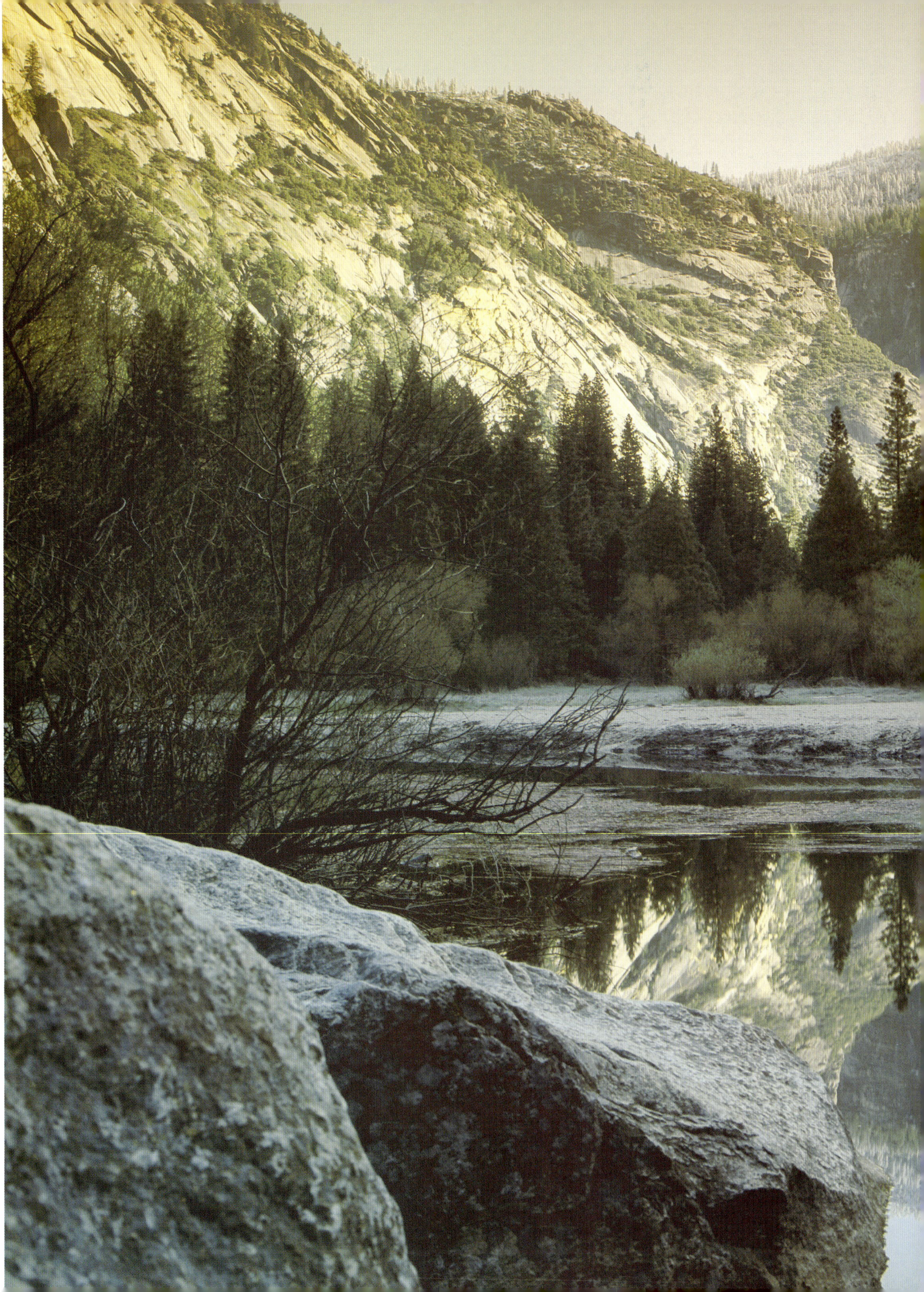

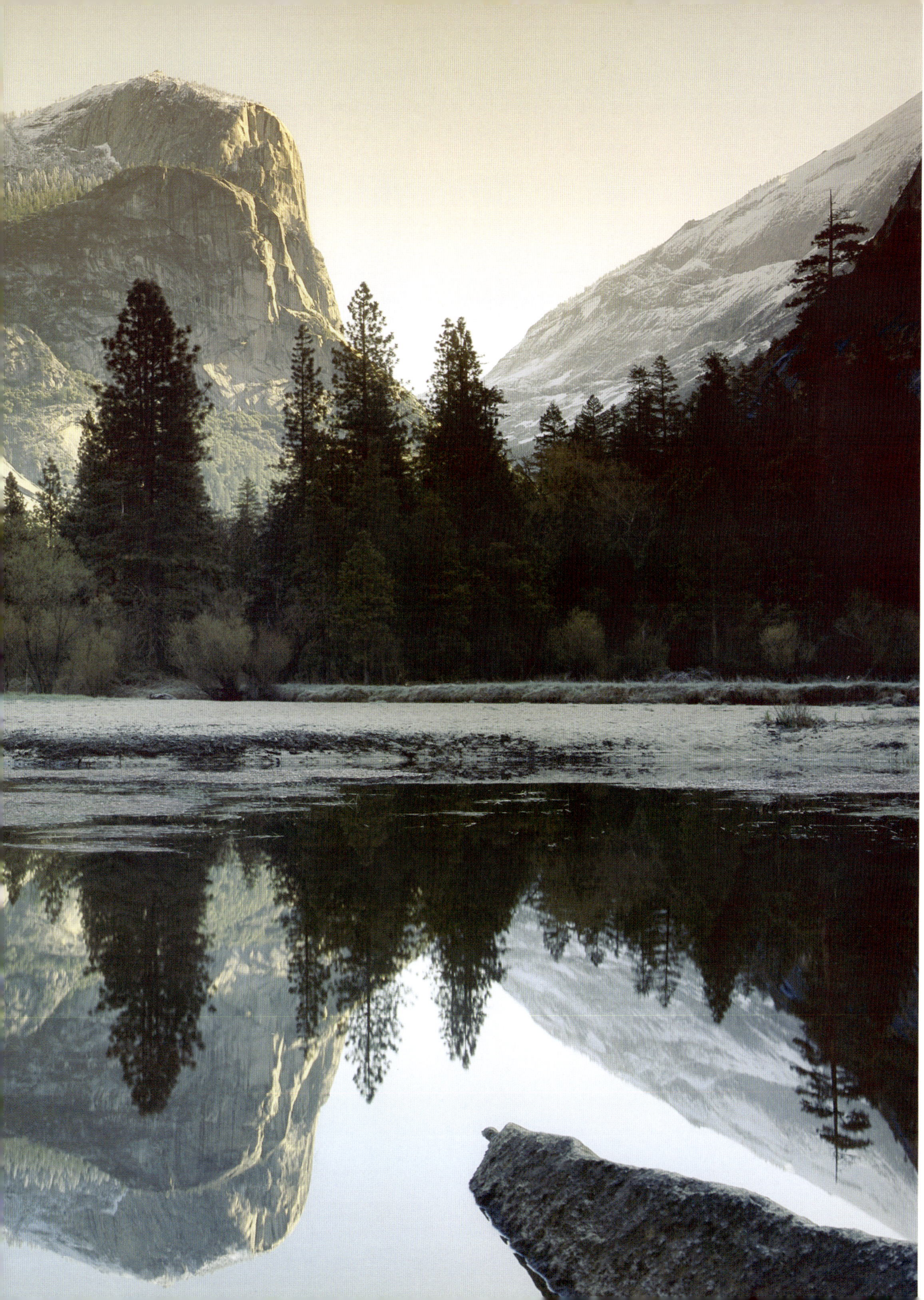

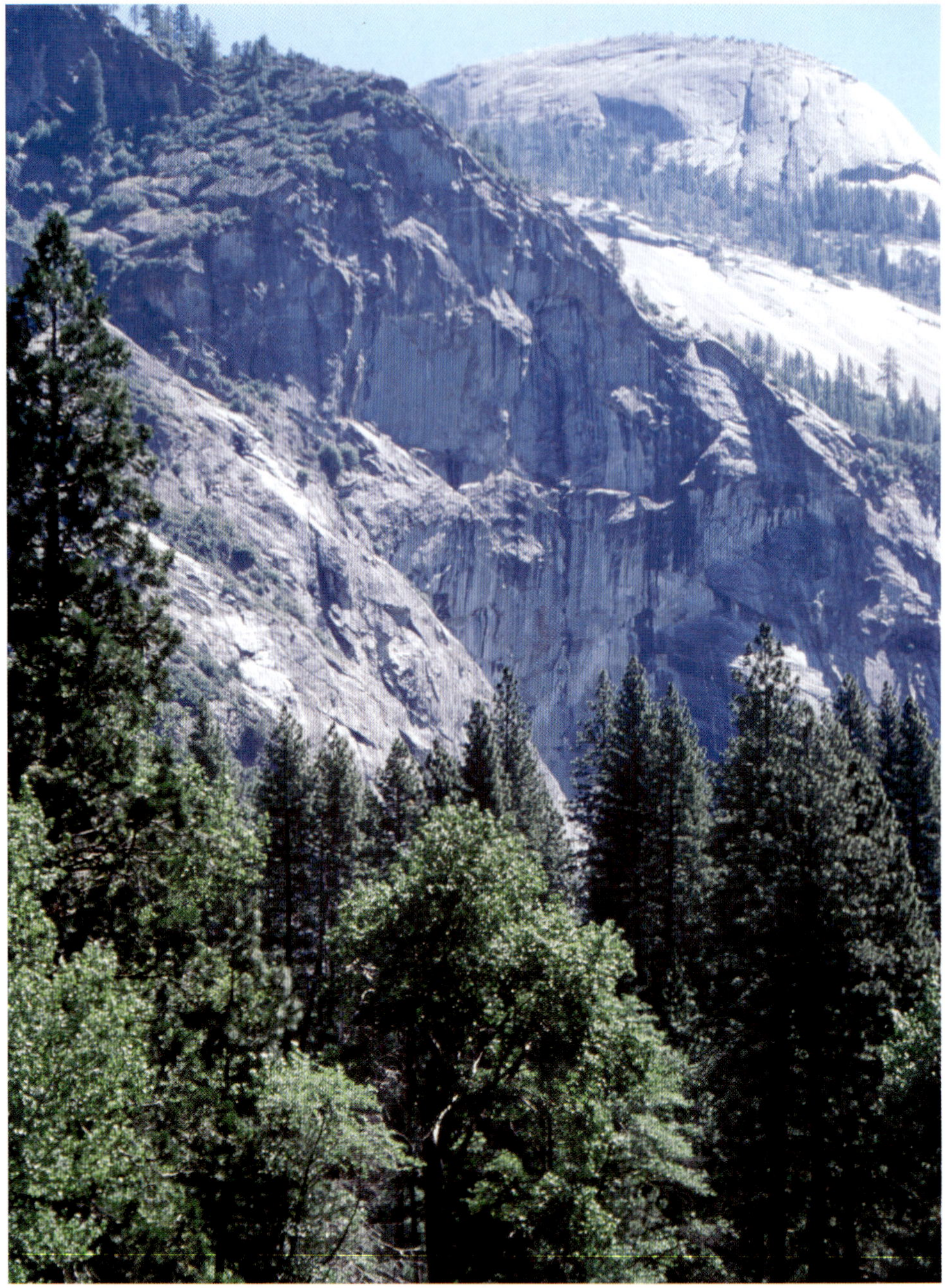

Above

NORTH DOME

Standing across from Half Dome, impressive North Dome rises 3,500 feet above the Yosemite Valley floor. The Ahwahneechee called it To-ko-ye, their name for an acorn basket. According to legend, To-ko-ye was a giant acorn basket turned upside down.

Right

SENTINEL ROCK

Standing out in bold relief from the granite walls around it, Sentinel Rock rises above the Merced River, on the south side of Yosemite Valley.

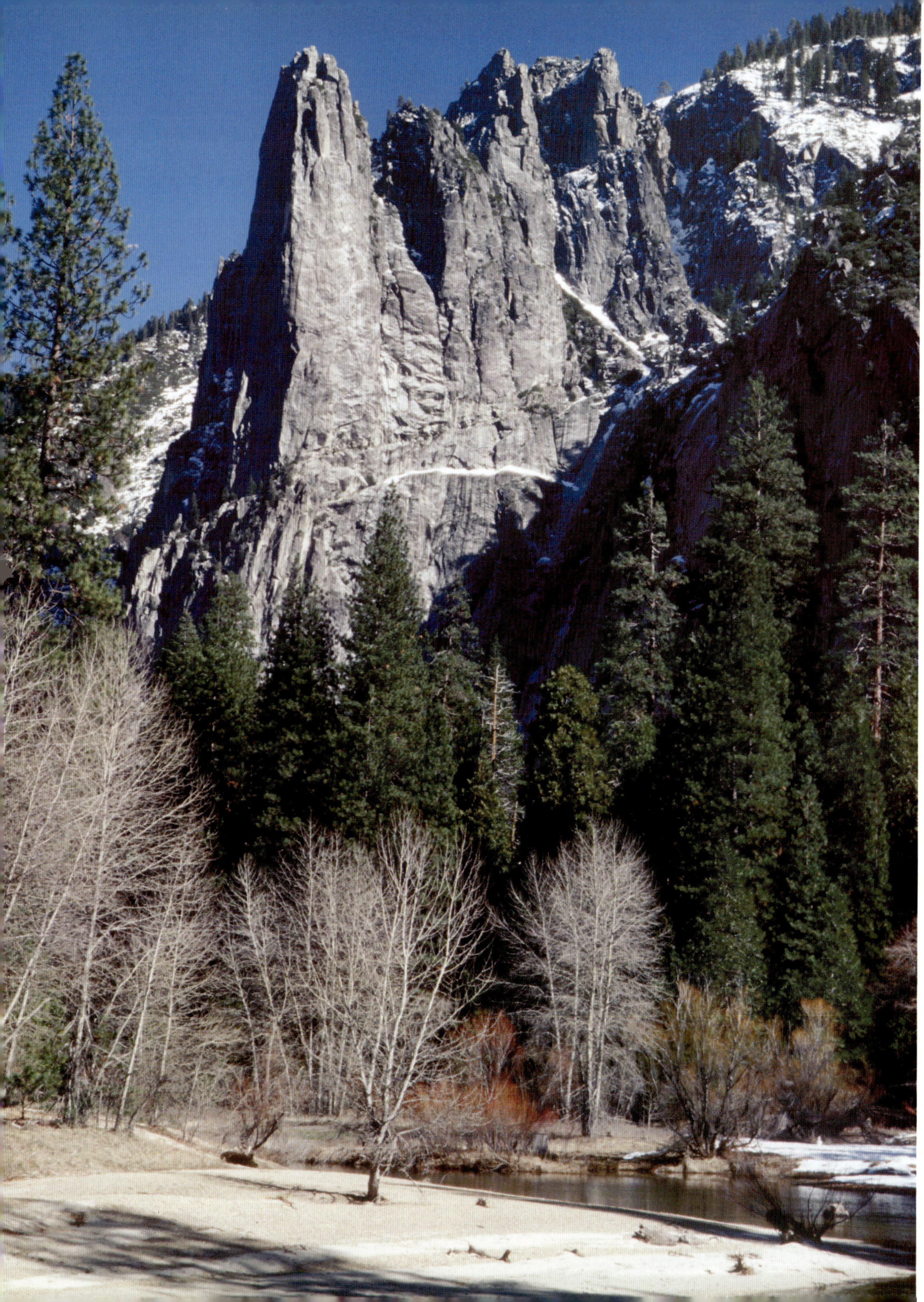

Below and right

UPPER AND LOWER YOSEMITE FALLS

The highest waterfall in North America, Yosemite Falls drop 2,425 feet in a series of three sections, known as the Upper Fall, Middle Cascade, and Lower Fall. The upper fall, at 1,430 feet, is more than 400 feet taller than the Eiffel Tower, in Paris, and a few feet shorter than Sears Tower in Chicago, Illinois, while the lower fall is 24 feet longer than a 100-yard football field.

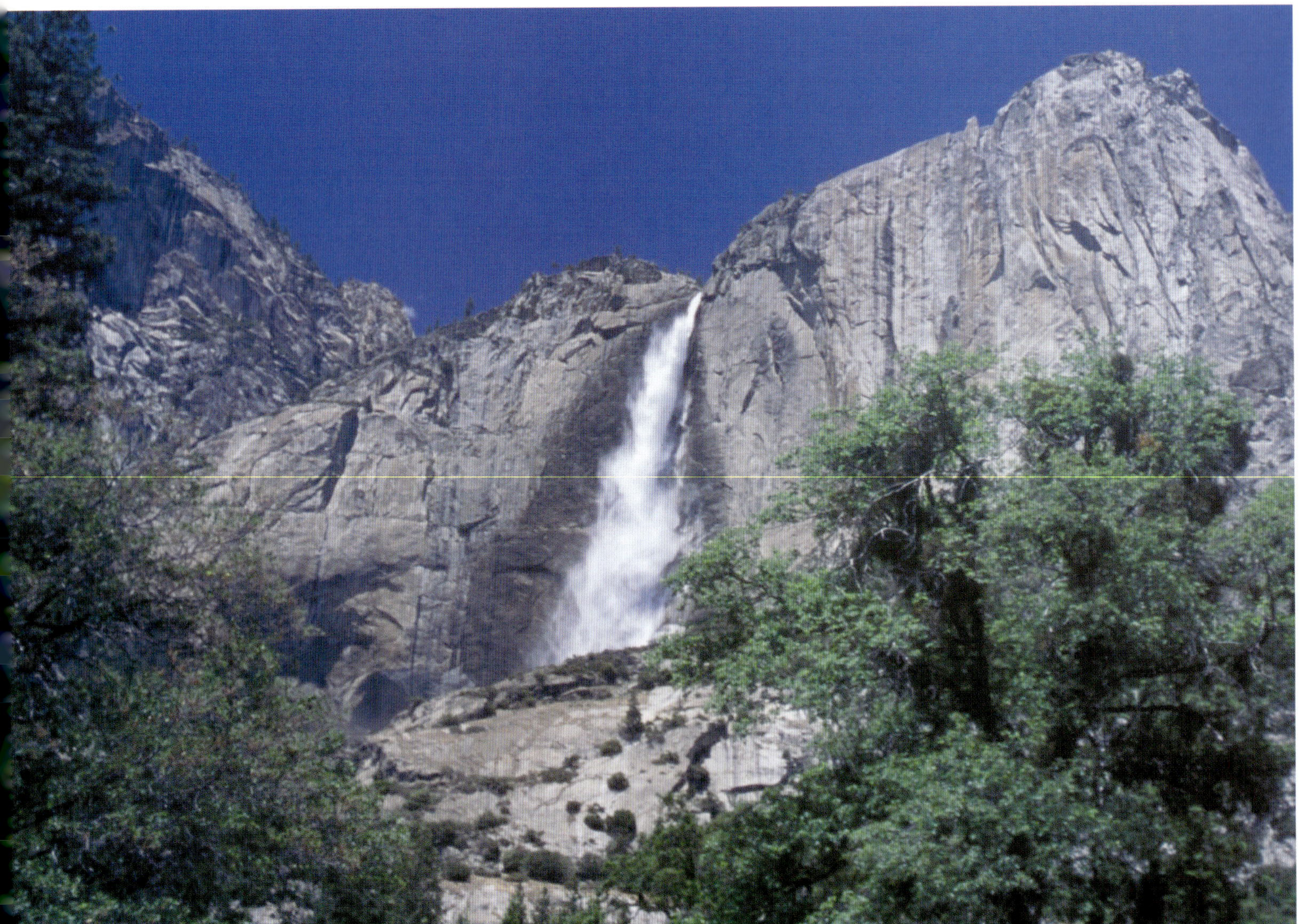

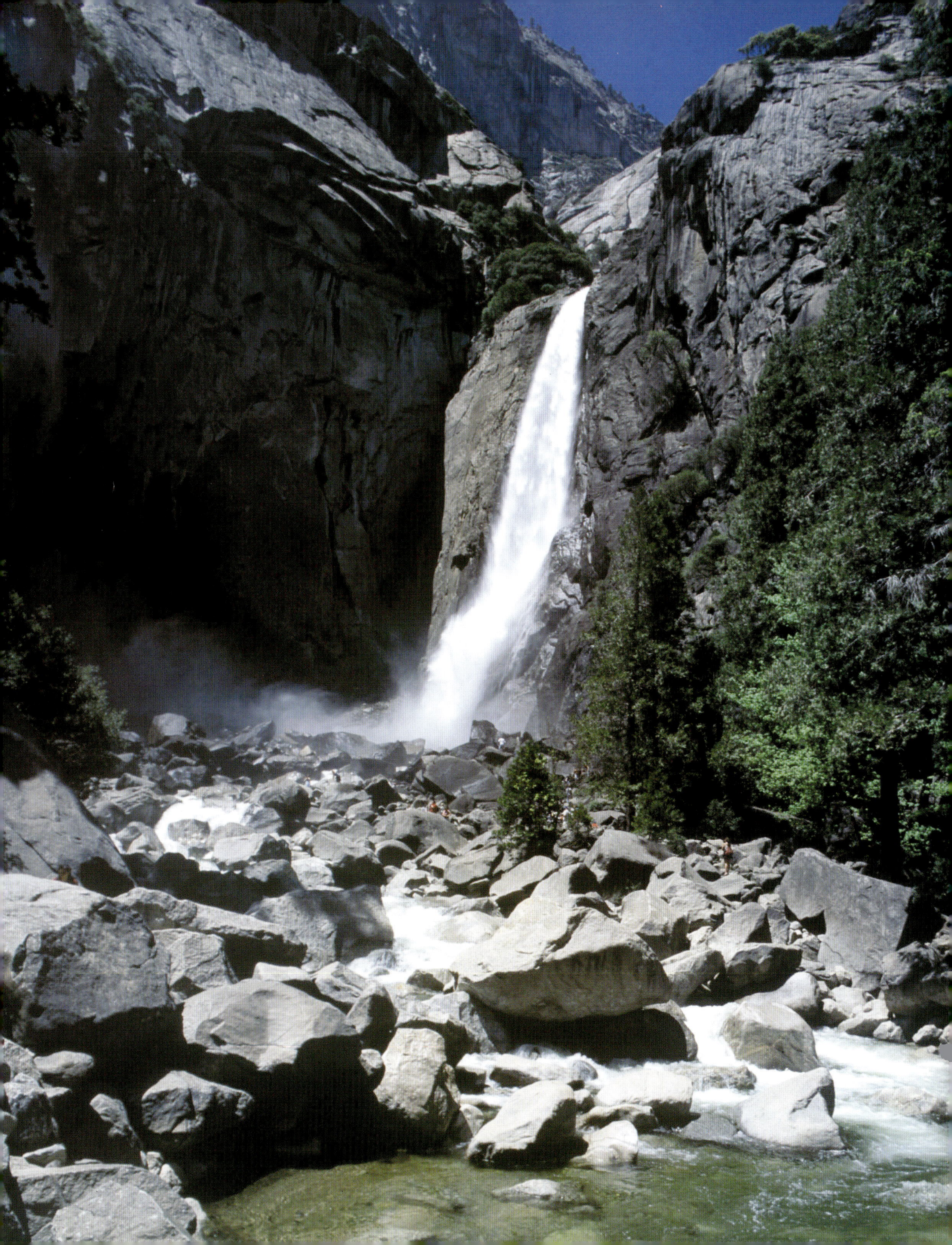

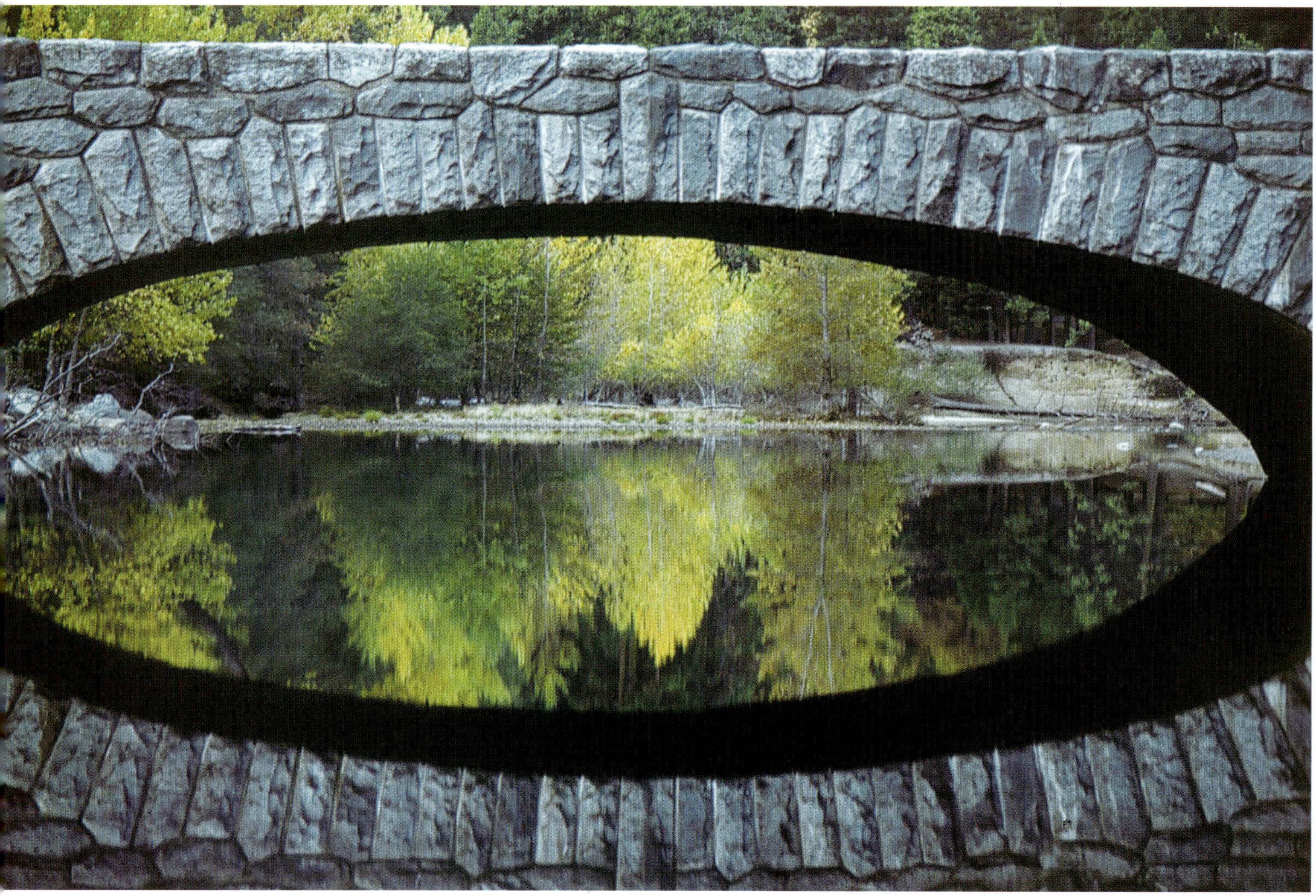

Above

STONEMAN BRIDGE

The graceful and rustic Stoneman Bridge, its facade fitted with rounded river stones, was constructed by the Park Service in 1933. The bridge crosses the Merced River near Curry Village.

Right

STONEMAN MEADOW

Beautiful Stoneman Meadow was probably named in honor of California governor George Stoneman. Overcrowded campgrounds in 1970 led to a riot in the meadow on July 4, 1970, between Vietnam anti-war protestors and park rangers. The next day the meadow was peaceful, and has served since then as a quiet haven between the Merced River and Curry Village. The western edge of the meadow offers a fine view of looming Half Dome.

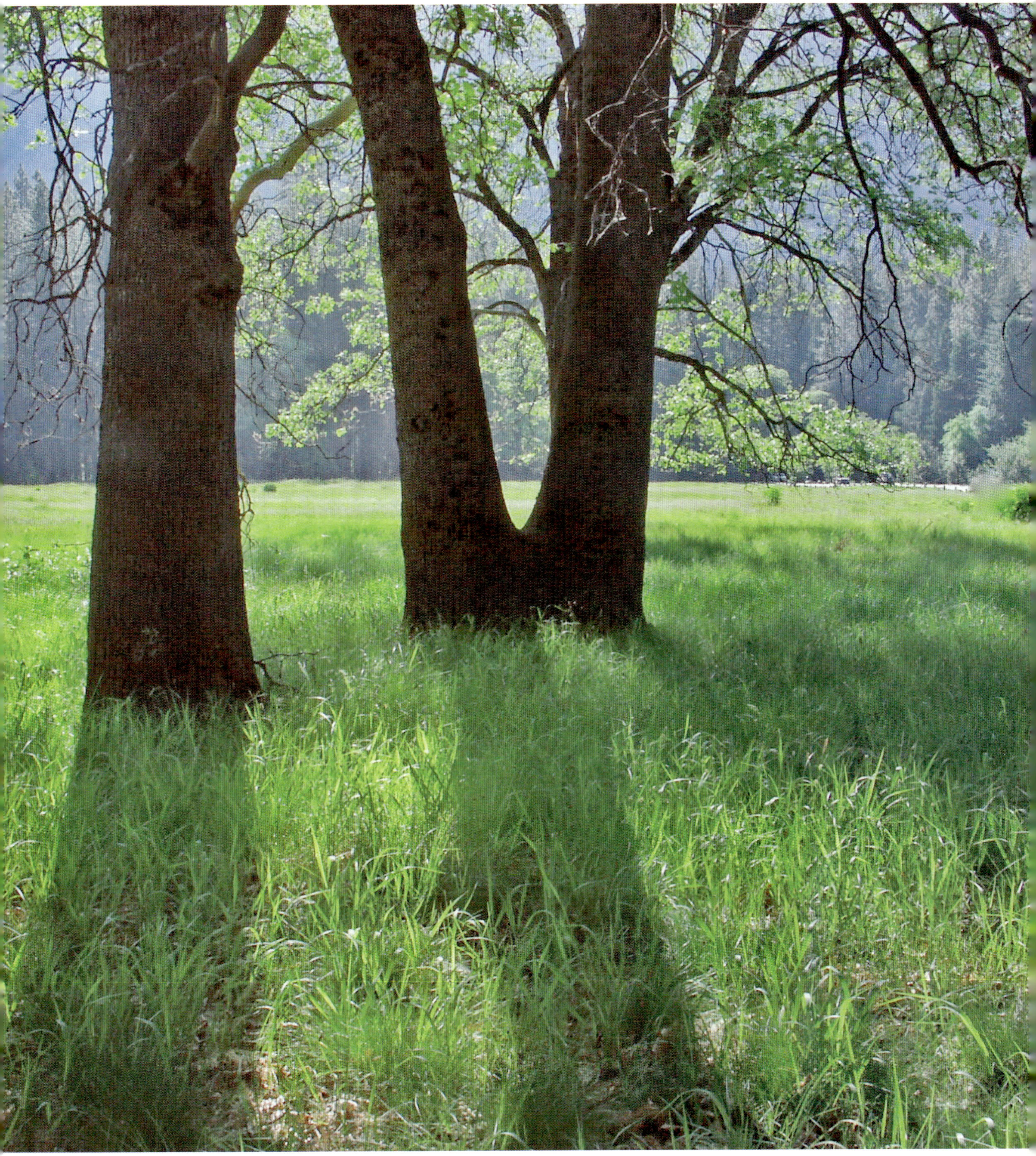

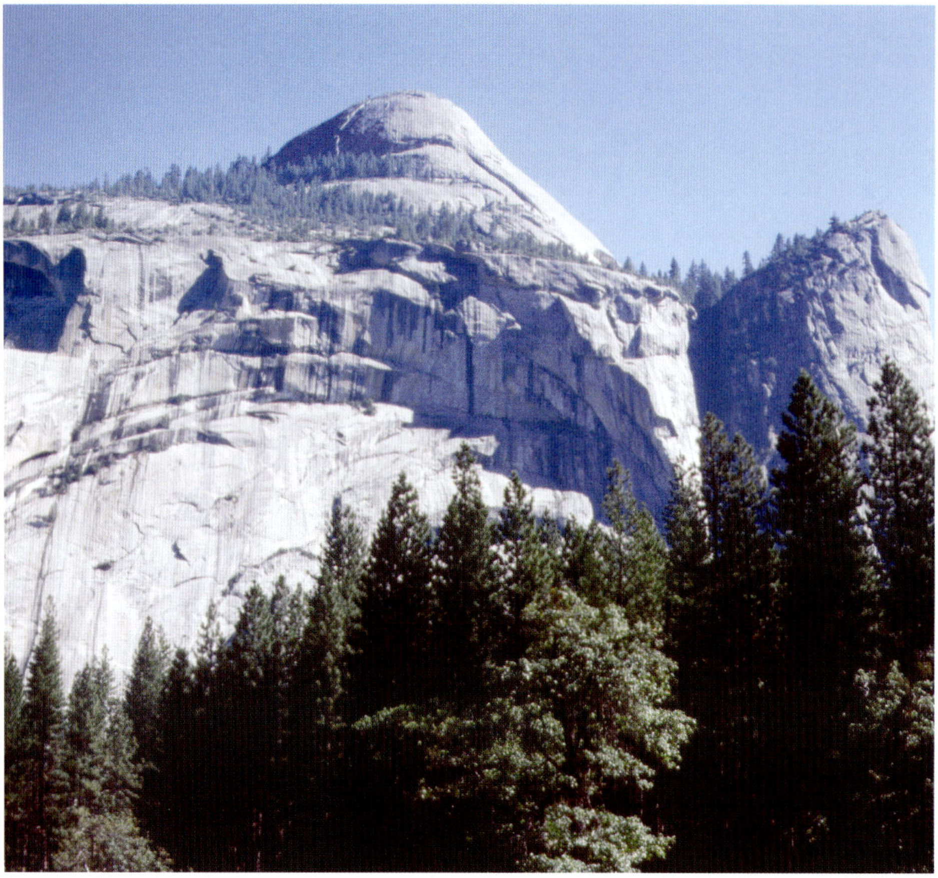

Above

WASHINGTON COLUMN WITH ROYAL ARCHES & NORTH DOME

North Dome overlooks Royal Arches, which were formed when various types of erosion, including rock fall and the grinding passage of glaciers, dropped and plucked the granite off the cliff face. Washington Column, with more than 2,300 feet of vertical granite, is a popular location for rock climbers.

Right

THE THREE BROTHERS

Three sharply slanting peaks, called Lower Brother, Middle Brother, and Eagle Peak, rise on the north side of Yosemite Valley. The trio of granite peaks were named during the Mariposa Indian War, after the capture of three Native American brothers.

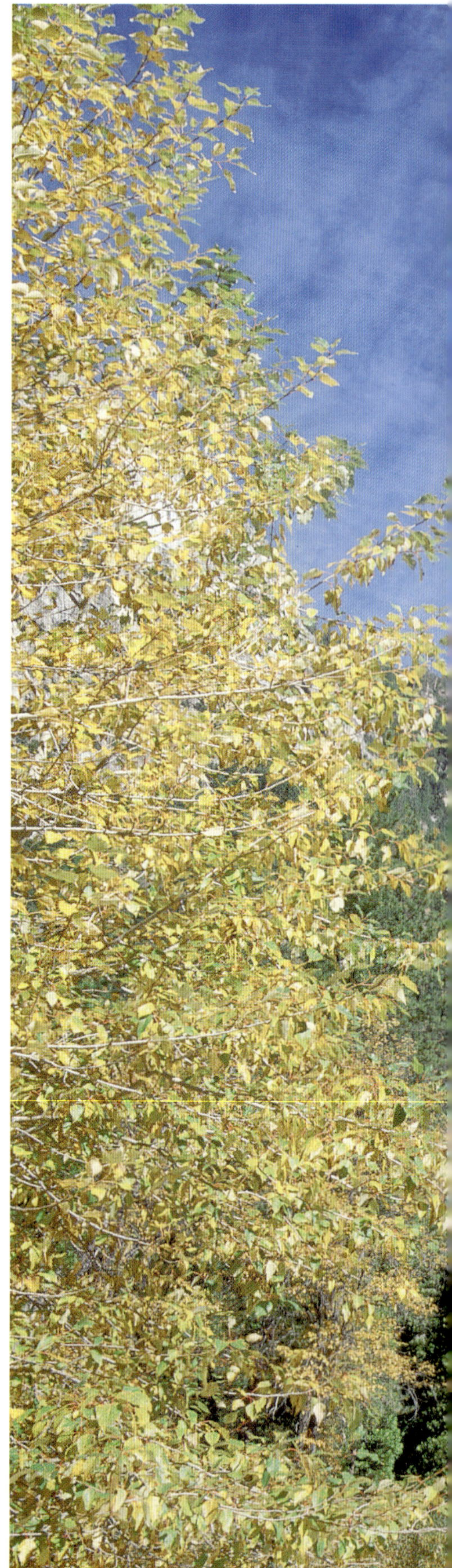

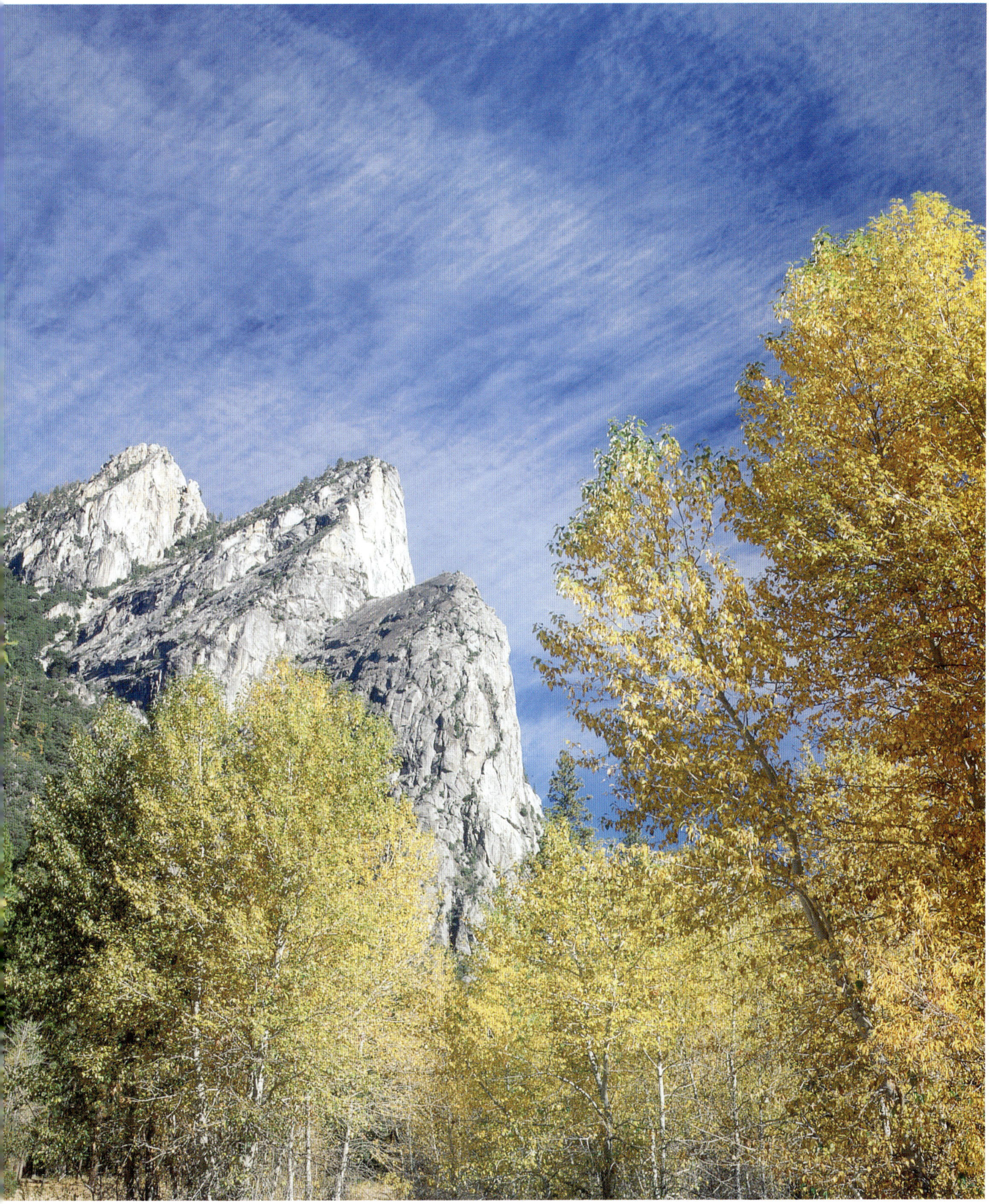

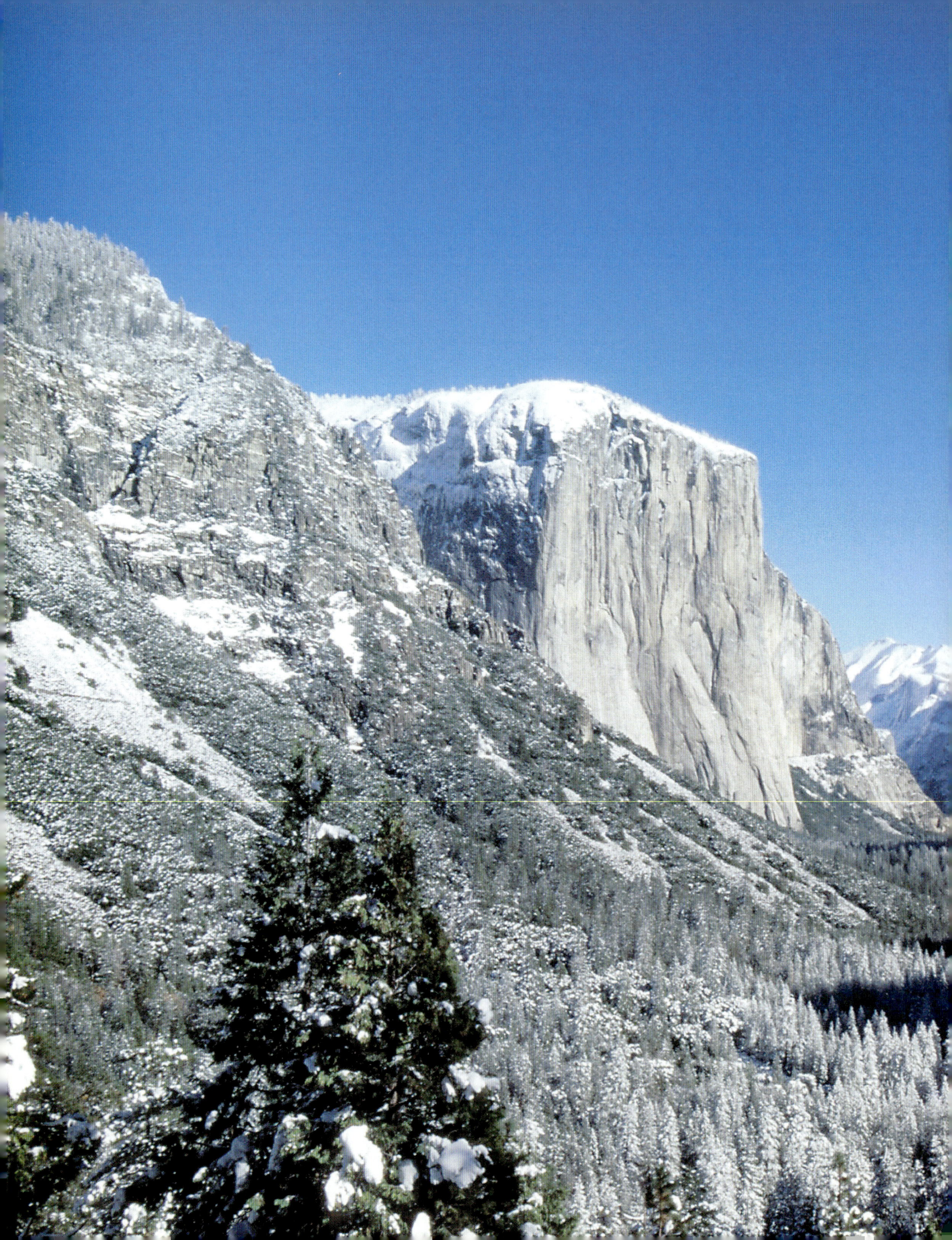

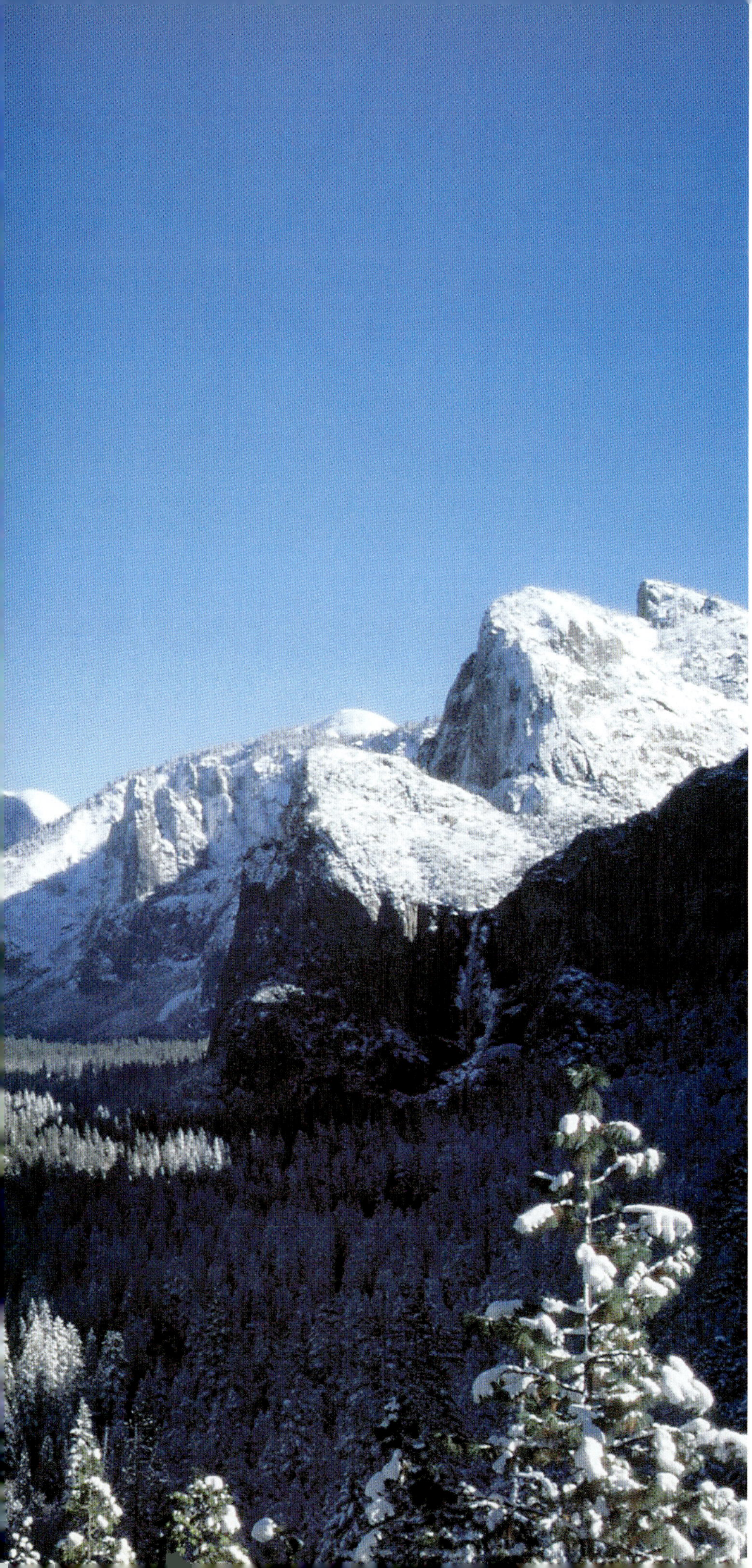

Left

VIEW FROM INSPIRATION POINT

The Wawona Tunnel travels a little less than a mile underground, burrowing beneath the hard granite of Turtleback Dome. Built in 1933, the tunnel bypasses the old, more difficult route over Inspiration Point, which traveled above Turtleback Dome. Now the view from the east end of the Wawona Tunnel provides the first look into the valley. A trail from the parking lot at the tunnel leads to Inspiration Point, less than 1,000 feet above. The views at both locations are both striking and remarkably similar. El Capitan rises majestically out of the forested valley floor on the left, while Bridalveil Fall plunges over an enormous, vertical granite wall on the right. Clouds Rest and Half Dome are in the center background of this panoramic view.

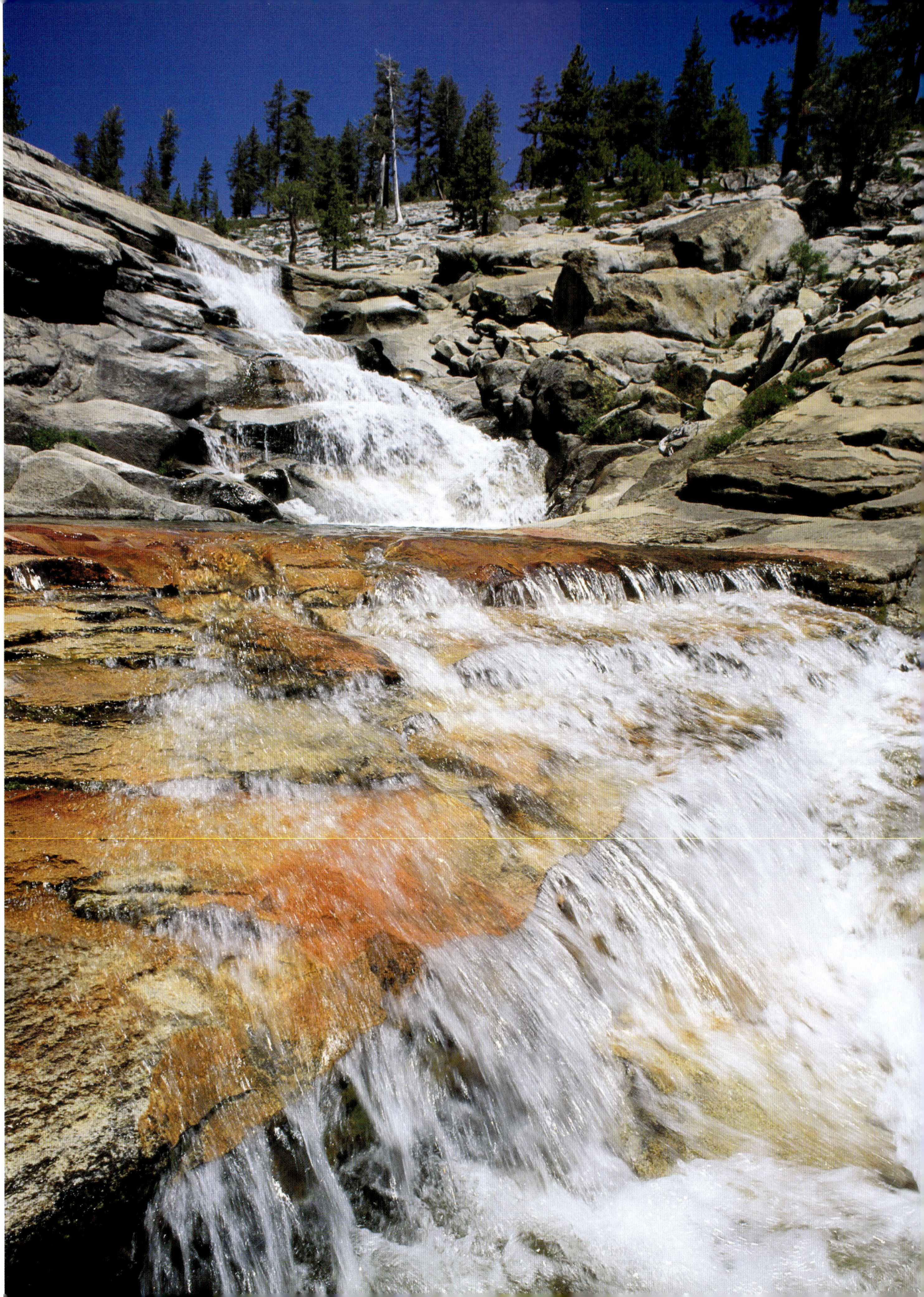

Left

TOP OF RIBBON FALL

With a drop of 1,612 feet, Ribbon Fall is the highest single-drop waterfall in North America, although Upper, Lower, and Middle Yosemite Falls together total a 2,425-feet drop. Ribbon Fall, seen here pouring over the lip of the valley just west of El Capitan, is usually dry by mid-summer.

Right

MOUNT WATKINS

Carlton Watkins first visited Yosemite in 1861, when he was 32 and already an established photographer. He made a series of stunning 18 x 22-inch landscape photographs, and he continued to photograph Yosemite for the next 20 years. Mount Watkins was named in honor of the photographer for his work with the California State Geological Survey.

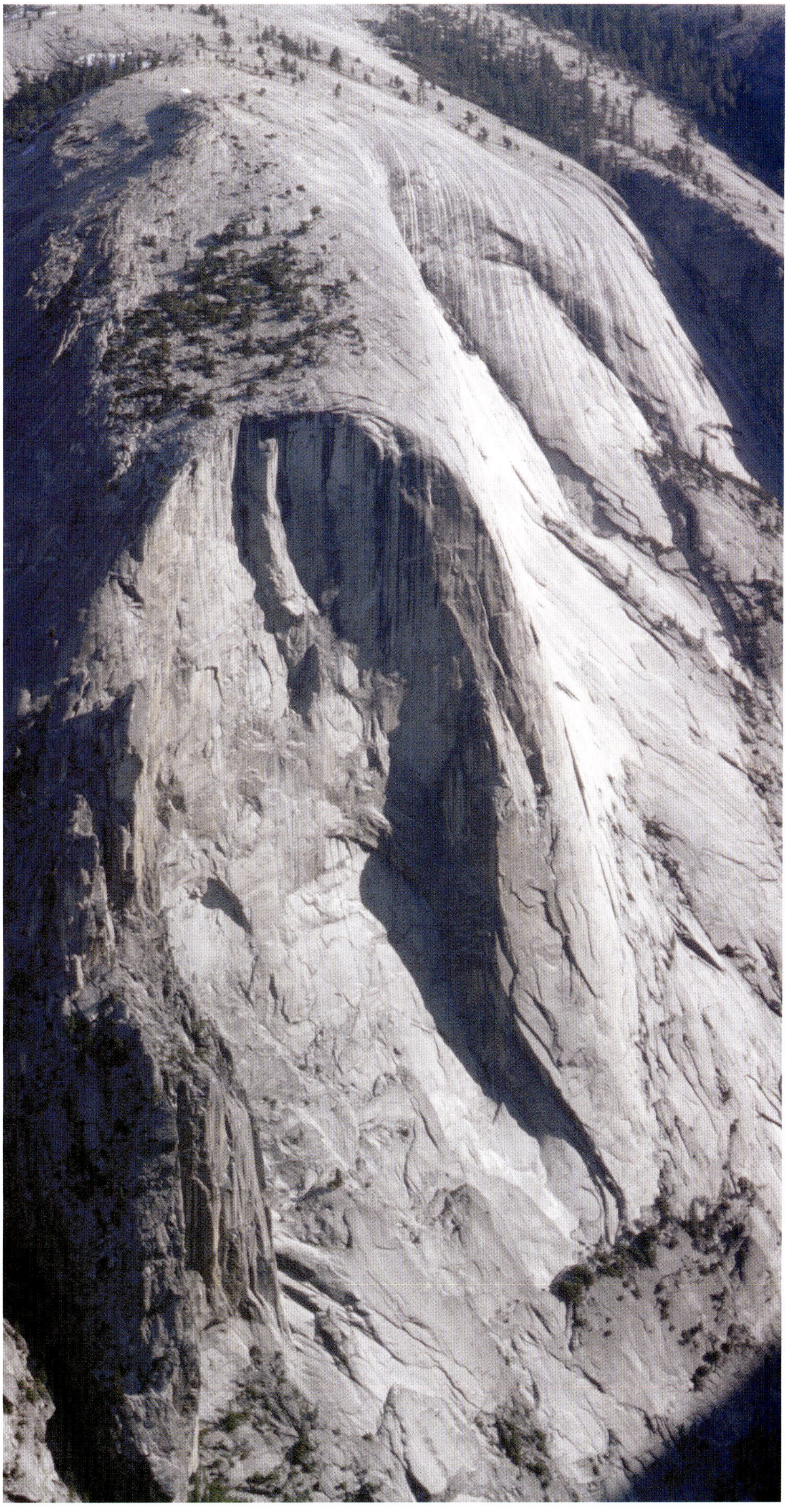

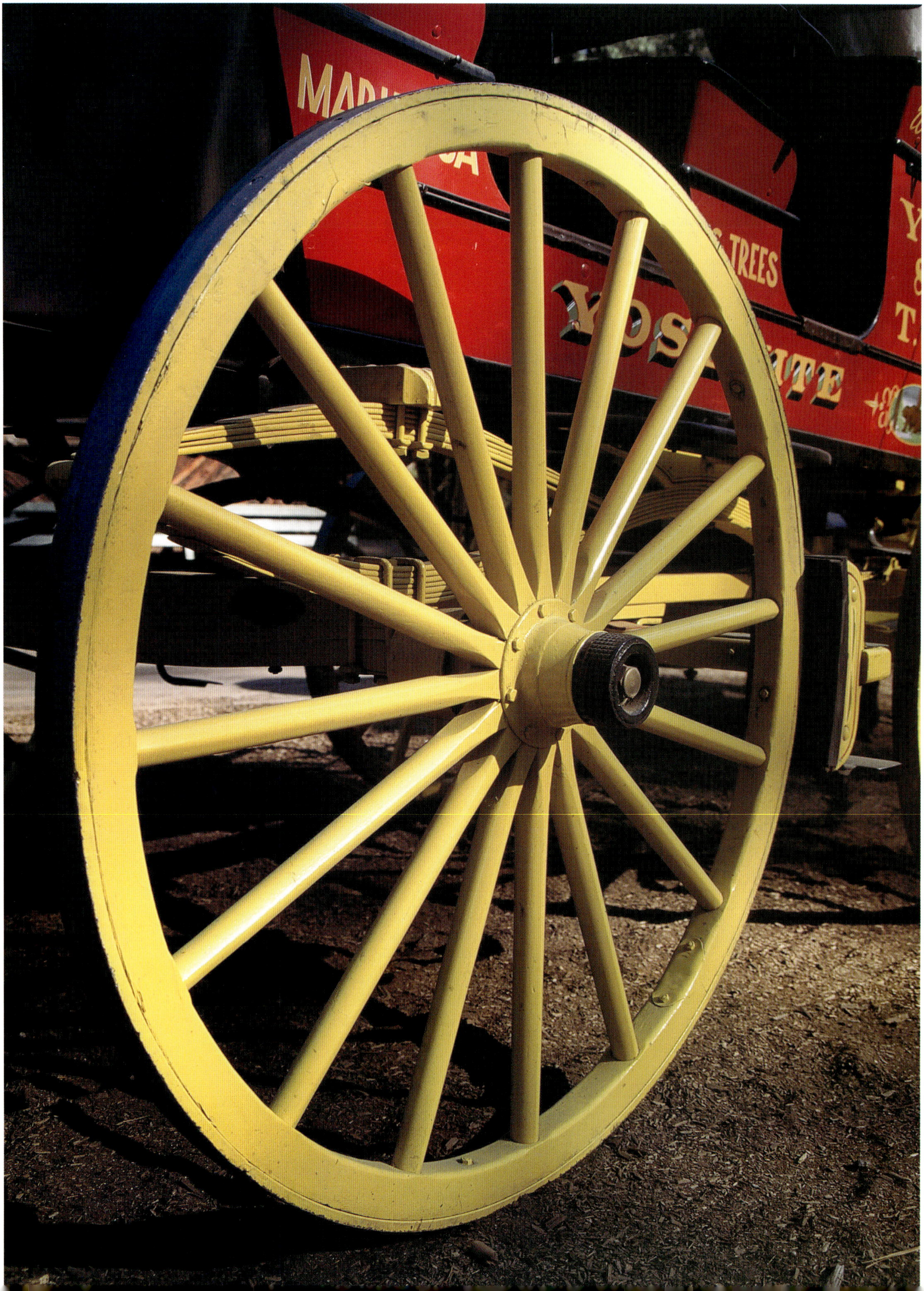
TREES

Left

STAGECOACH

Tourists traveling to and from Yosemite in the nineteenth century and into the early twentieth had to endure a bumpy ride over mountainous roads in horse-drawn stagecoaches. The Yosemite Stage and Turnpike Company operated a fleet of 40 coaches. The last stagecoach to make a run to Wawona left Yosemite Valley in May, 1916, with "Stonewall Jackson" Ashworth at the reins.

Below

MOORE COTTAGE, WAWONA HOTEL

The charmingly Victorian-era Wawona Hotel includes two larger buildings and six "cottages." The Moore Cottage, named after one of the hotel owners and shown here, was built in 1891. Guests can relax on the wide verandas that offer views of the Wawona Meadow, the surrounding forests, and the nine-hole golf course, an unusual feature for a national park.

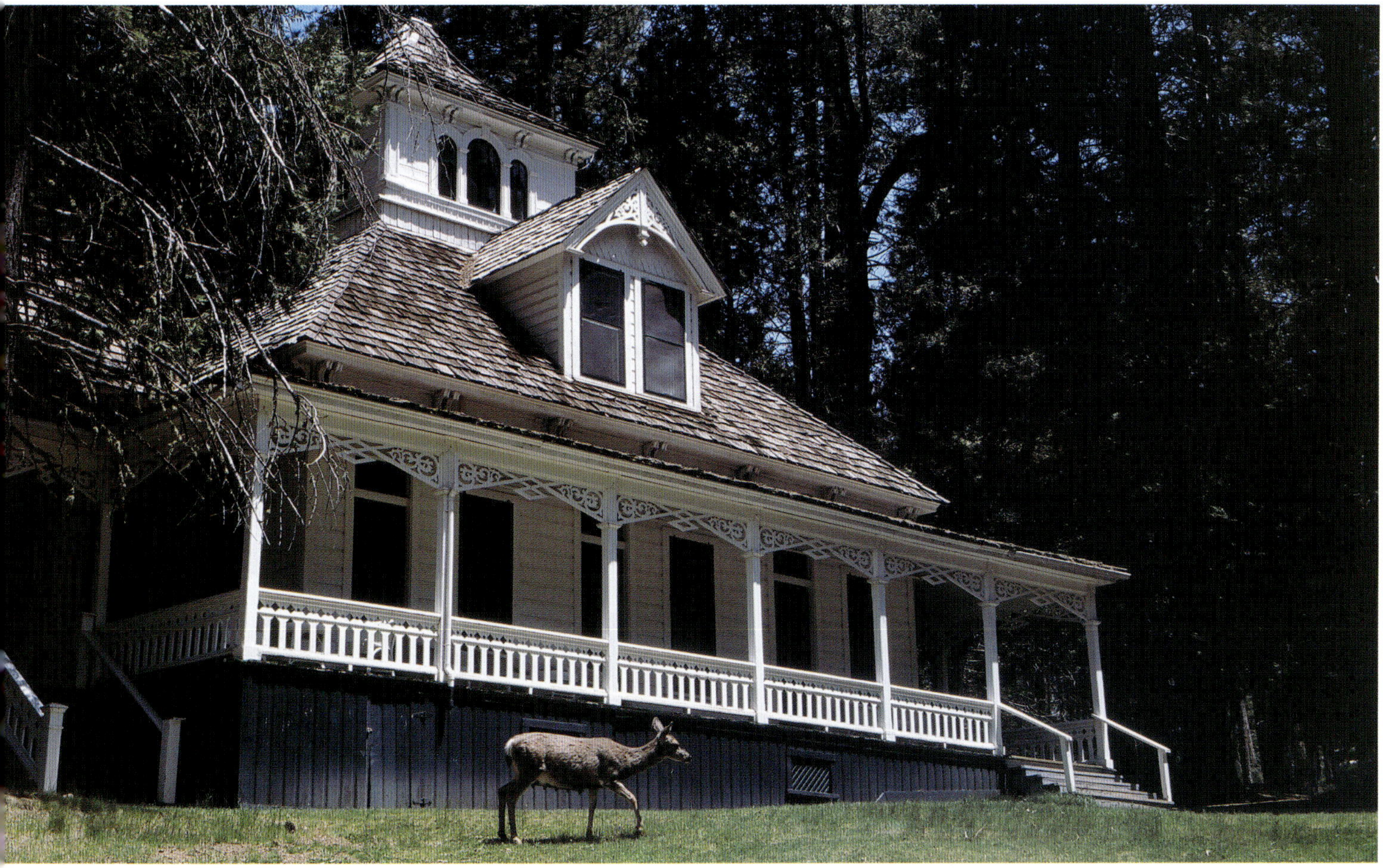

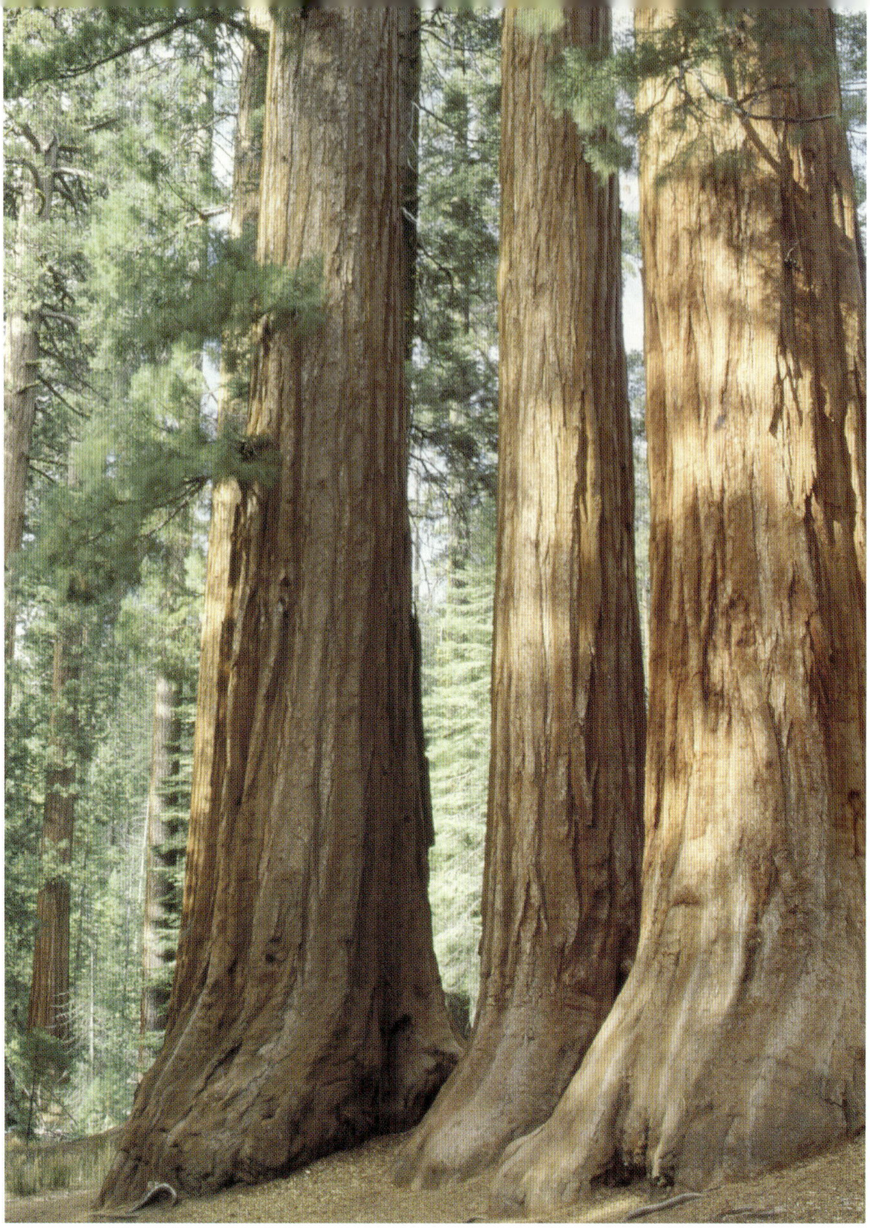

Above

GIANT SEQUOIAS

There are three groves of sequoias in the park. The Mariposa Grove is near the south entrance station and about seven miles from Wawona. The less accessible Merced and Tuolumne Groves are near Crane Flat, off Highway 120.

Right

MARIPOSA GROVE GIANT SEQUOIAS

Yosemite Valley and the Mariposa Grove of Giant Sequoias made up the original Yosemite Grant, which was created by the federal government in 1864. California was directed to administer the grant until Yosemite National Park was created in 1890. The grove is located a few miles off Highway 41, near the south entrance to the park. Sometimes called redwoods, and similar to the redwoods found along the coast of California, sequoias in Yosemite can reach as high as 250 feet above the ground.

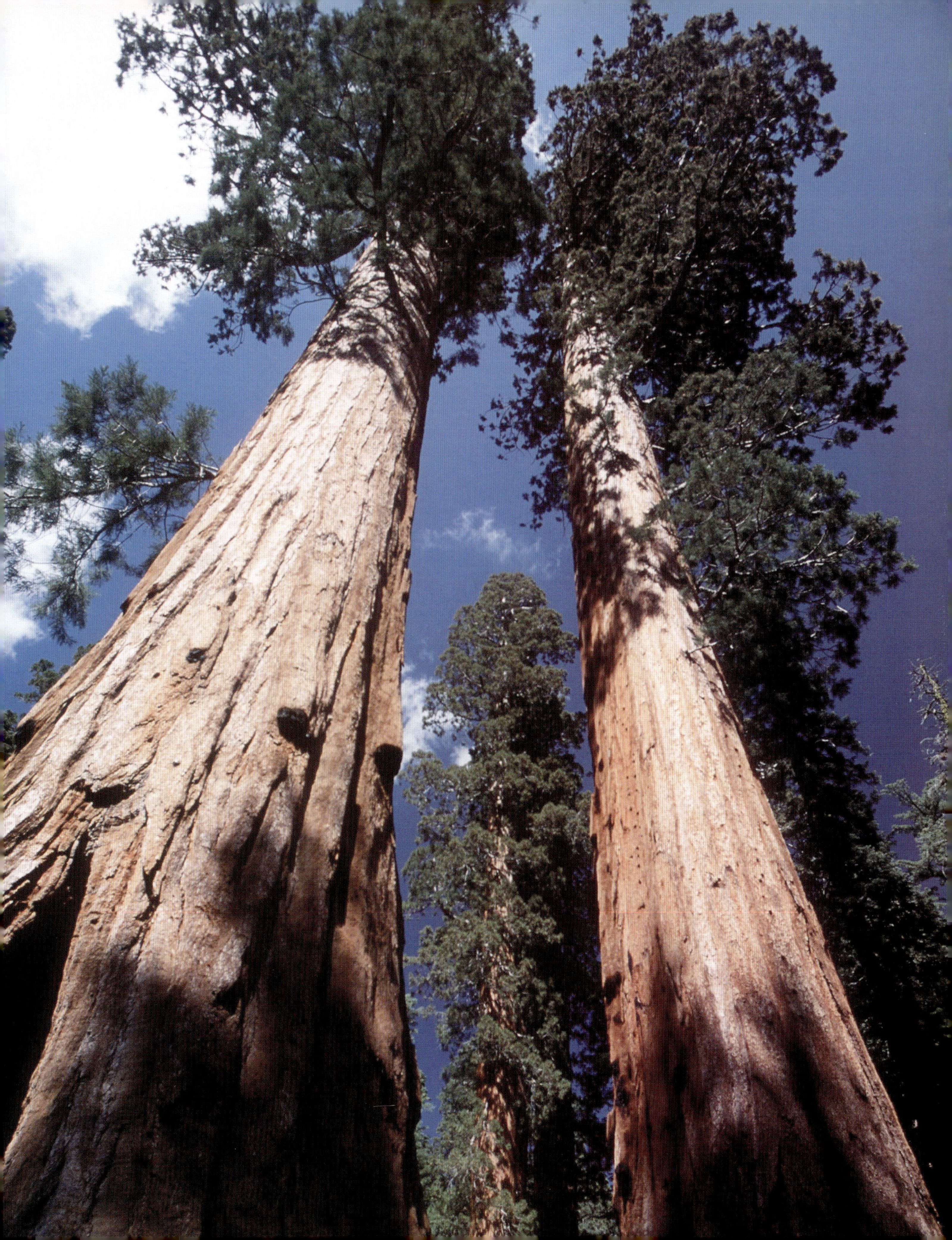

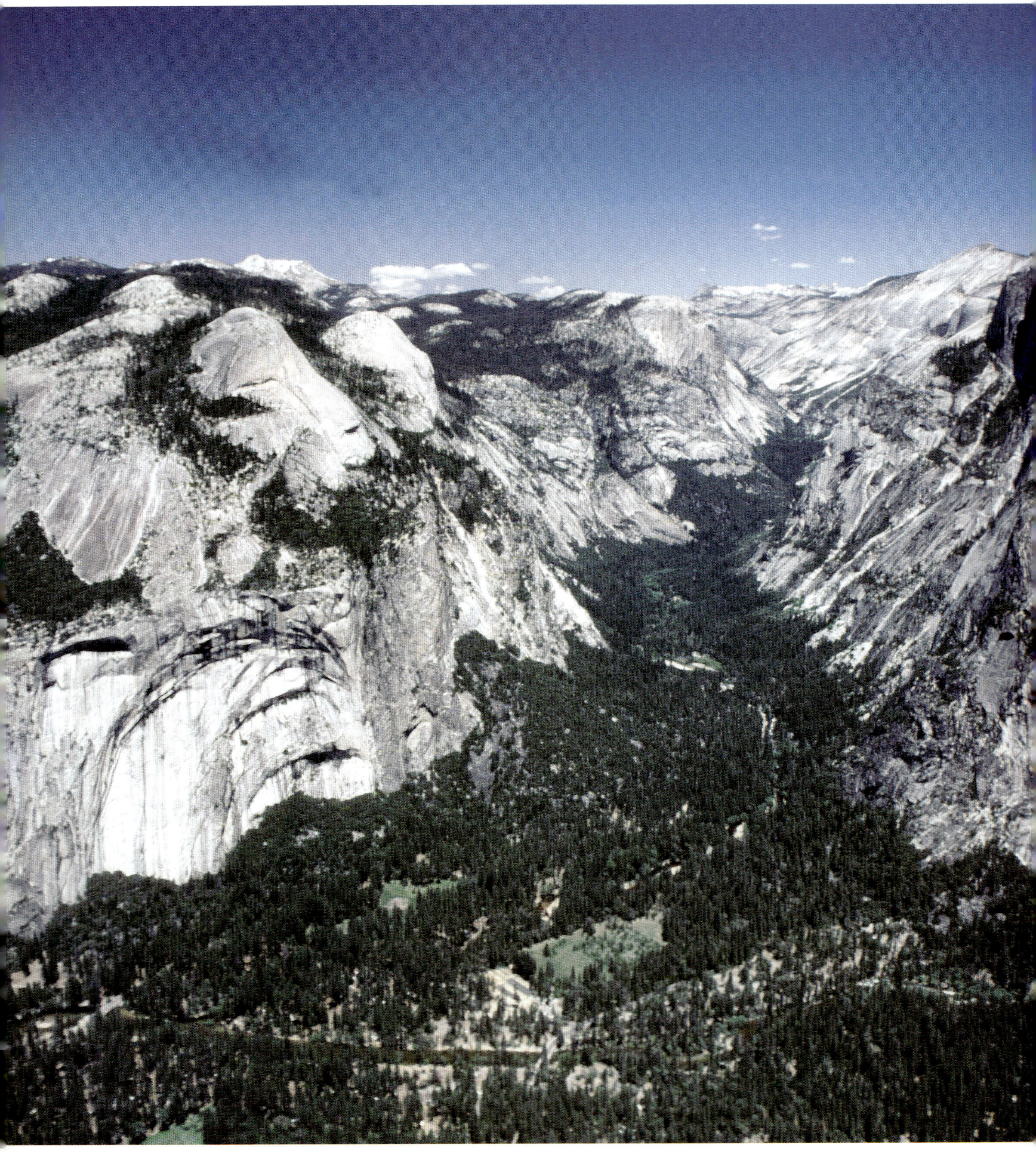

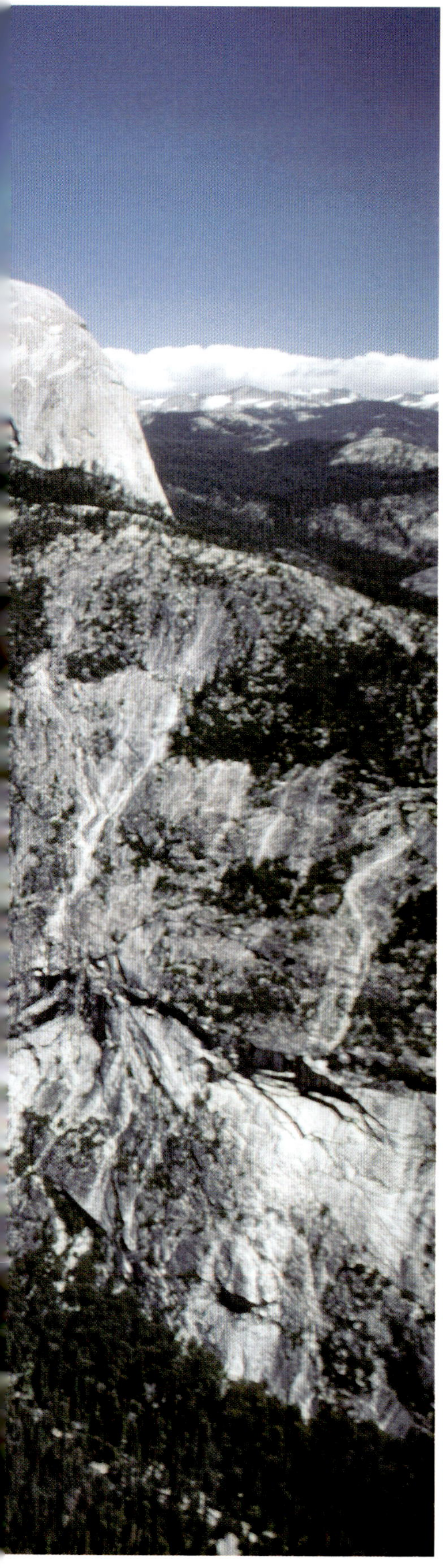

Left

VIEW FROM GLACIER POINT

Glacier Point offers a panoramic view over the High Sierra and into Yosemite Valley, more than 3,000 feet below, and is one of the best places to enjoy Yosemite's landmark rock formations. The most striking feature on view is massive Half Dome.

Below

GLACIER POINT

Glacier Point offers grand views of Yosemite Valley and the high country. The summit, atop spectacular granite cliffs, can be reached by hiking up the arduously steep "Four Mile Trail" from Yosemite Valley, or by road, traveling 32 miles from Yosemite Valley. The park concessionaire offers a bus service for those who don't want to drive or who want to start from the top or the bottom of the trail but not make a round trip on foot.

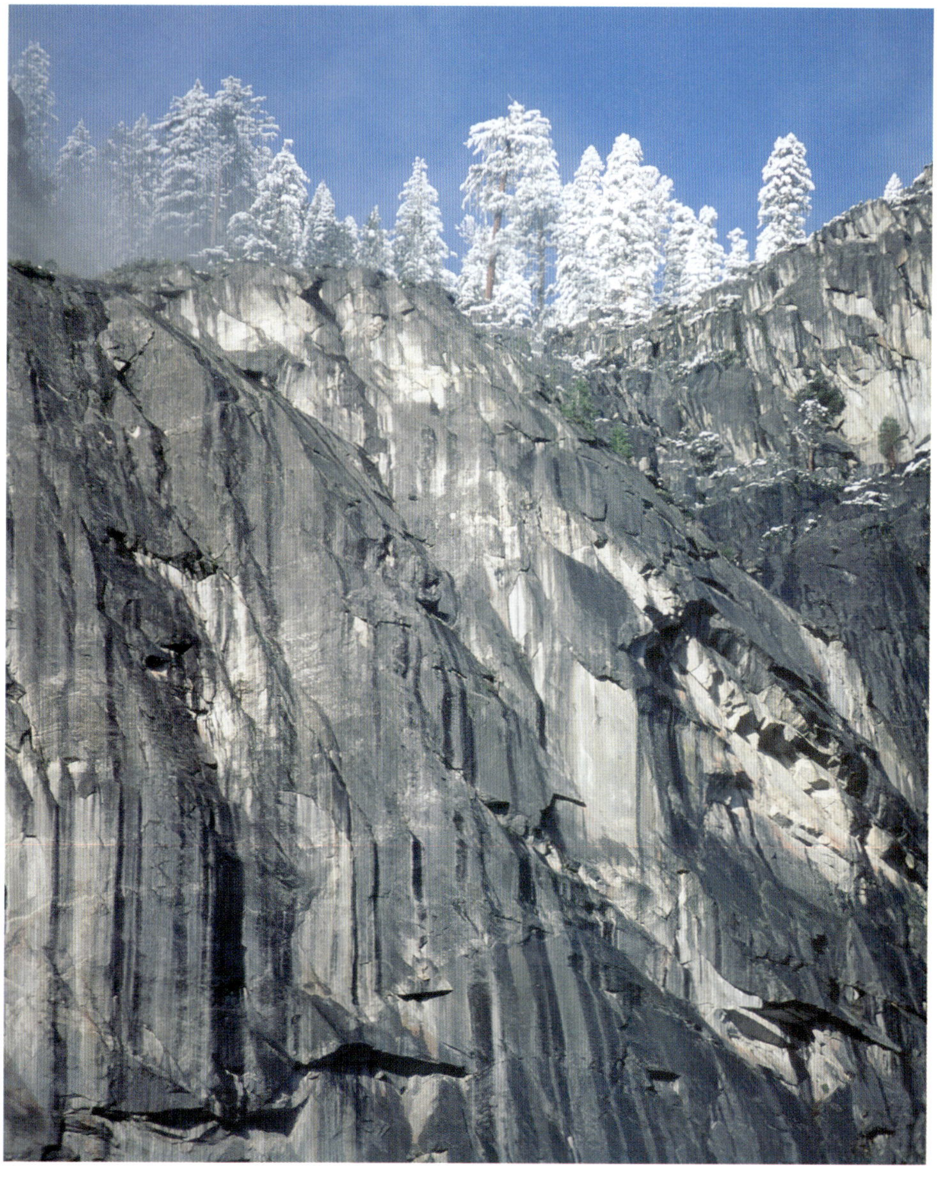

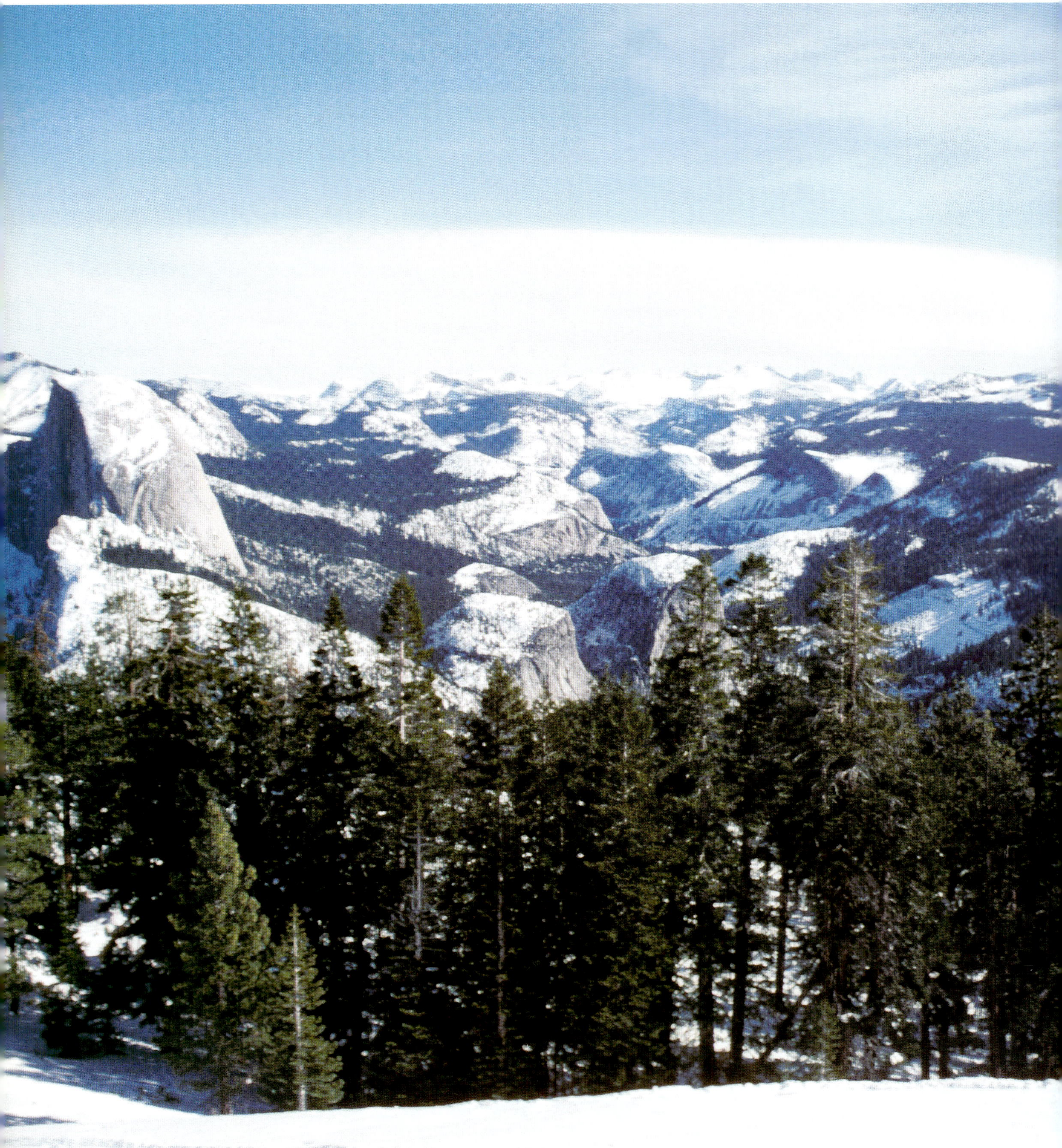

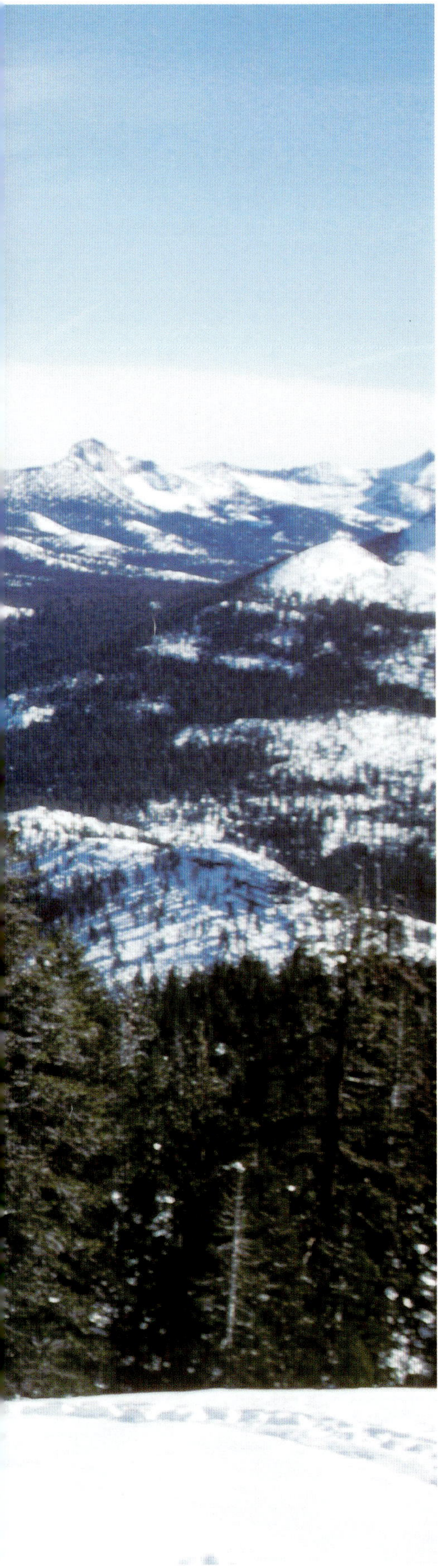

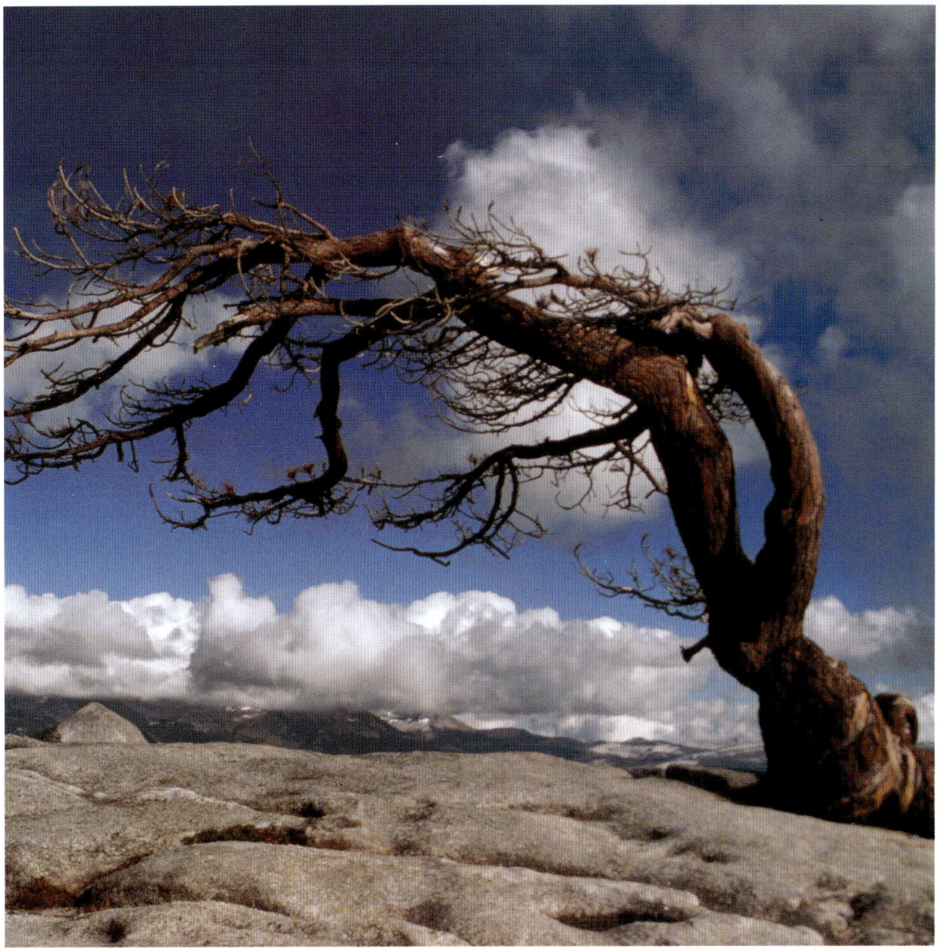

Left

VIEW FROM SENTINEL DOME

Much of Yosemite Valley and portions of the high country are visible from the top of Sentinel Dome. The view includes Half Dome, as well as Vernal and Nevada Falls.

Above

SENTINEL DOME

An easy hike leads from the parking lot along Glacier Point Road to the base of Sentinel Dome. From there it's a slight scramble up the northeast side to reach the top of the dome. The signature Jeffrey pine atop the dome, made famous by photographers such as Ansel Adams and Galen Rowell, has toppled over; however, the view makes the 2.2 mile ascent from parking lot to summit, with it's all-encompassing views of Yosemite Valley and portions of the high country, worth the ascent.

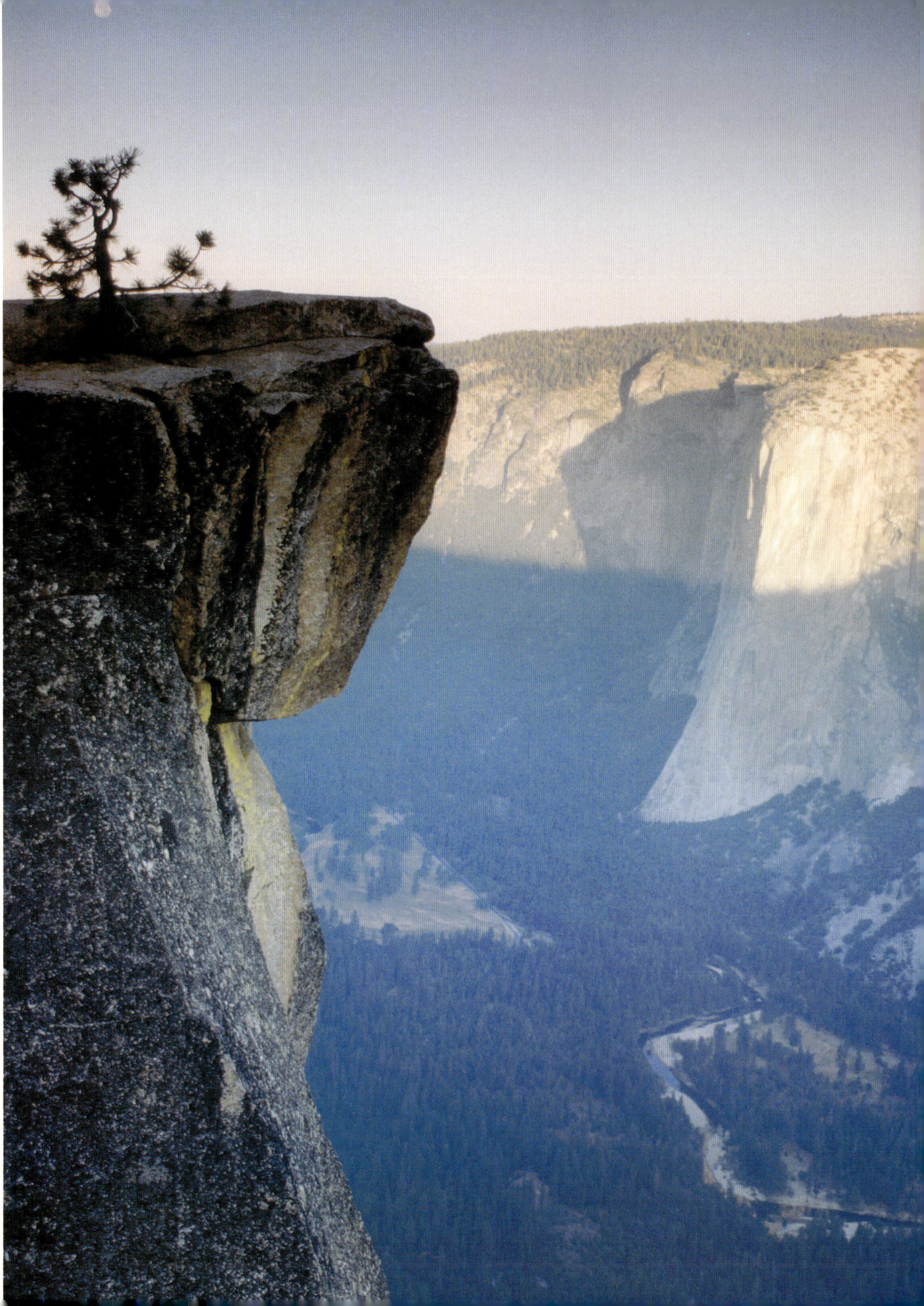

Left

TAFT POINT

Set on the southern rim of Yosemite Valley, Taft Point offers amazing views of the valley, 3,000 feet below.

Below

EICHORN PINNACLE

Climber Conrad Anker stands atop the Eichorn Pinnacle, on the west side of Cathedral Peak. The impressive granite spire was named for Julius Eichorn, who climbed it in 1931. Eichorn Pinnacle and the places explored over the next several pages all require leaving automobiles behind and call for sometimes strenuous walks or climbs of more than a mile. Some of these places are not far above the floor of Yosemite Valley, while others are found in remote locations in the upper reaches of the park.

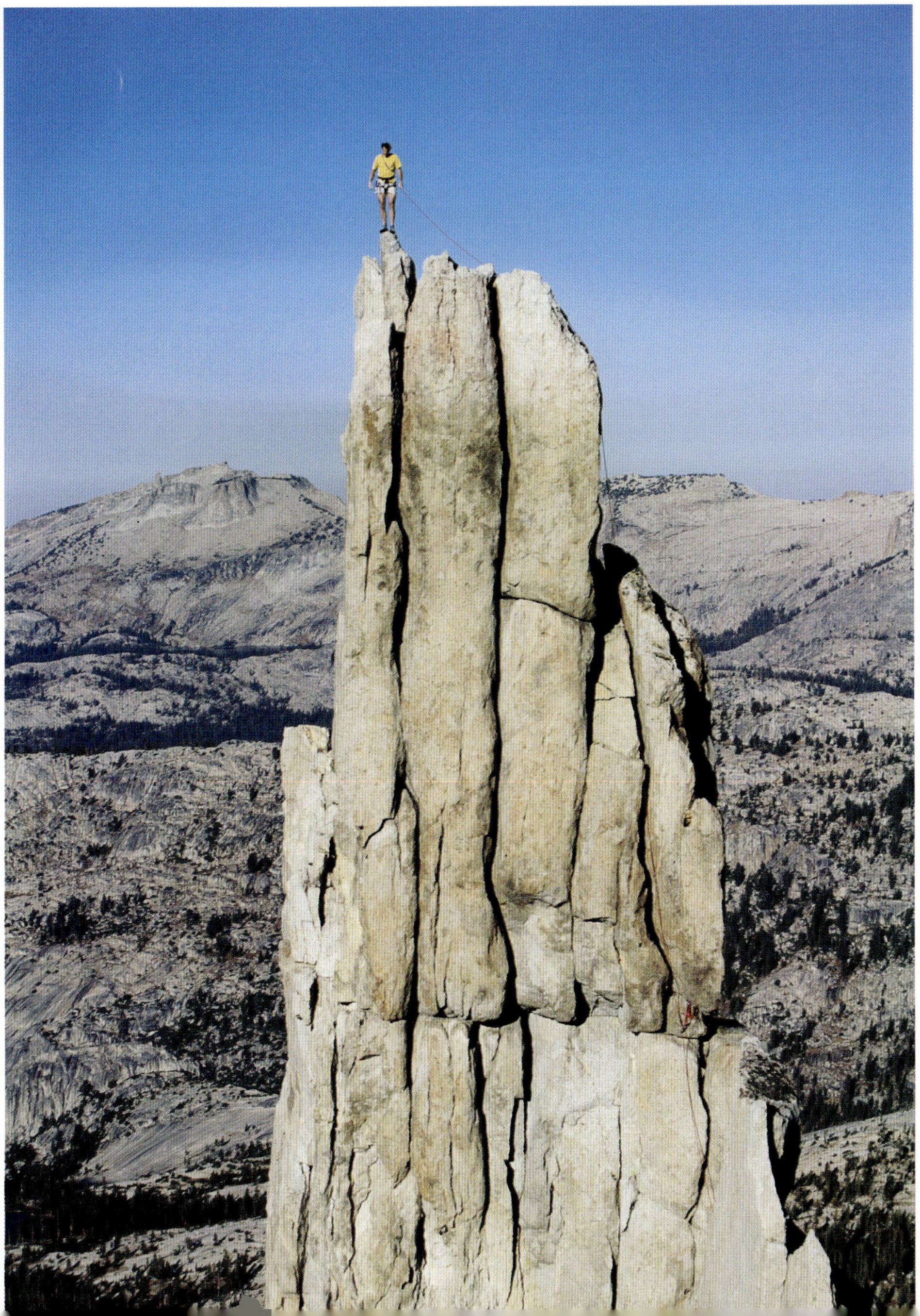

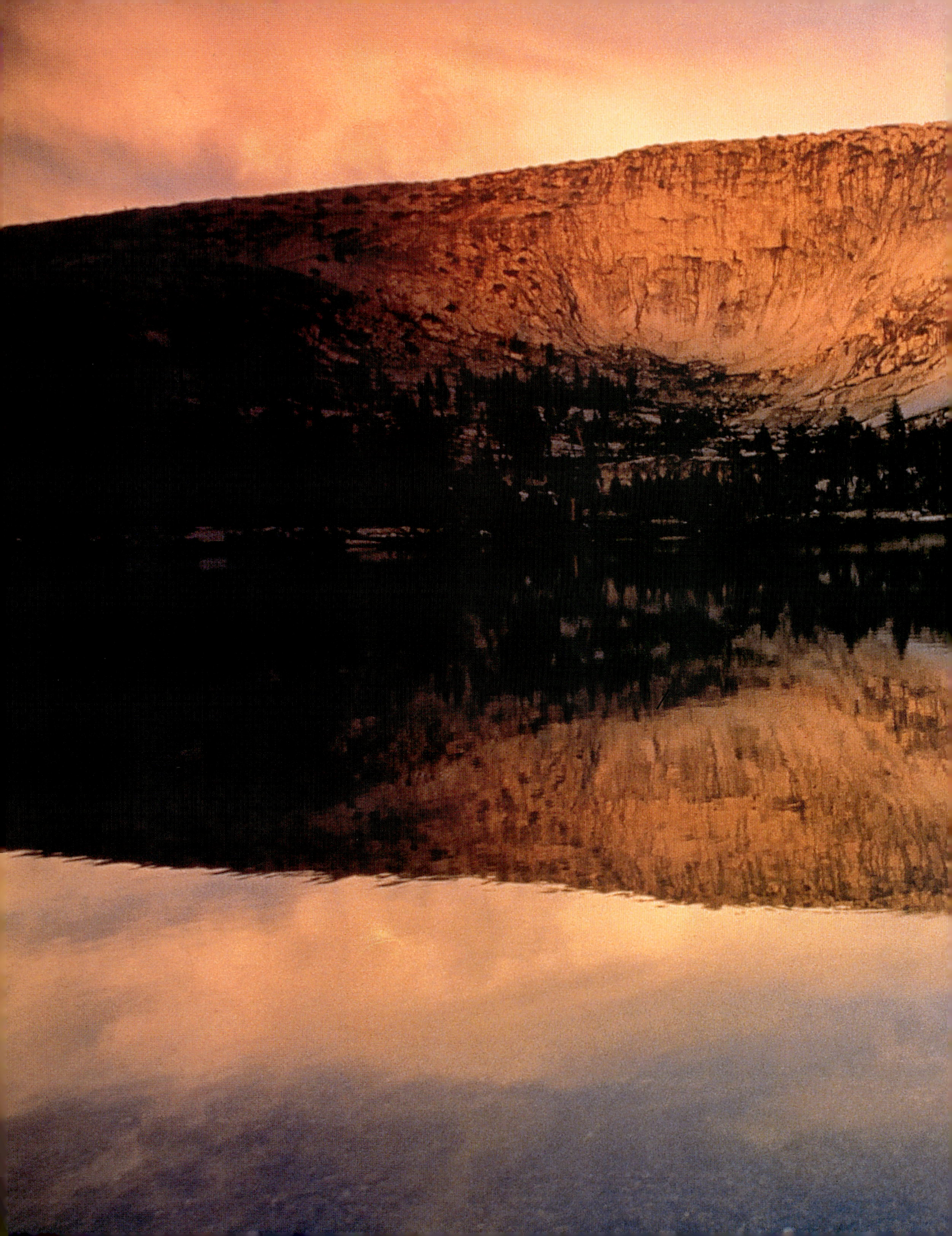

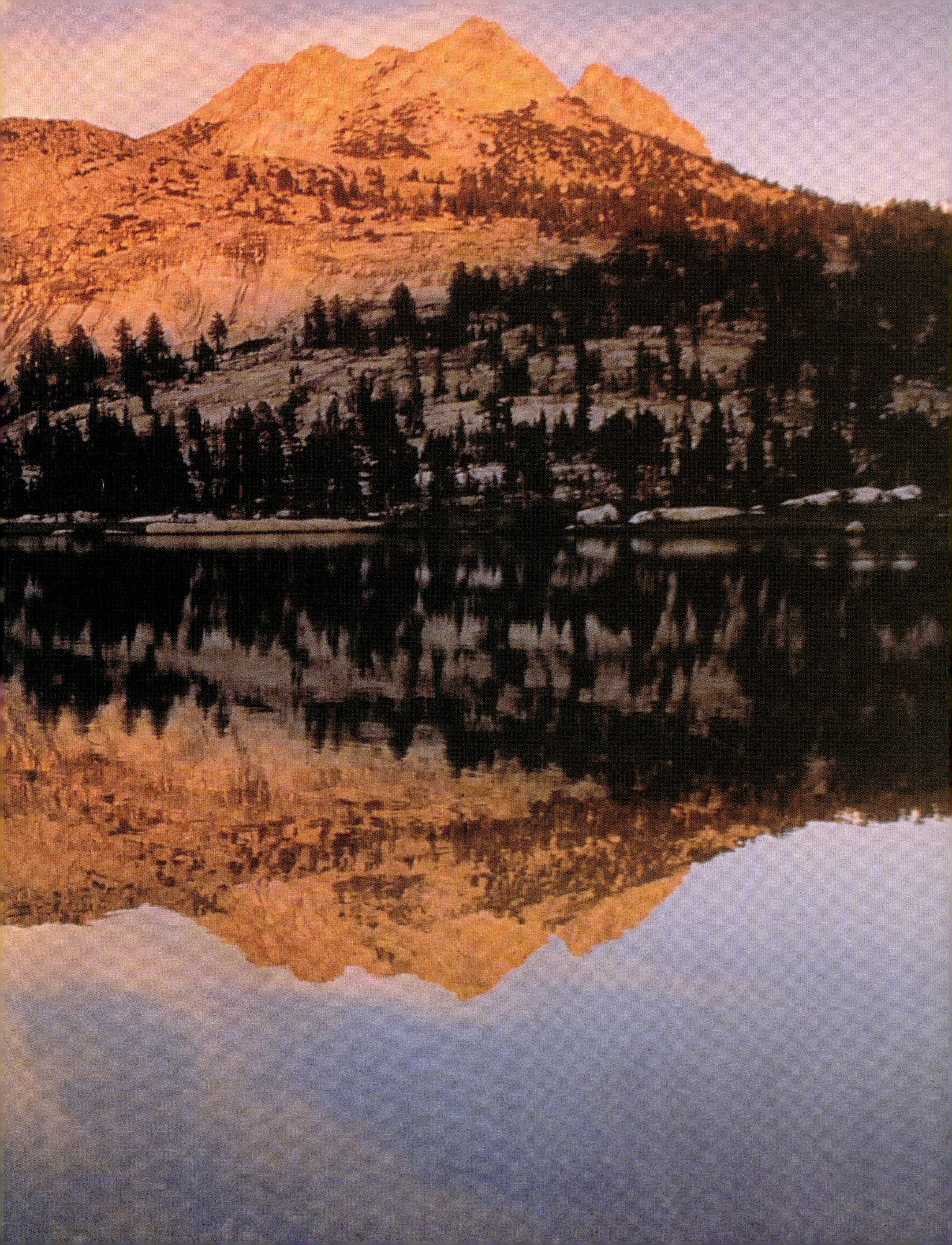

Previous

CATHEDRAL LAKE

Sierra Nevada granite turns from its usual gray color to gold in the fading light of the setting sun at Upper Cathedral Lake.

Right

CLARK RANGE

Looking south from the summit of Mount Hoffman, massive Clouds Rest (center) and Half Dome (right) are visible in the middle distance. The Clark Range is in the far distance in the upper left; this collection of impressive and remote peaks was named for Galen Clark, who came to the park in 1855 and was the first designated Guardian of Yosemite.

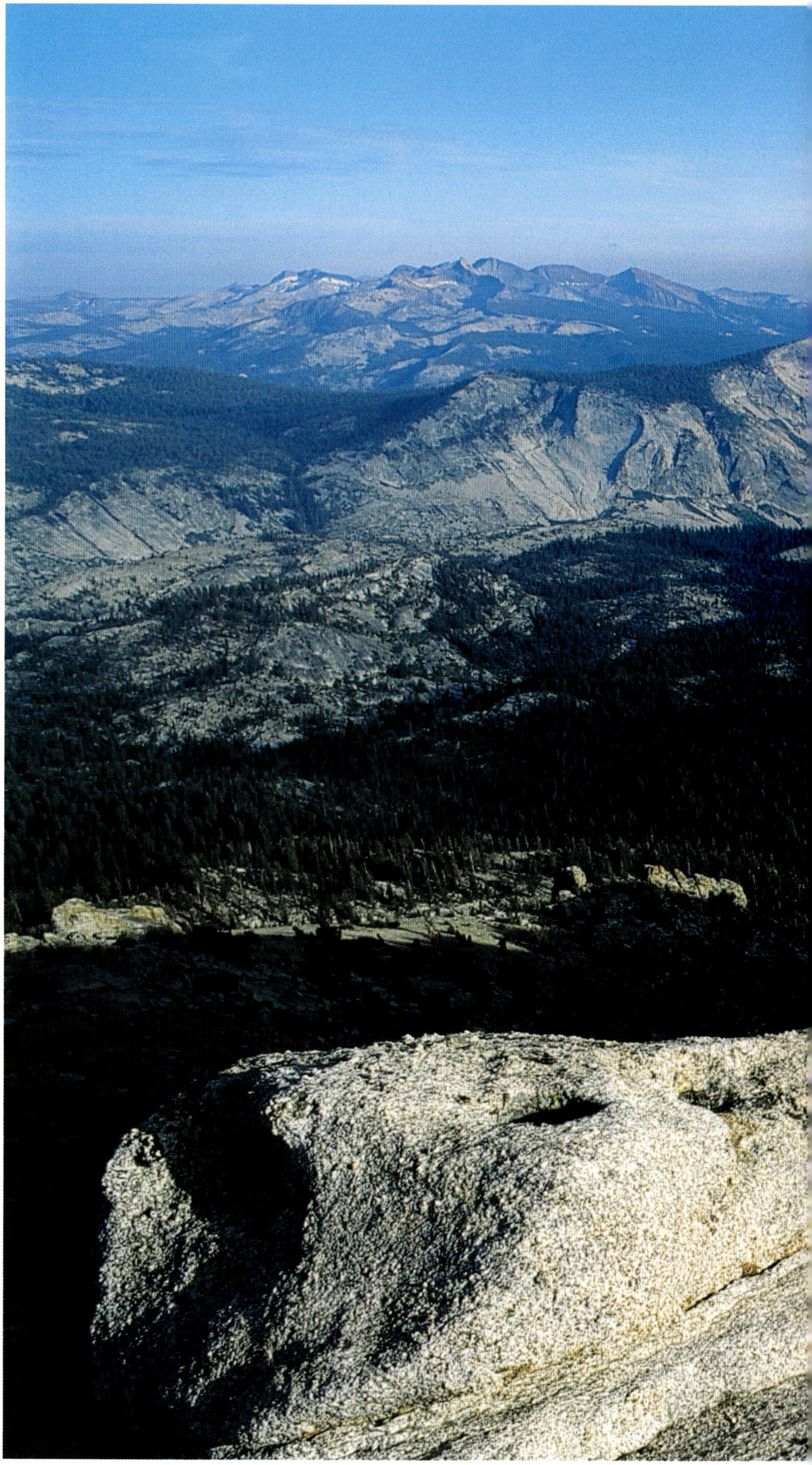

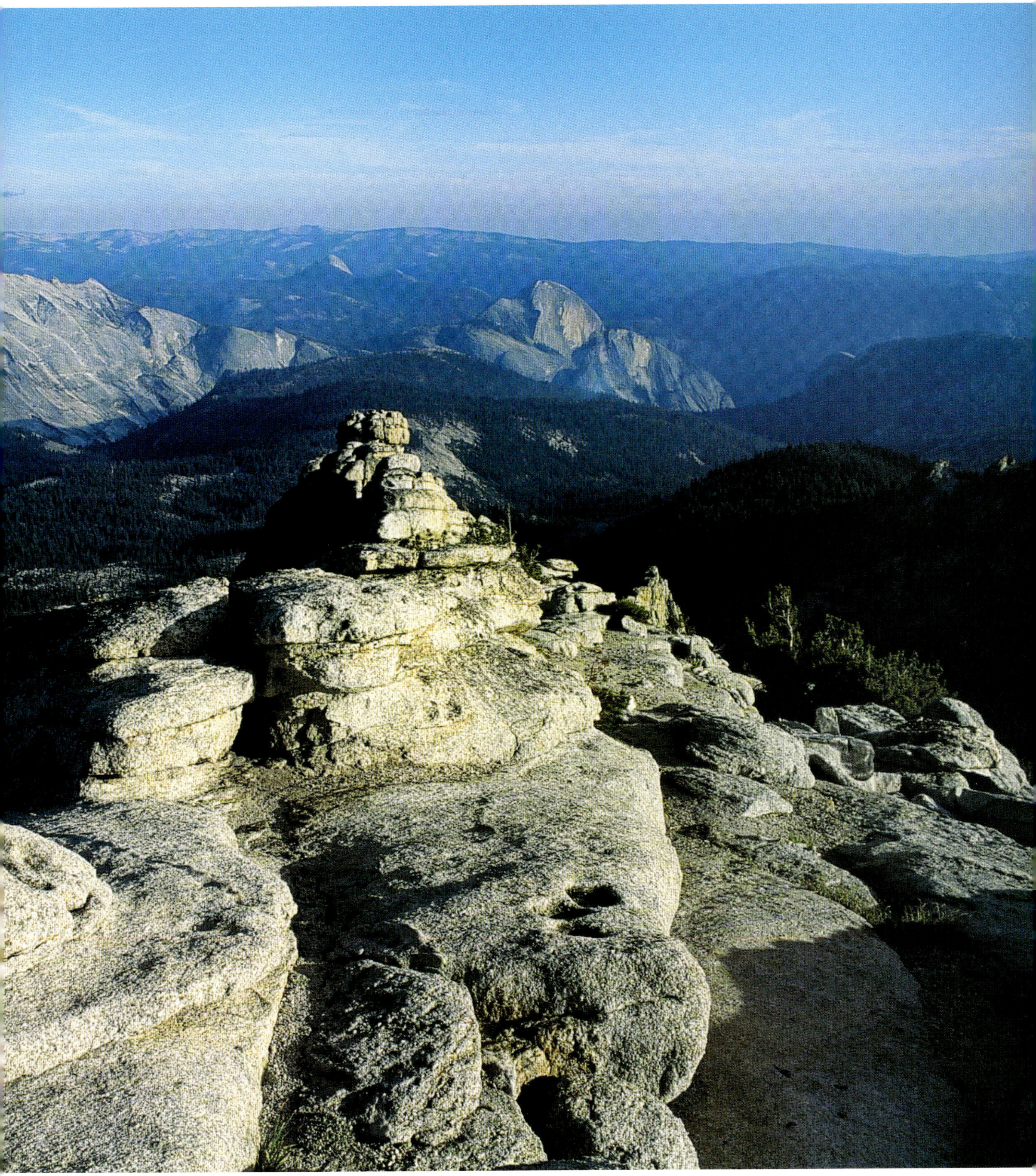

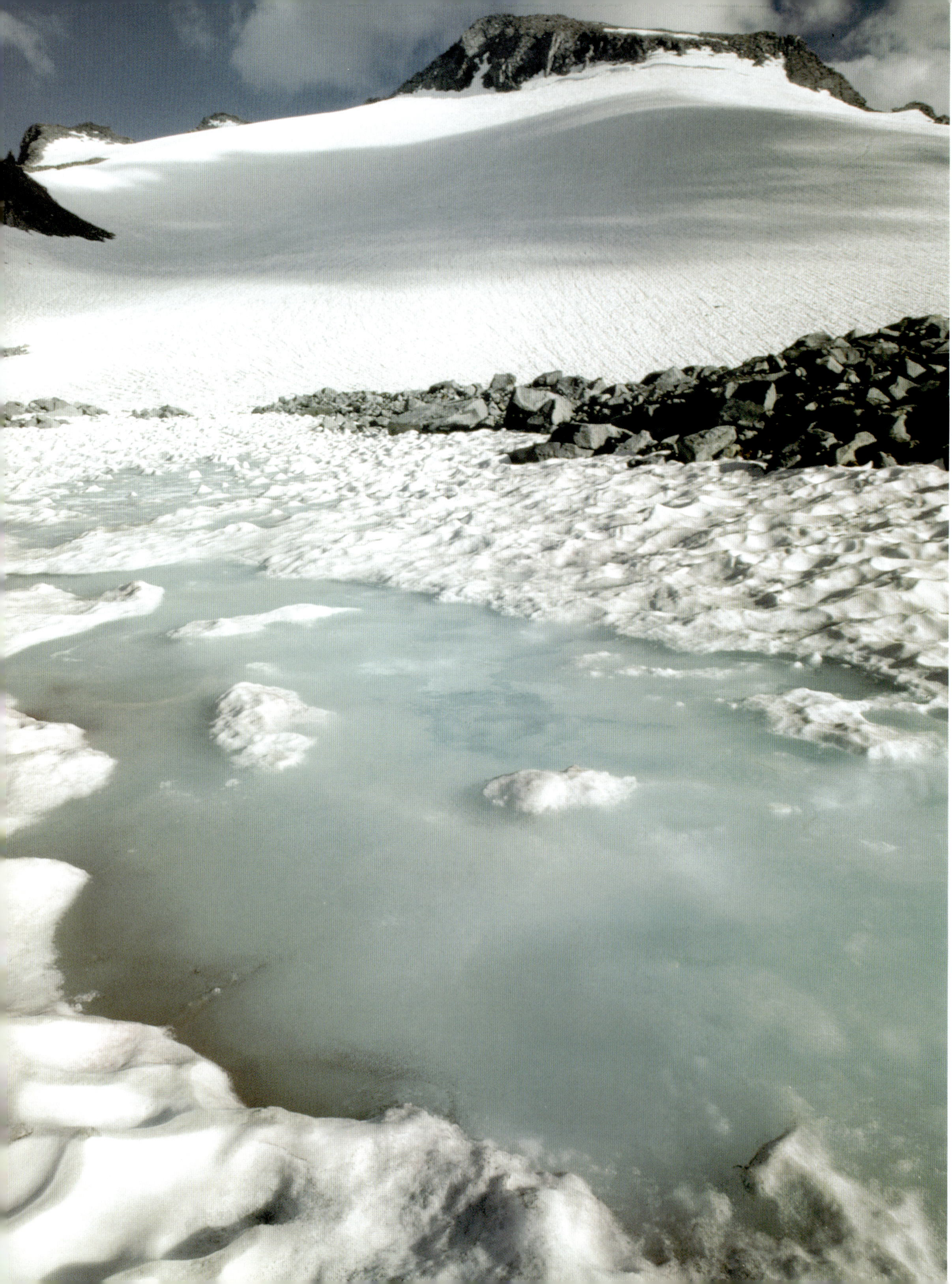

Left

LYELL GLACIER

Situated on the northern flank of Mount Lyell, the highest mountain in the park at 13,144 feet above sea level, the Lyell Glacier is the largest glacier in the park.

Right

NEVADA FALL

As with Vernal Fall, Lafayette Bunnell gave Nevada Fall its name in 1851, when he entered Yosemite with the Mariposa Battalion. He chose the name because Nevada Fall, which drops 594 feet, was "closest to the Sierra," and because he considered the name a "wintery companion" for Vernal Fall. The top of Nevada Fall is in the mouth of Little Yosemite Valley.

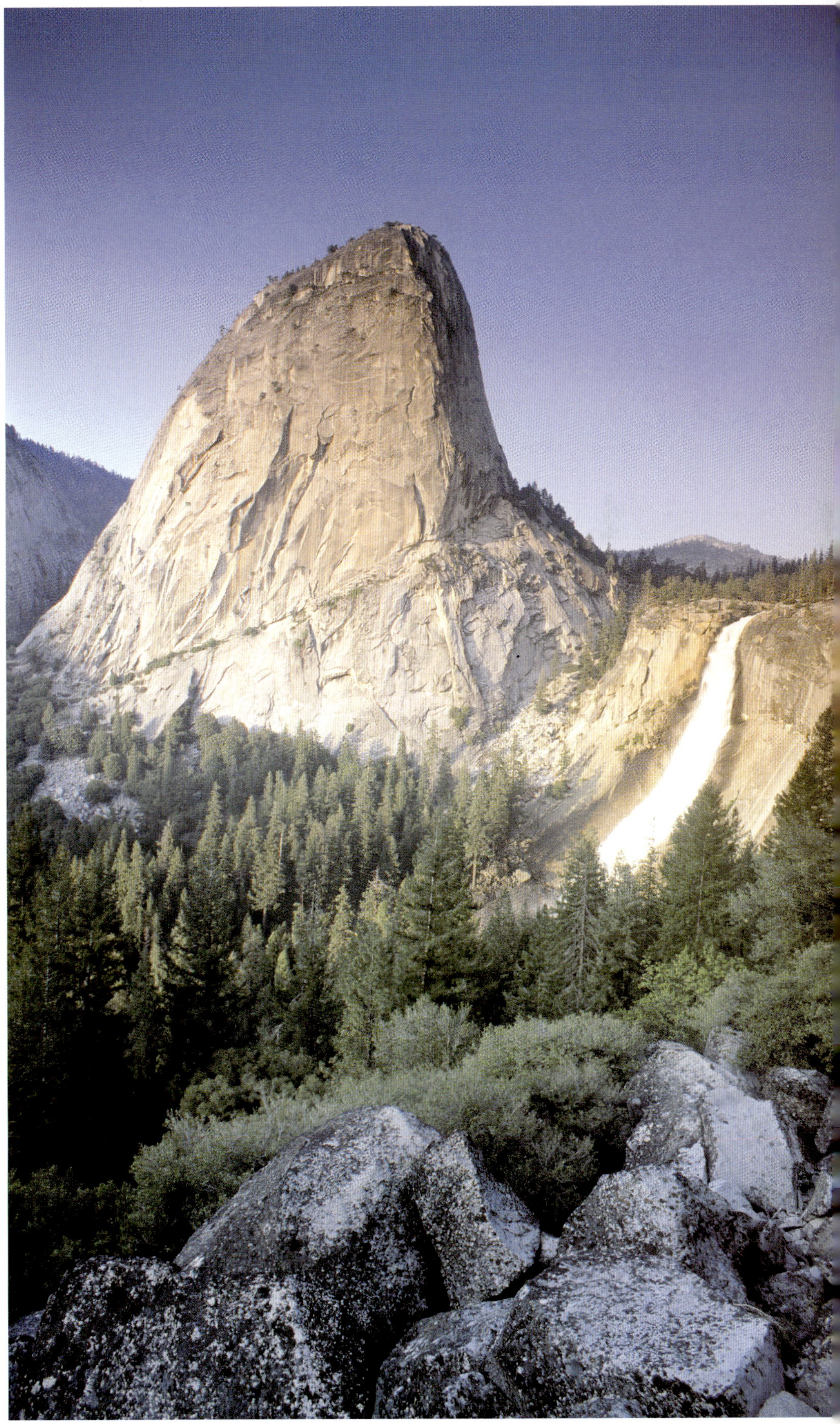

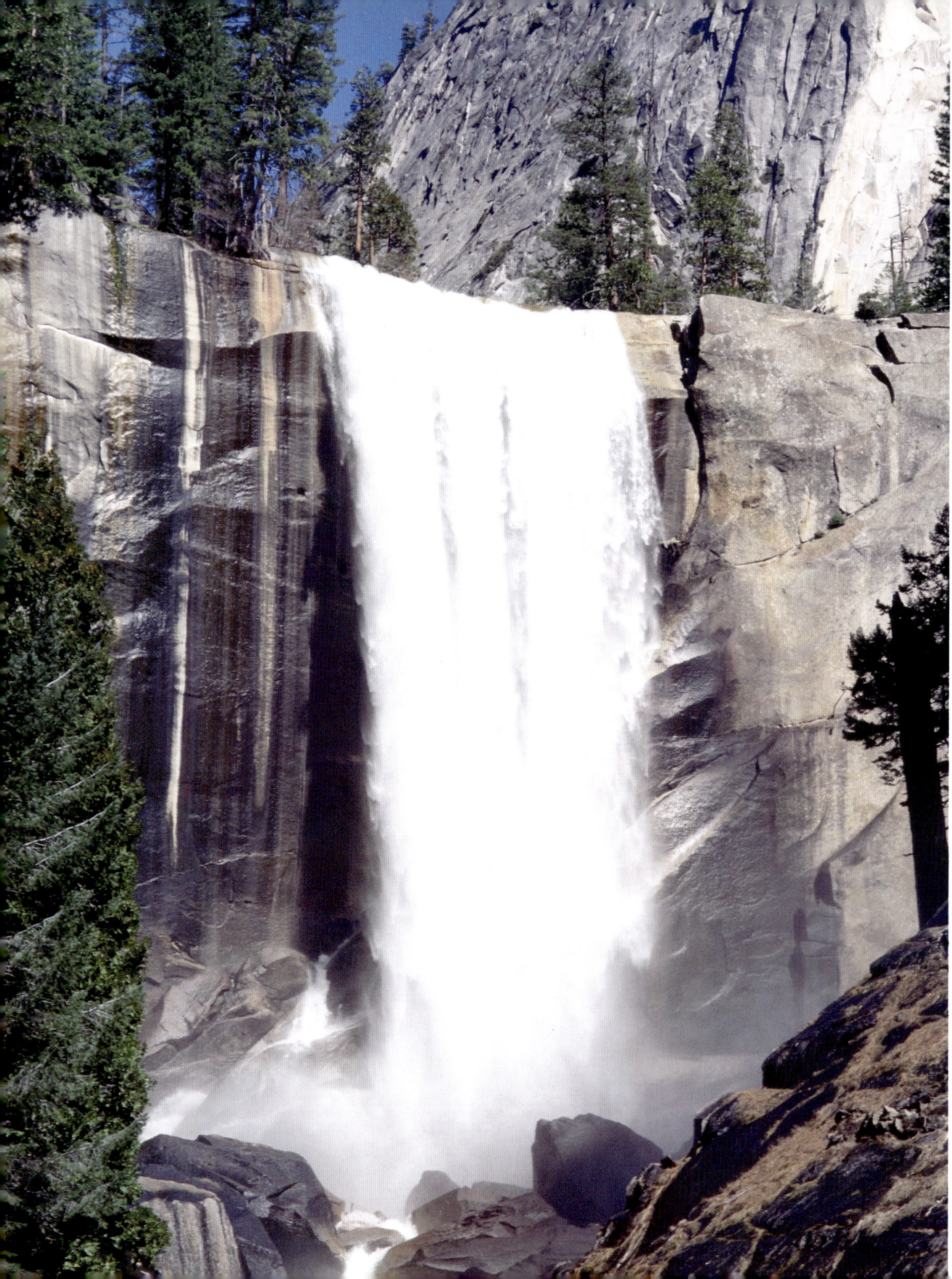

Left

VERNAL FALL

The 0.7-mile walk to the viewpoint of Vernal Fall from Yosemite Valley begins at Happy Isles, where two small islands break the flow of the Merced River. Vernal Fall makes a drop of 317 feet. Lafayette Bunnell named the fall in 1851, writing some years later that the spray during the heat of summer reminded him of an April rain shower. The steep walk to the top of the fall, known as the Mist Trail, includes a staircase of 600 granite steps. In spring and summer, the spray off Vernal Fall can feel like a hard rain, but by late summer the water is sometimes reduced to a trickle.

Below

WATERWHEEL FALL

Waterwheel Fall is actually a steep cascade in a canyon of granite located 1,500 feet below Tuolumne Meadows, in the Grand Canyon of the Tuolumne River. The shape of the granite causes the cascade to throw out a series of "waterwheels" that reach 20 feet into the air.

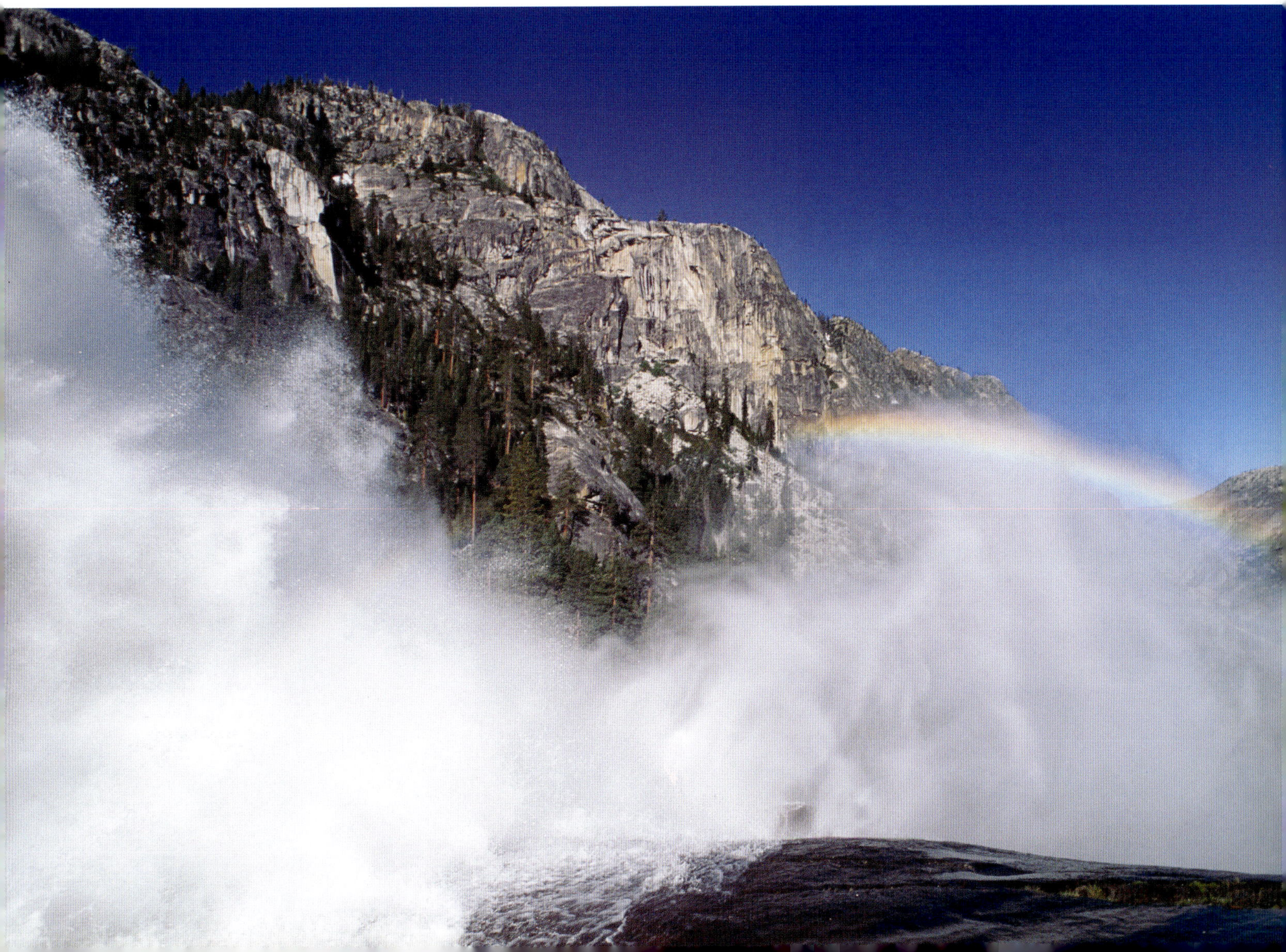

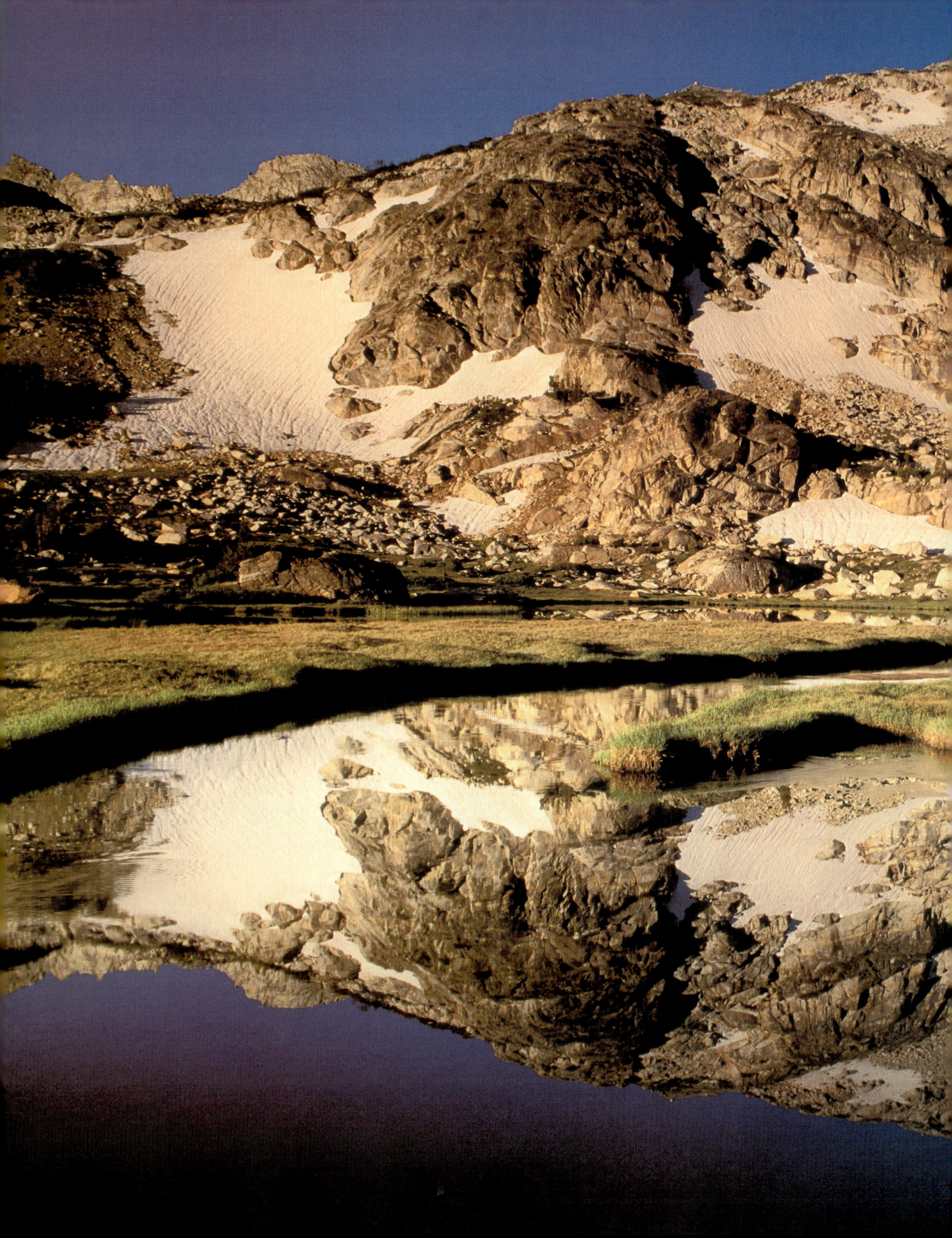

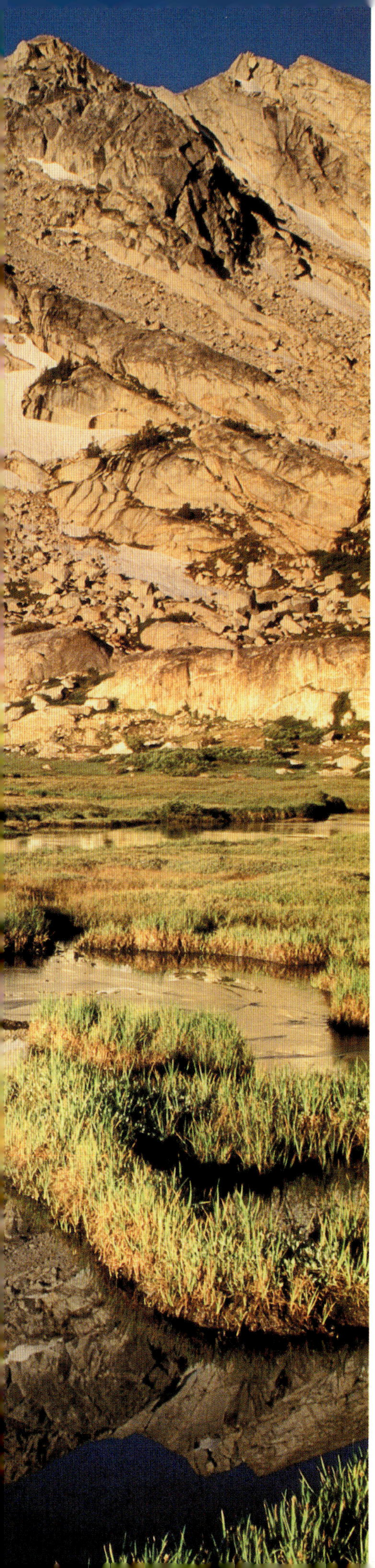

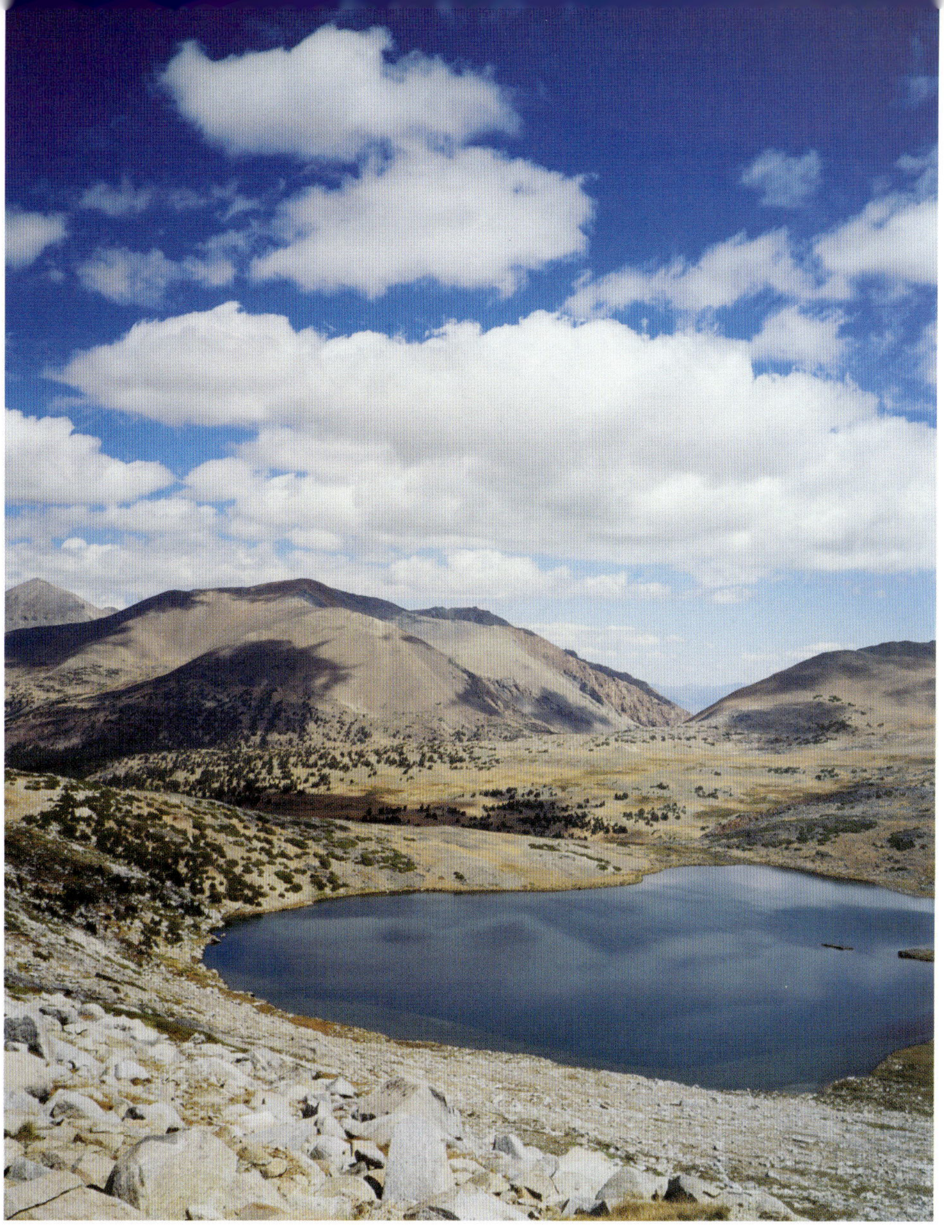

Above

HELEN LAKE

Helen Lake is nestled beneath Mount Lyell, in the southeastern region of Yosemite. The lake was named for the daughter of George Otis Smith, the director of the United States Geological Survey.

Left

MOUNT CONNESS

Mount Conness is not only a tall peak (12,590 feet), it's also a massive mountain. Named for John Conness, a United States senator from California and a native of Ireland, the remote mountain rises along the crest of the High Sierra, in the northeast corner of the park.

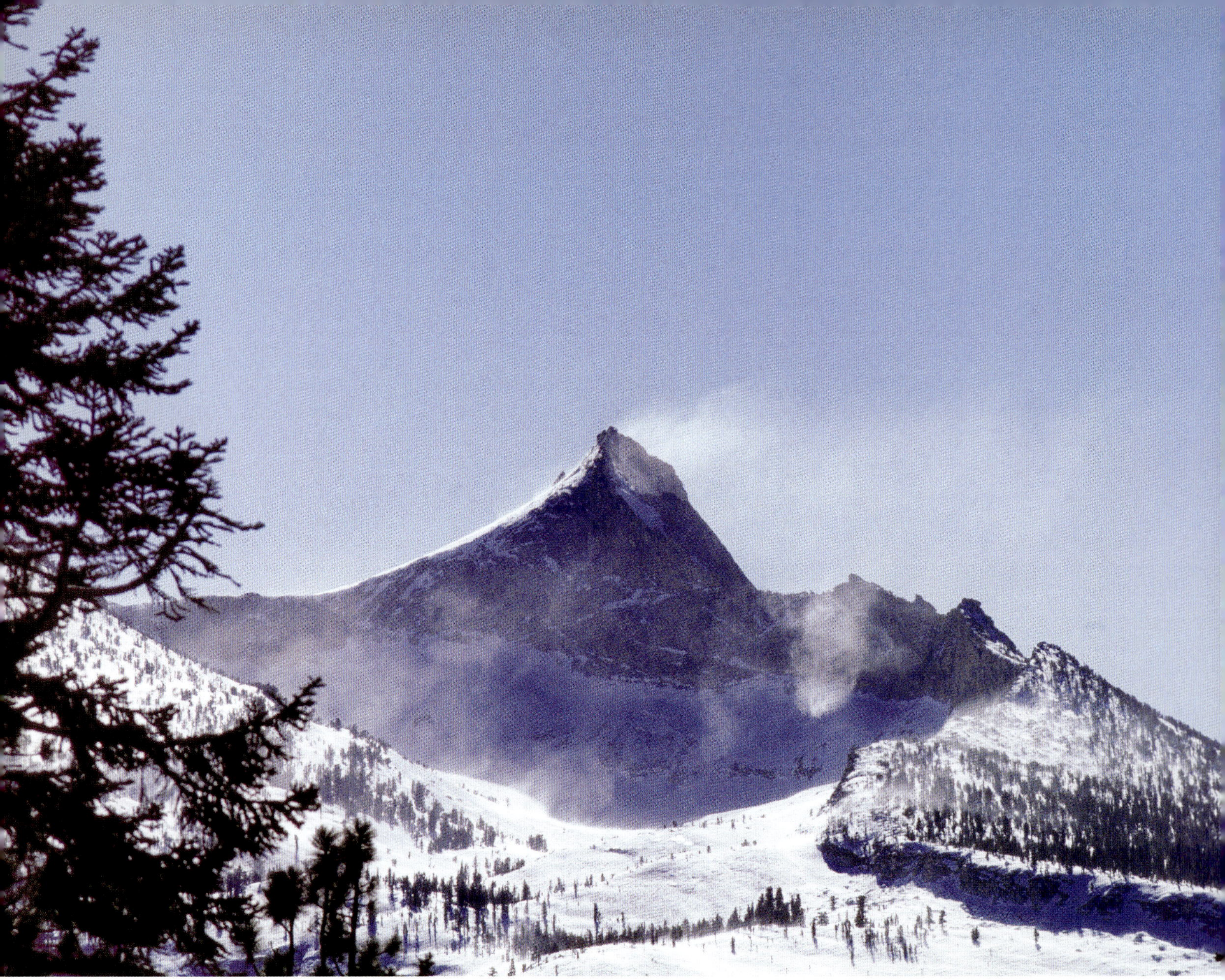

Above

MOUNT CLARK

Once known as the Obelisk, for its sharp features, Mount Clark was first climbed in 1866 by members of the California Geological Survey. In 1878, Lieutenant M. M. Macomb Mount ascended the peak; he set up his surveyor's transit to help produce what would become the most accurate map of Yosemite for many years.

Right

LITTLE YOSEMITE VALLEY AT SUNSET

The aptly named Little Yosemite Valley was, like Yosemite Valley, shaped by glaciers. There are good campsites for people who have backpacked up from Yosemite Valley, on their way to and from deeper regions in the back country. Black bears are on the prowl here; these ordinarily shy creatures will try to grab unattended backpacks in hopes of enjoying a free meal.

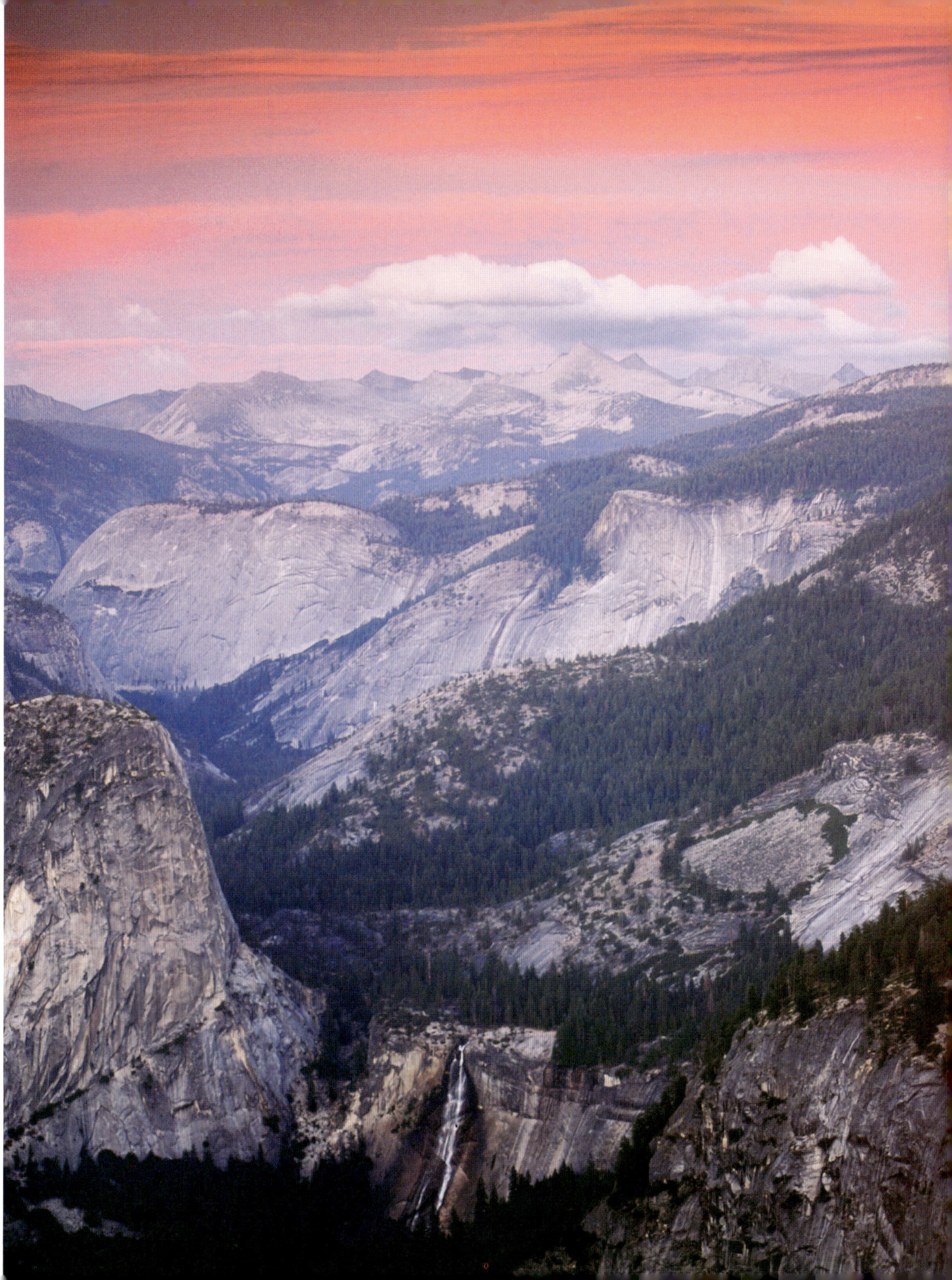

Right

CLOUDS REST

Boulders known as glacial erractics—carried by a glacier and then deposited on top of the granite dome when the ice melted—lie in the foreground near Olmstead Point. Mighty Clouds Rest is in the background. The steep, treeless slopes high on the mountain reveal concave sheets of granite.

Below

GAYLOR LAKE

Adjacent to Gaylor Peak, this pretty little alpine lake was named for Andrew J. Gaylor, a national park ranger in Yosemite early in the twentieth century.

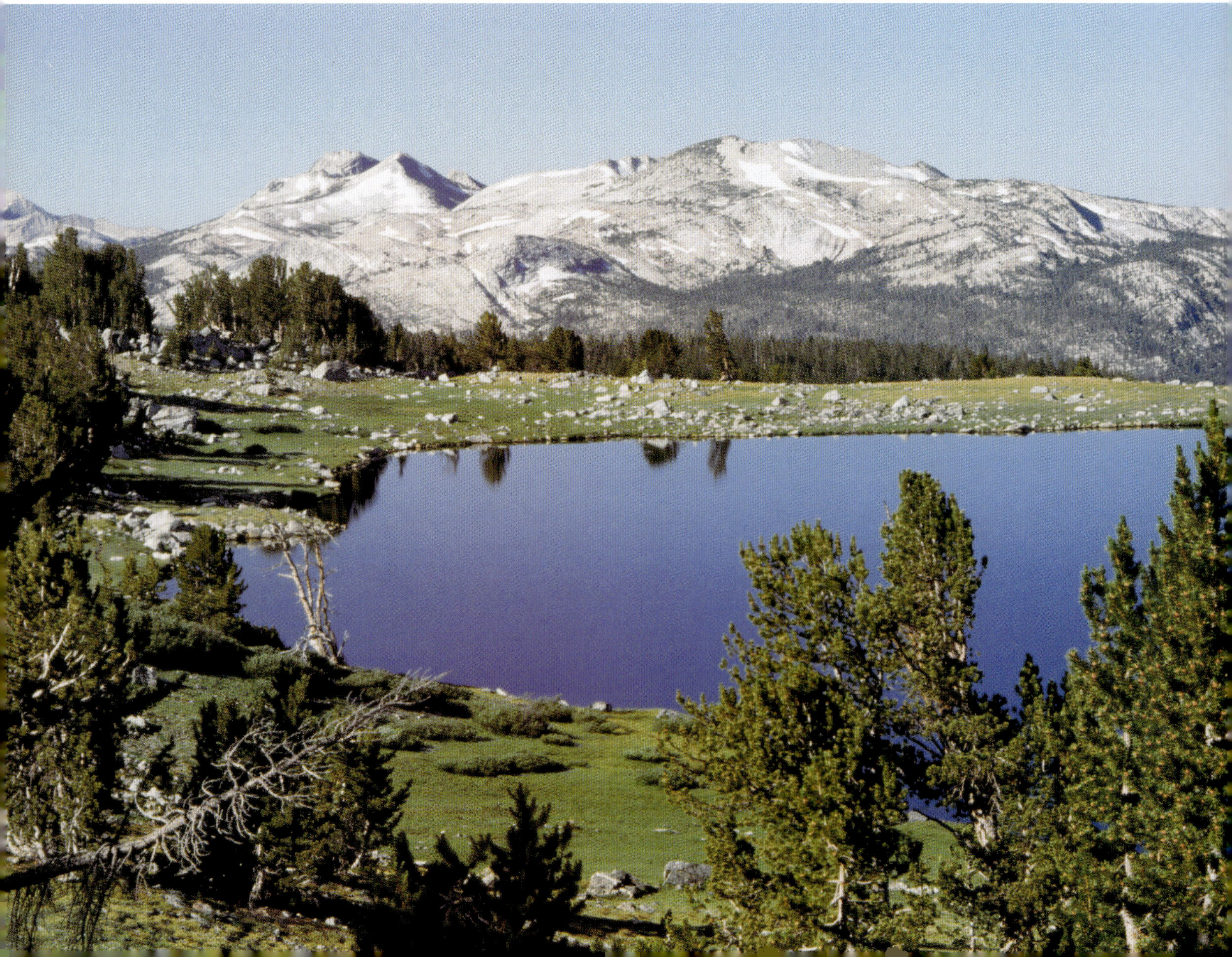

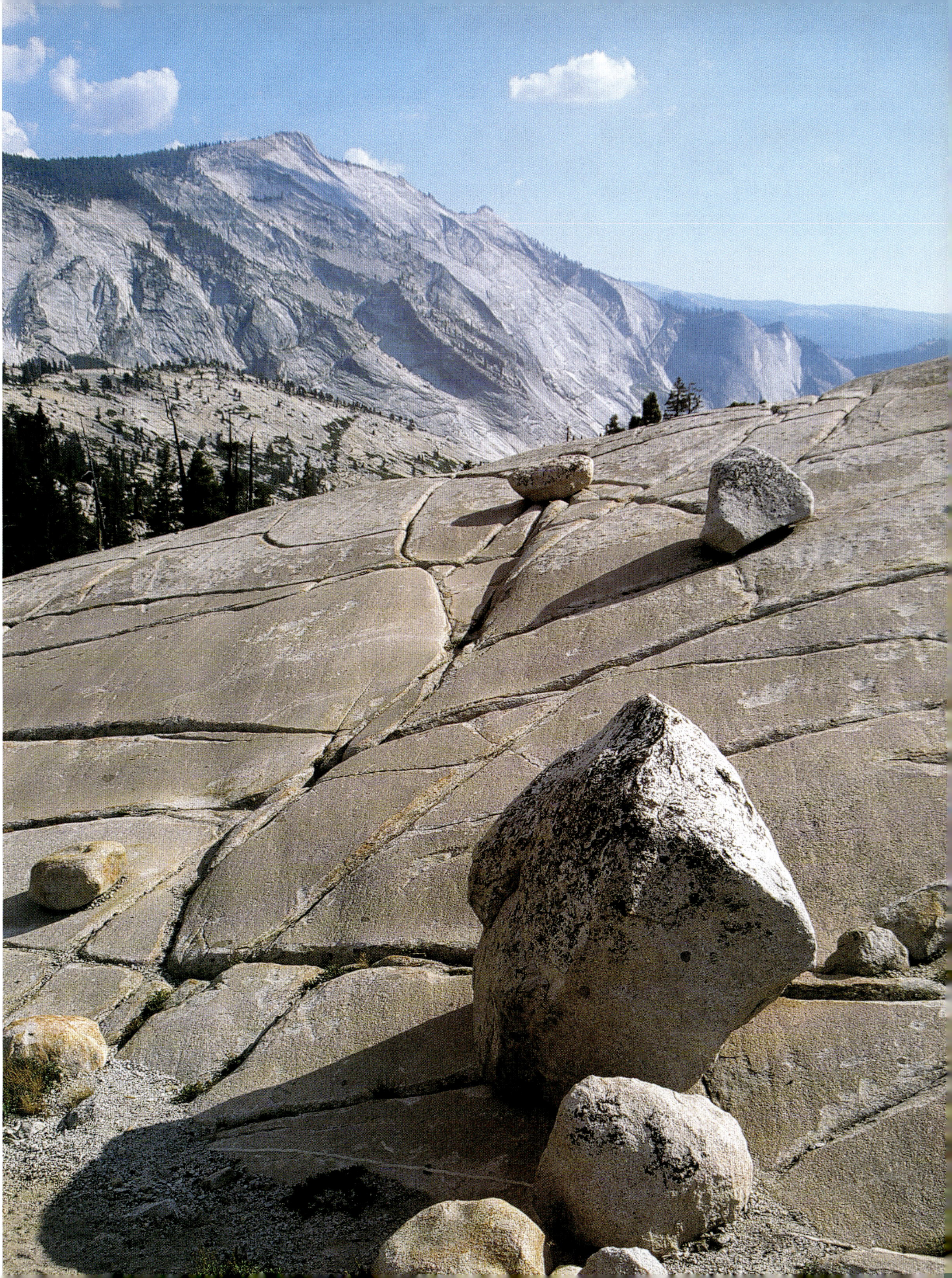

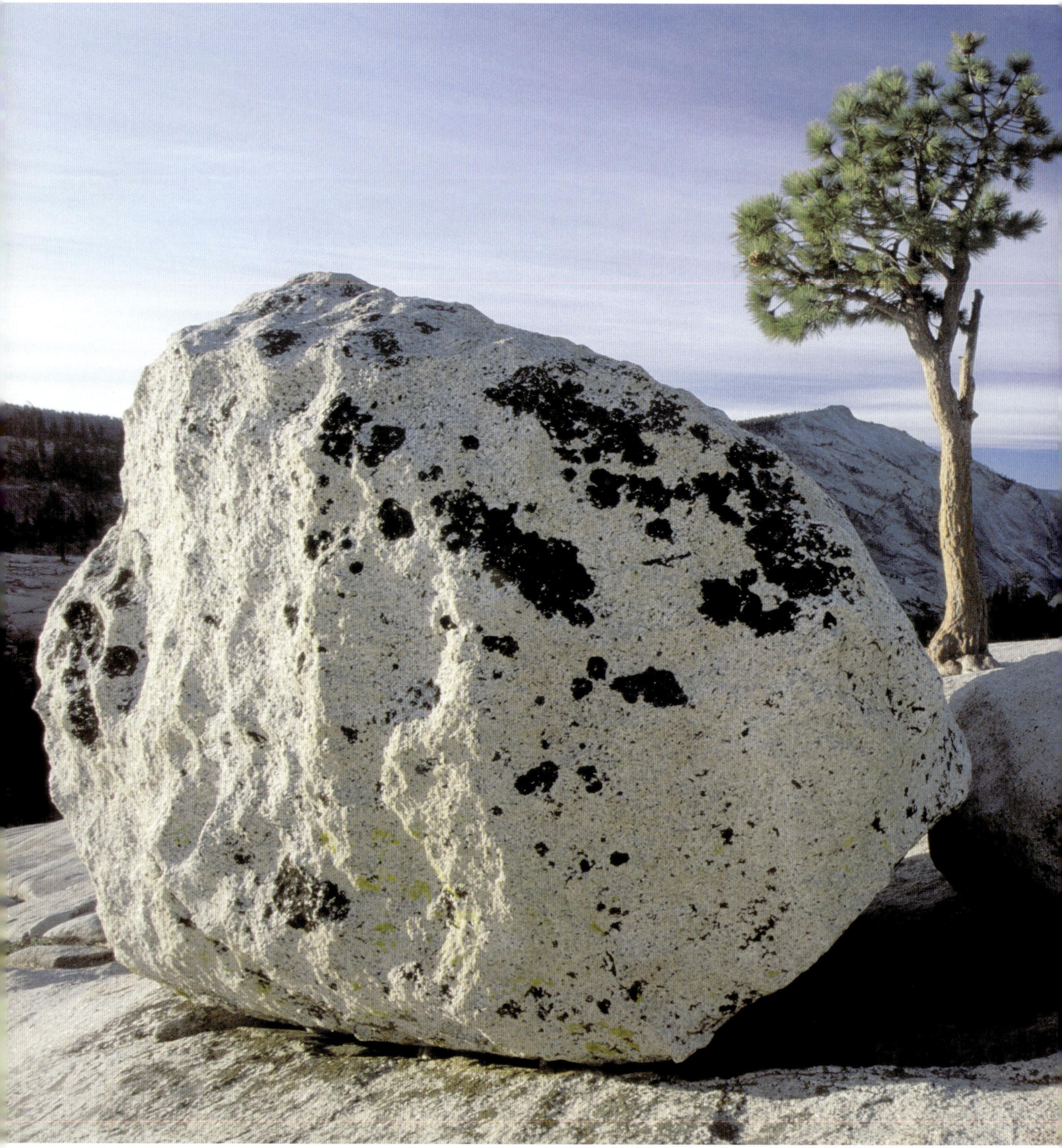

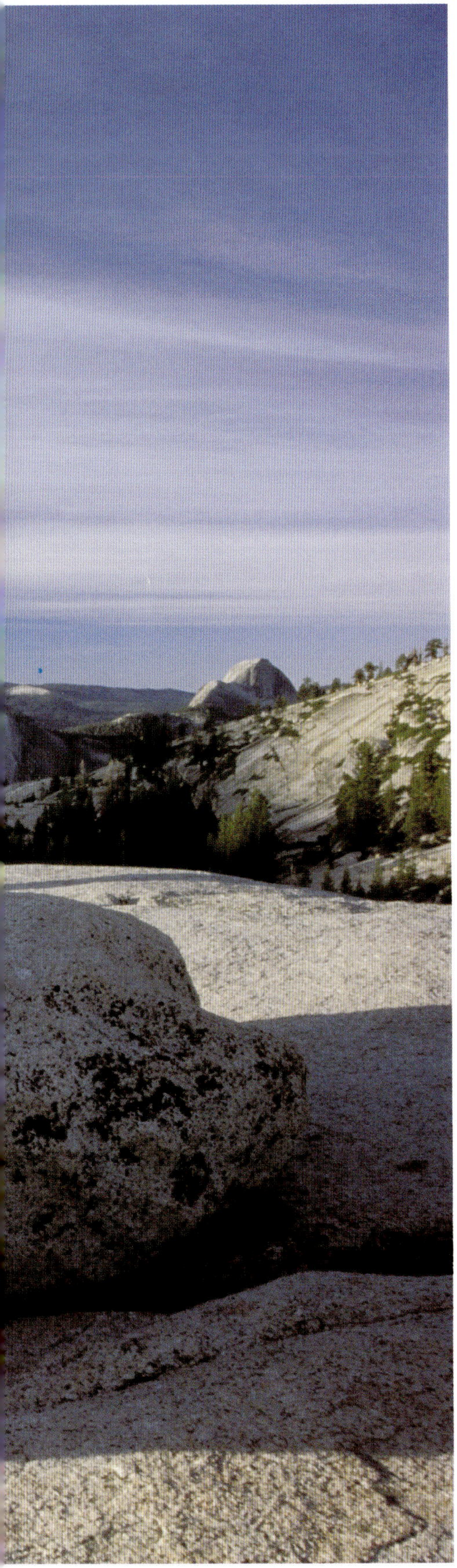

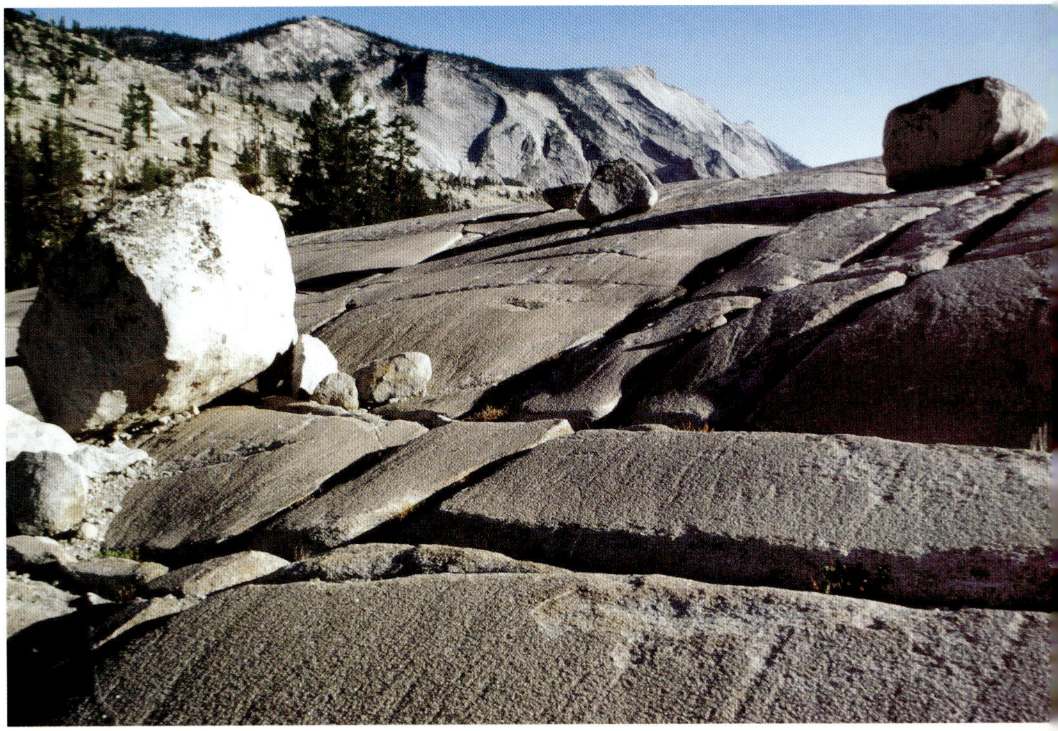

Above and left

OLMSTEAD POINT

The overlook at Olmstead Point along Highway 120 (Tioga Road) takes in the view down Tenaya Canyon, as well as the long granite ridge that culminates with Clouds Rest and a distant Half Dome. Olmstead Point is a good place to view glacial erratics; boulders which were carried by glaciers—sometimes for miles—and then deposited on the Sierra Nevada bedrock after the ice melted. Olmstead Point and the places pictured on the following pages were all taken from locations in high country along or near Highway 120, above Yosemite Valley.

Overleaf

TENAYA LAKE

Located on Tioga Road about seven miles west of Tuolumne Meadows, Tenaya Lake was formed by a glacier that carved a path through the Tuolumne Canyon about 15,000 years ago, leaving a depression in the granite. Tenaya, at 8,149 feet above sea level, is surrounded by peaks and domes; it is also one of the larger lakes in Yosemite, about one mile in length and half a mile in width. Beaches and picnic tables invite visitors to linger. The water, while cold, attracts brave swimmers throughout the summer.

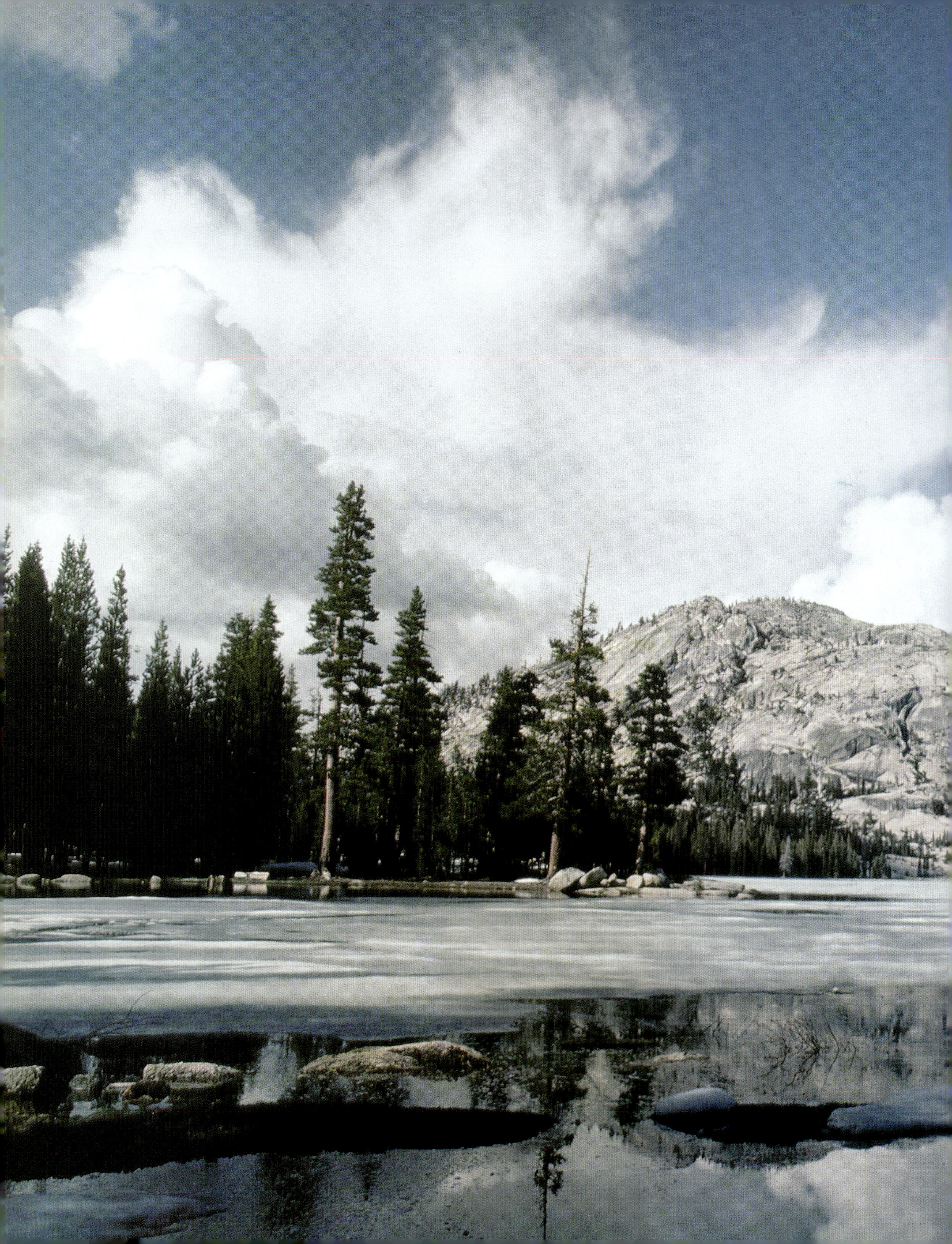

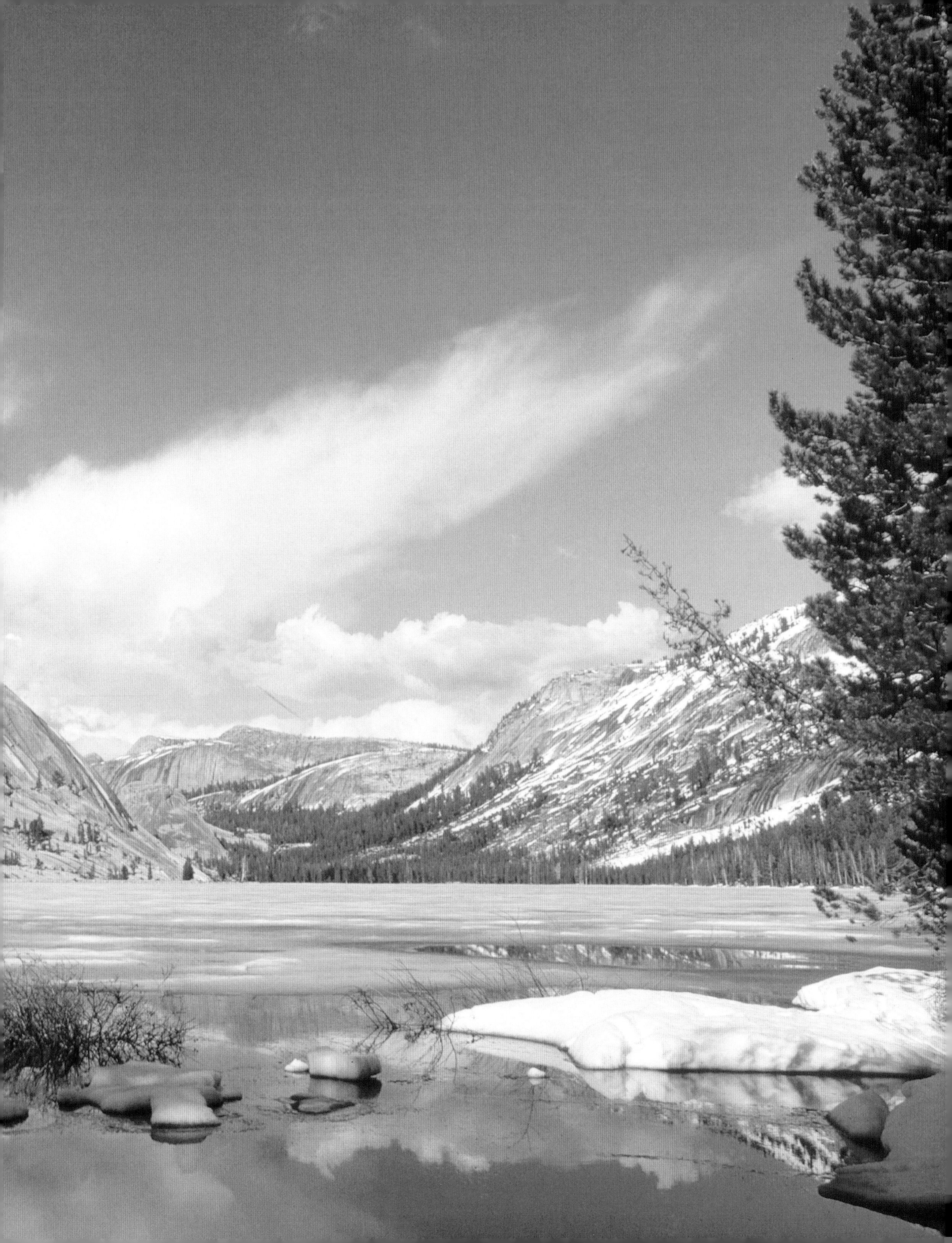

Right

TENAYA VALLEY

The slow but inexorable power of the glaciers that swept through Yosemite is on full display in Tenaya Canyon, where the rivers of ice carved their way through massive amounts of granite bedrock in the Sierra Nevada Mountains.

Below

TIOGA PASS

Tioga Pass, the eastern gateway to Yosemite, is the highest trans-Sierran pass at 9,441 feet in elevation. The view from the entrance station includes alpine peaks and meadows. Trails near the pass lead into the back country. While several roads cross the Sierra Nevada to the north, no road to the south, until Walker Pass, makes the crossing for 160 miles.

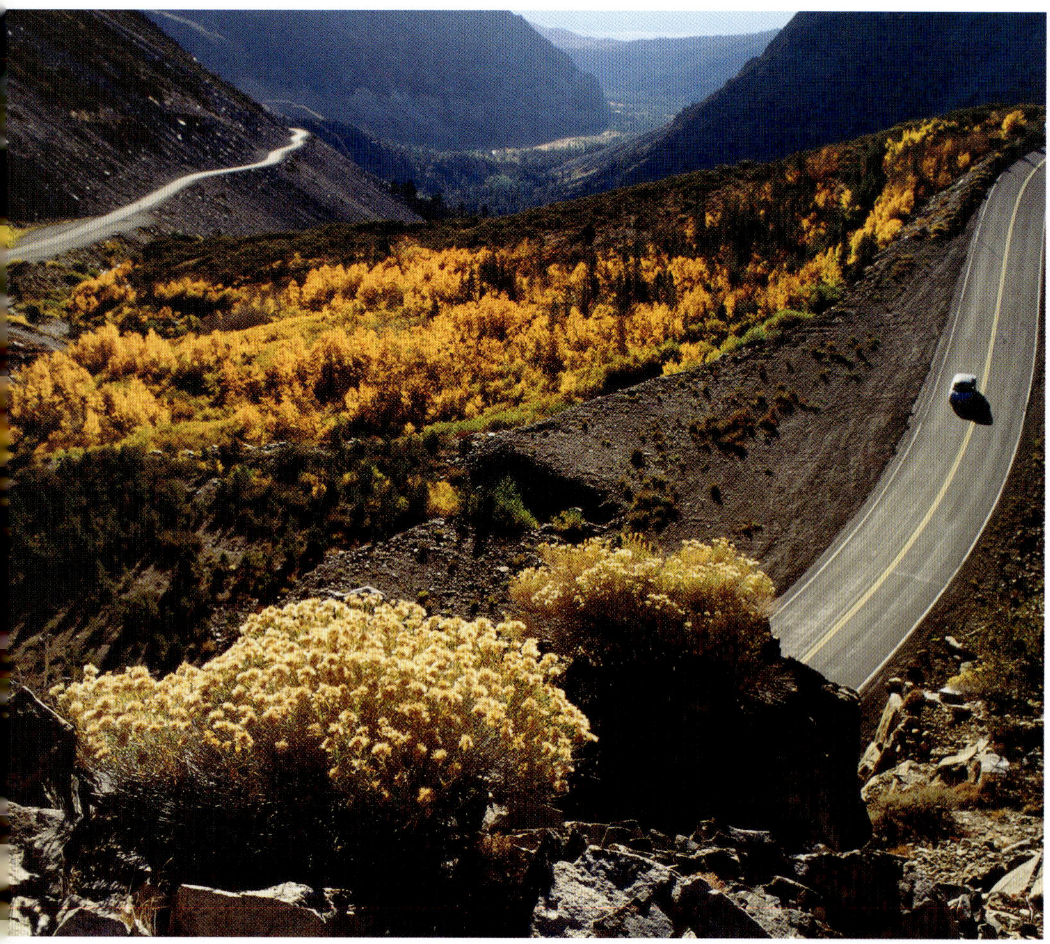

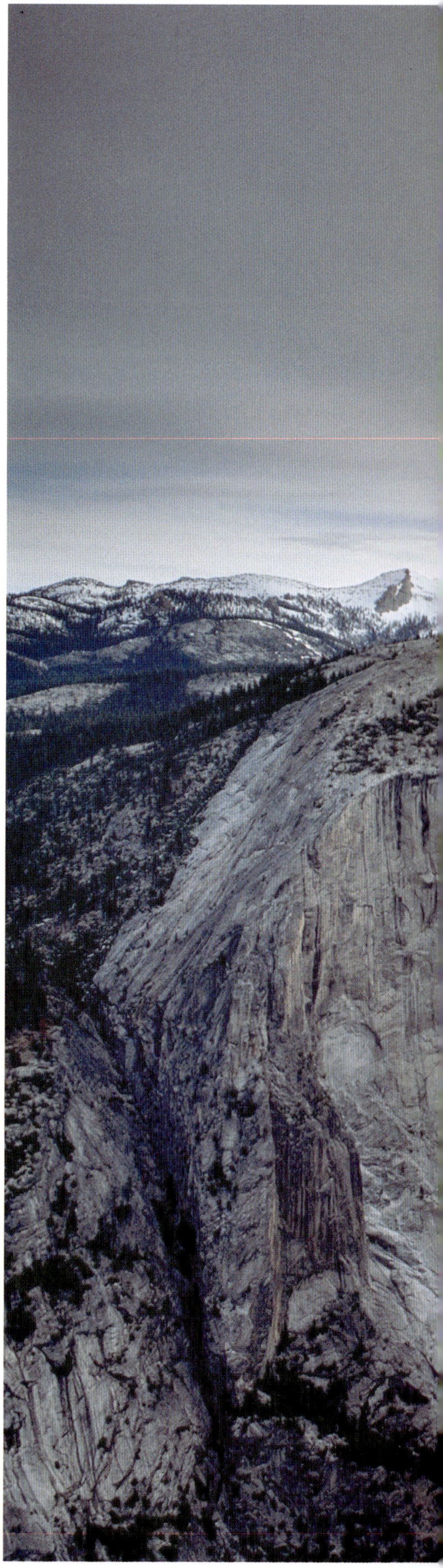

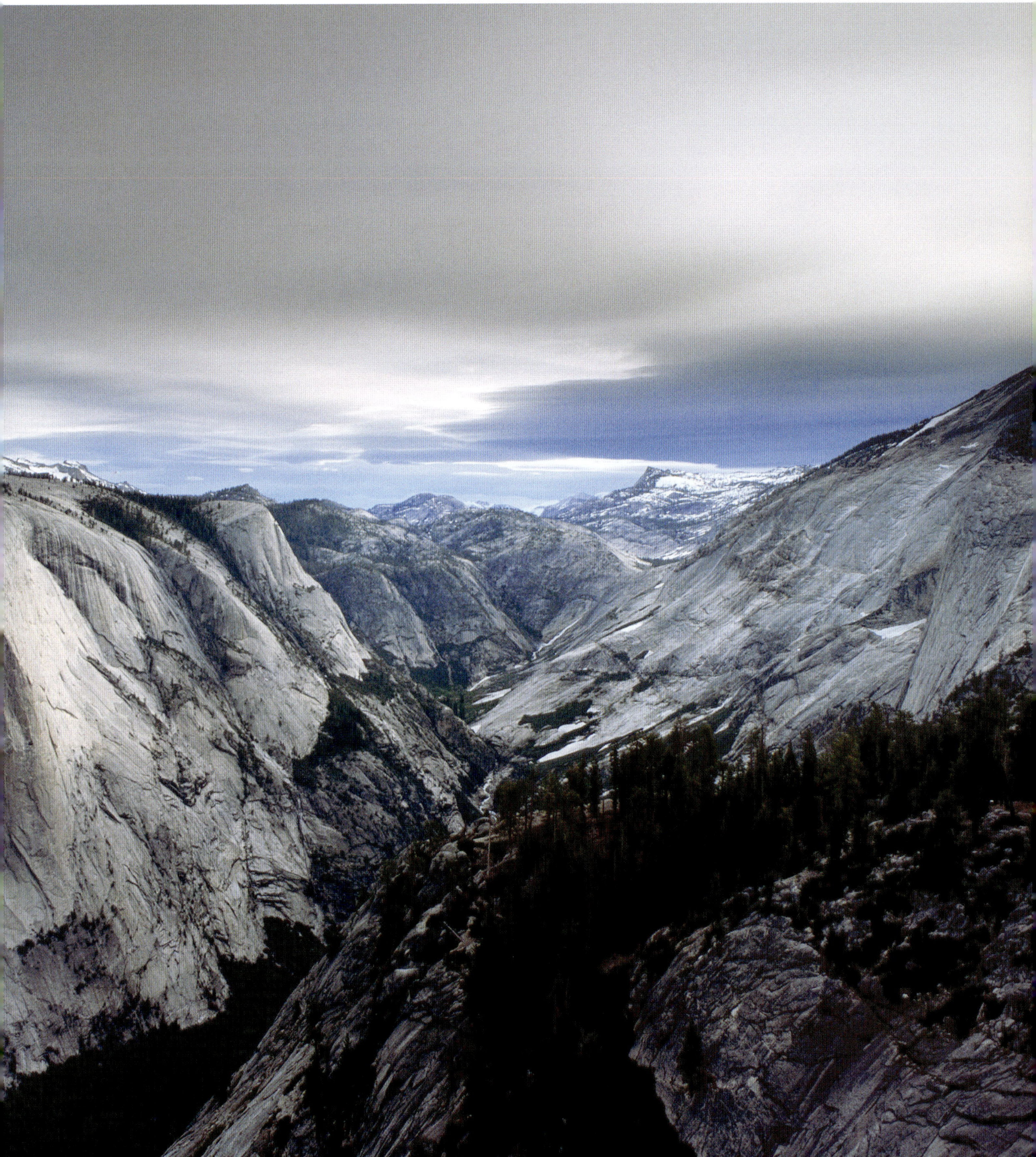

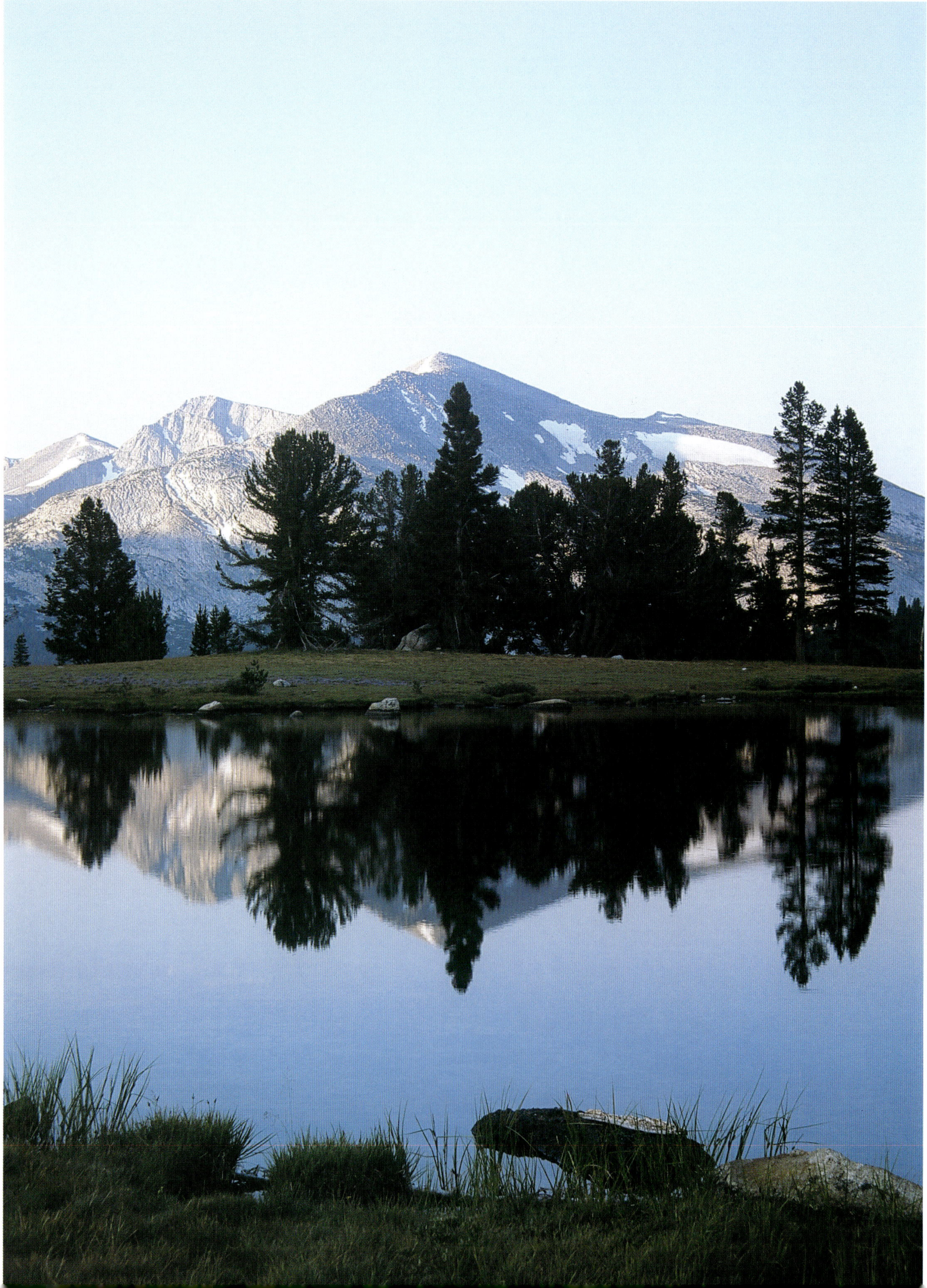

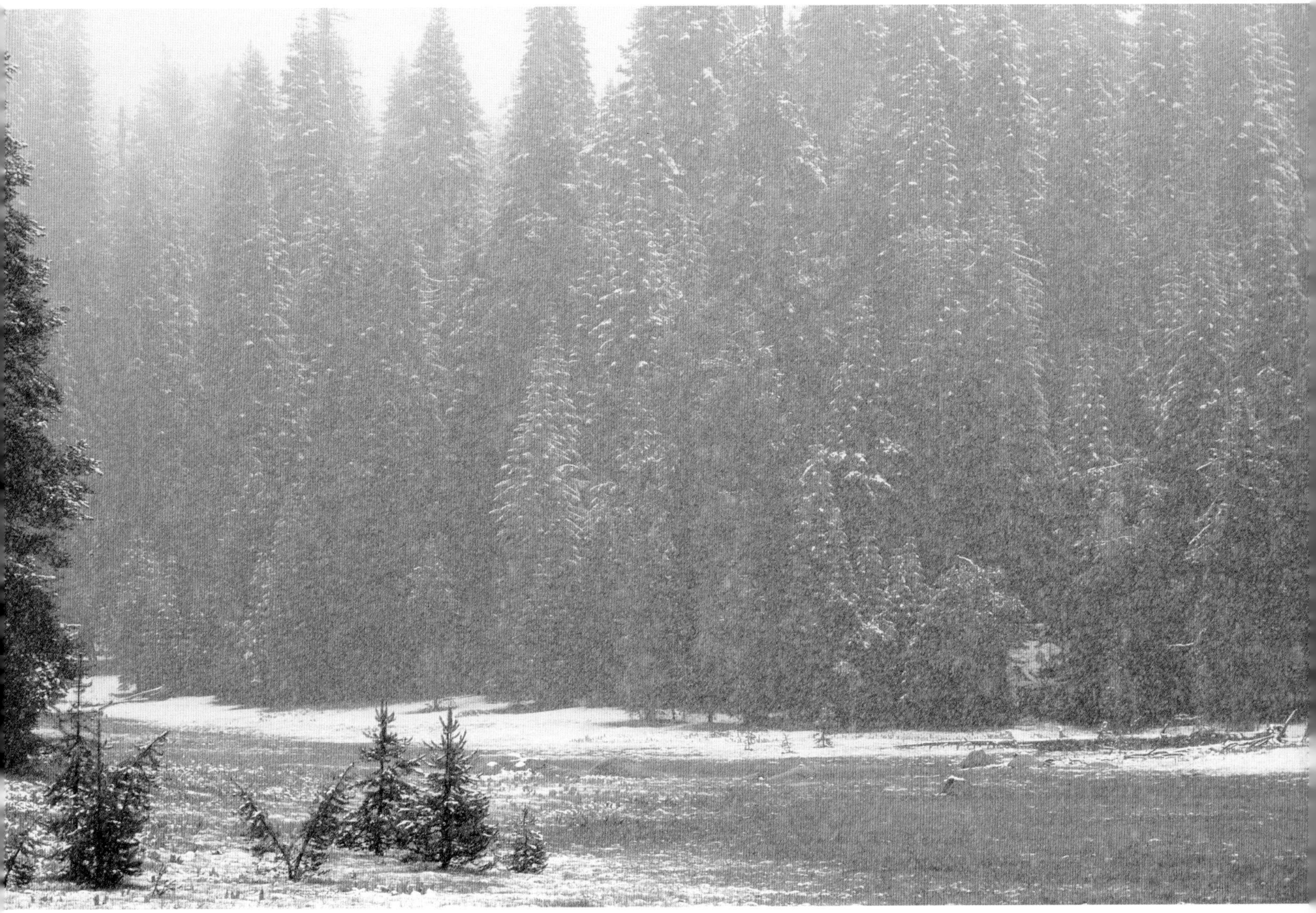

Above

CRANE FLATS

Beautiful meadows, a comfortable campground, a little store, and a gas station are located at the junction of the Big Oak Flat Road and the Tioga Road, about half an hour's drive from Yosemite Valley. The Tioga Road is closed to motorized vehicles in the winter, but cross-country skiers like to explore along the snow-covered highway and the adjacent meadows.

Left

TIOGA LAKE

Just outside the park boundary, little Tioga Lake reflects a beautiful view of the High Sierra, including Mammoth Peak and Kuna Crest.

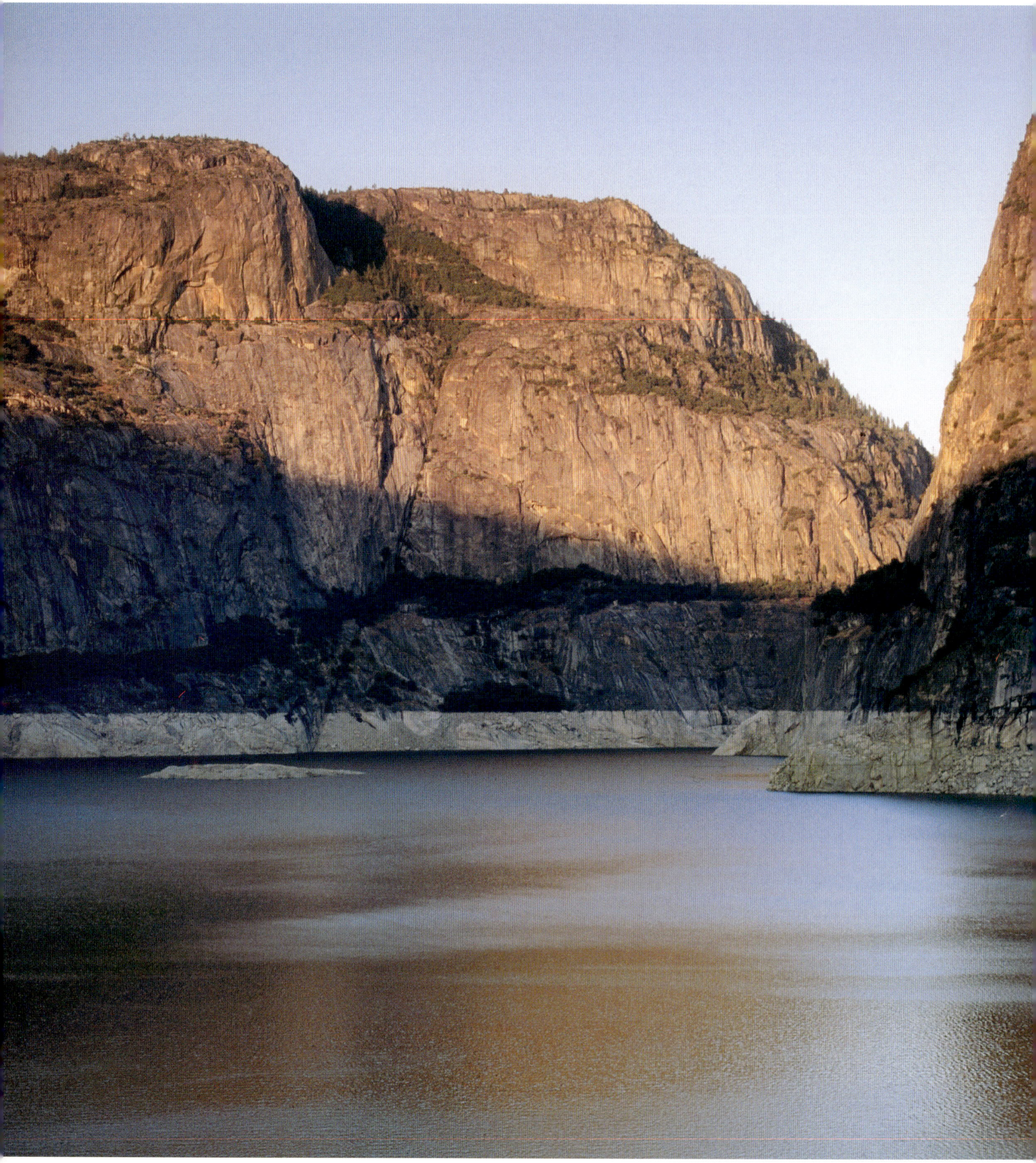

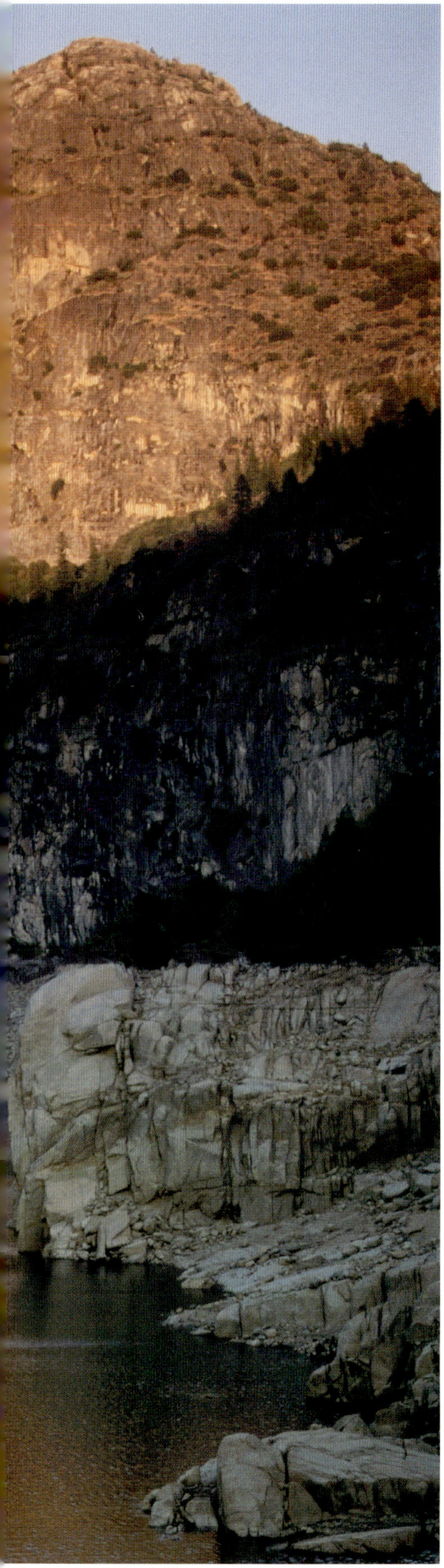

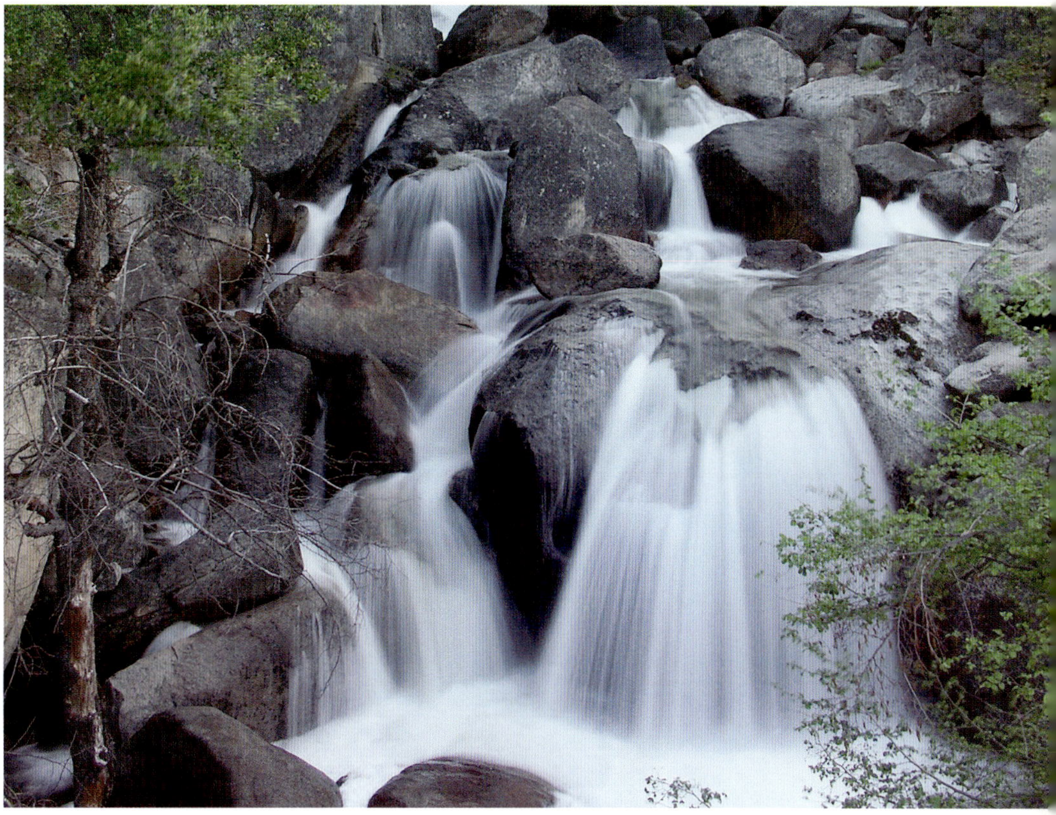

Above

CASCADE CREEK

During spring and early summer, Cascade Creek thunders down the side of the mountain and under a bridge along Big Oak Flat Road. It reaches a raging junction with nearby Tamarack Creek a few hundred feet below the bridge. Two small parking areas allow visitors to view both creeks from either side of the bridge.

Left

HETCH HETCHY DAM

Hetch Hetchy (the Native American meaning of the name of the valley is not known) was the smaller and northern "twin" of Yosemite Valley, complete with towering cliffs, massive domes, and spectacular waterfalls. Early in the twentieth century, the city of San Francisco wanted to dam the Tuolumne River where it flowed out of Hetch Hetchy, and use the captured water to generate hydroelectric power. John Muir led a spirited opposition, writing: "Dam Hetch Hetchy! As well dam for water-tanks the people's cathedrals and churches, for no holier temple has ever been consecrated by the heart of man." But the United States Congress passed a special law in 1913, allowing San Francisco to build the 312-foot-high O'Shaughnessy Dam.

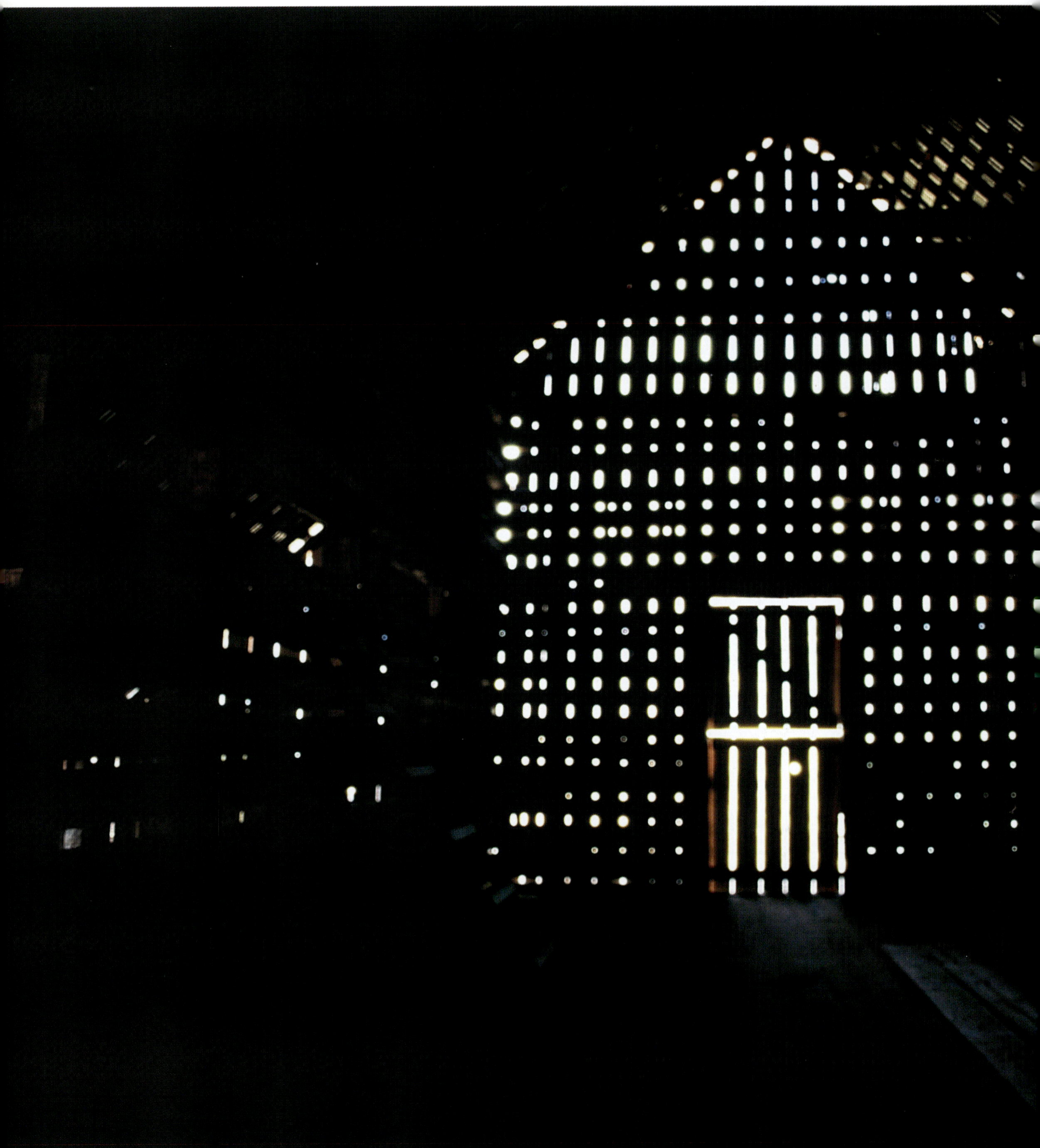

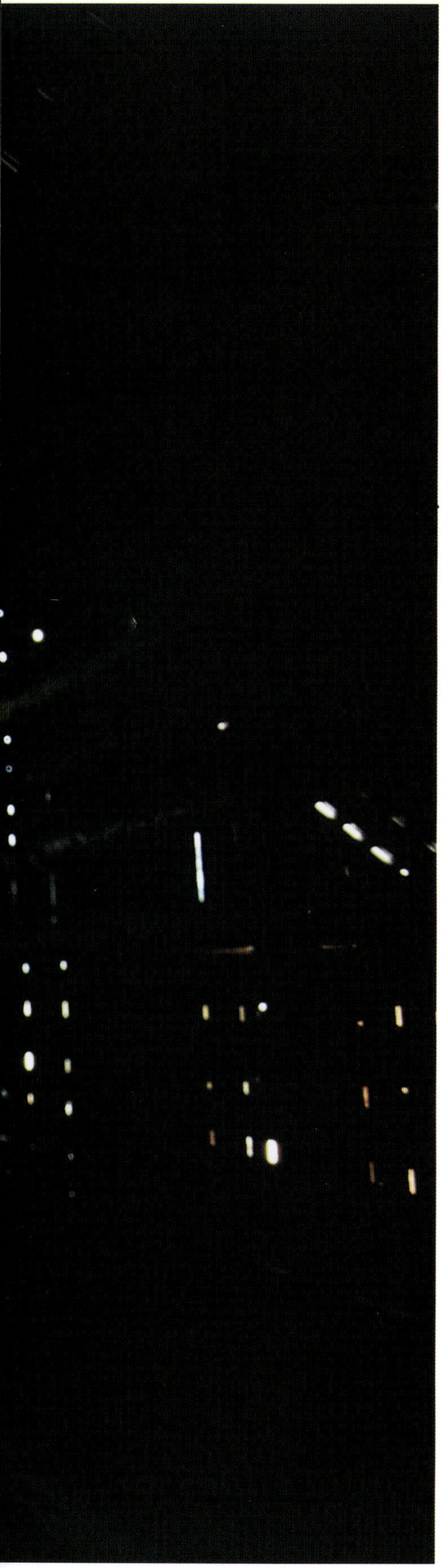

Below

FORESTA BARN

There are two historic barns in Big Meadow, in the little community of Foresta, about five miles from Yosemite Valley, on Foresta Road (and off Big Oak Flat Road). Listed in the National Register of Historic Places, the newer barn, pictured here, was constructed in the late 1880s, while the crib barn (left) was built about ten years earlier. Foresta is a small community of homes that are part of a private inholding inside Yosemite National Park. The Old Coulterville–Yosemite Road, the first road into Yosemite, which opened in 1875, runs through Foresta.

Left

FORESTA BARN INTERIOR

The Meyer crib barn stored hay for the horses and cattle on the ranch. The interior of the crib admits light through countless chinks in the wooden walls.

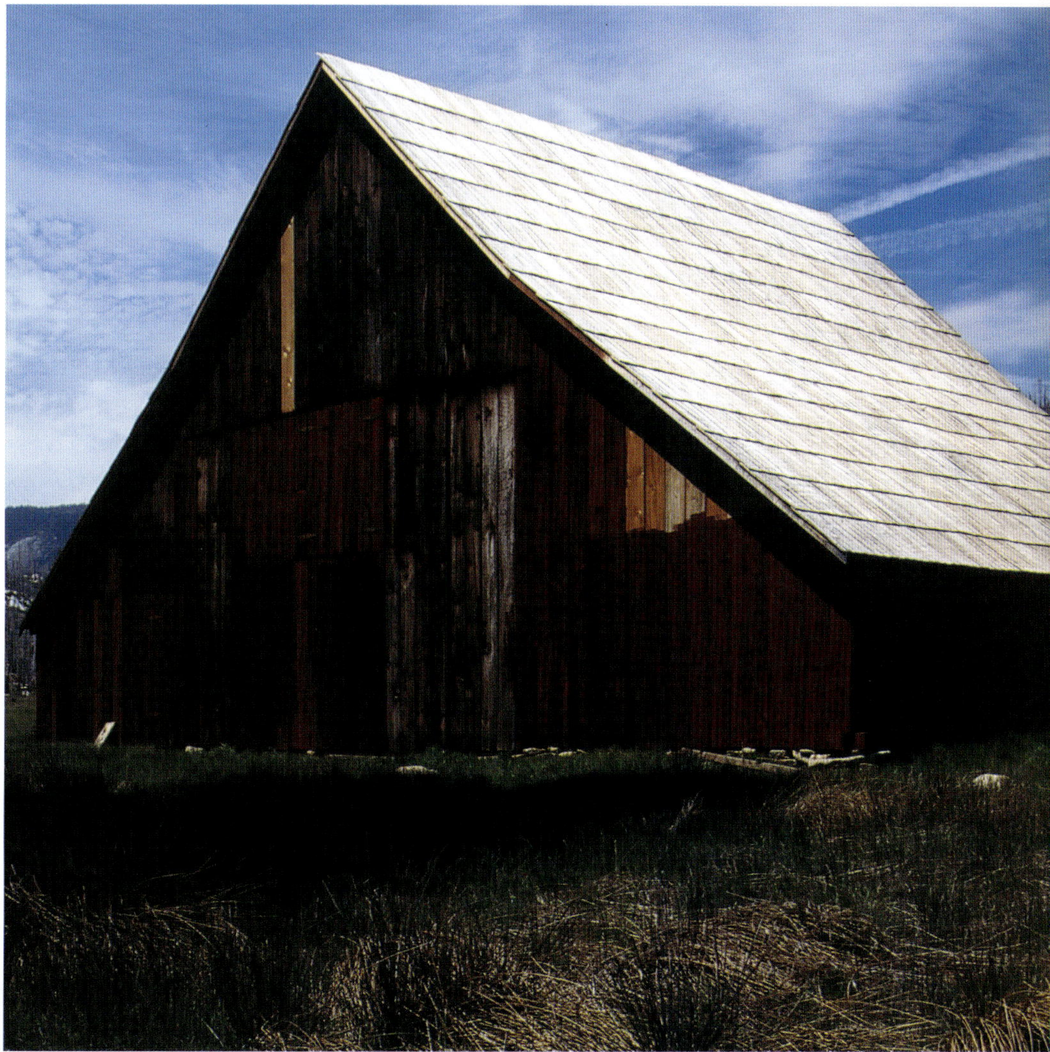

Right

MOUNT DANA AND MOUNT GIBBS

Named for prominent mid-nineteenth century scientists, two prominent peaks, Mount Dana and Mount Gibbs, are on the east side of Yosemite National Park. They are particularly conspicuous when viewed from the west, coming from Tuolumne Meadows; the alpine summits of Dana and Gibbs reach high above tree line. Gibbs is almost 13,000 feet in elevation, while Dana breaks that height by less than 100 feet.

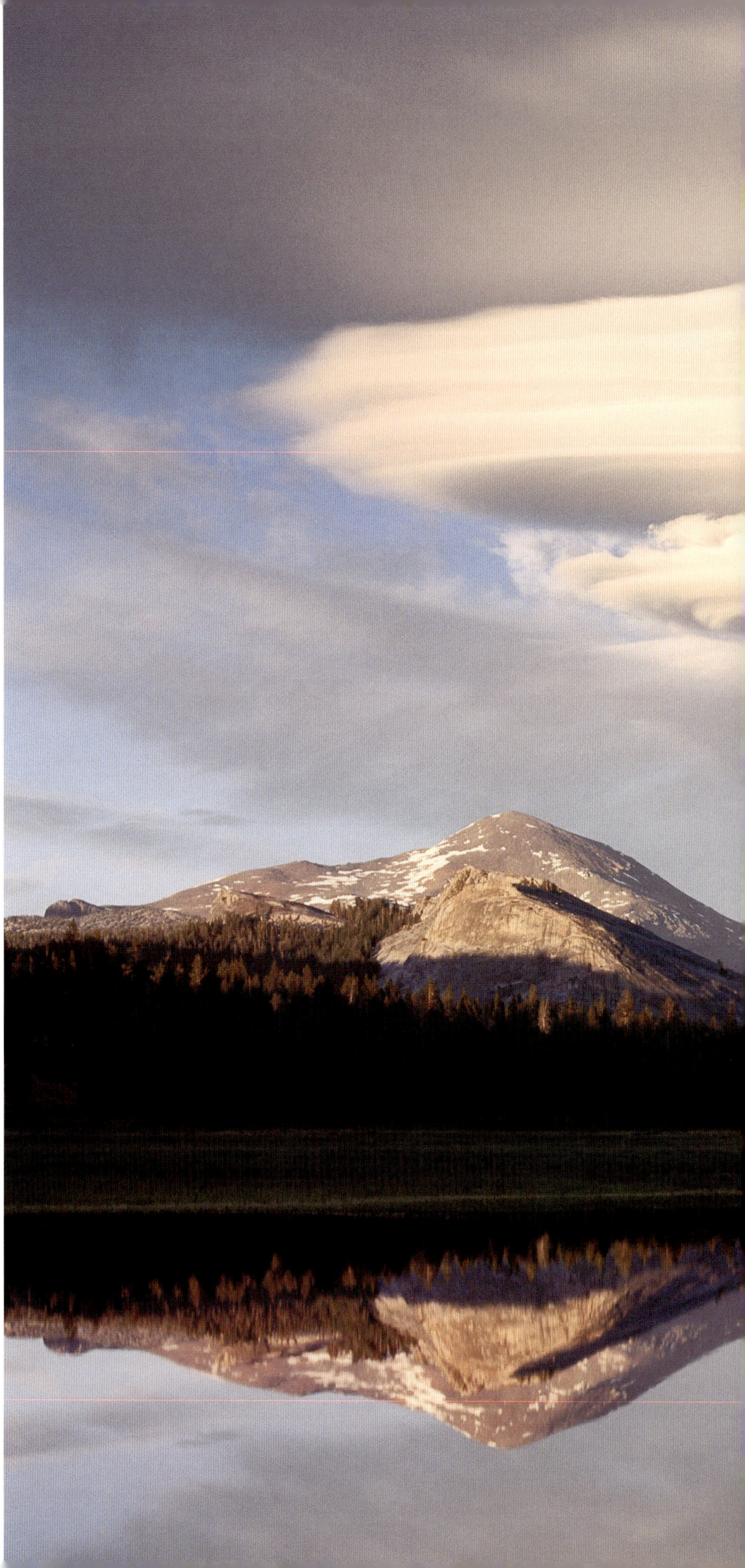

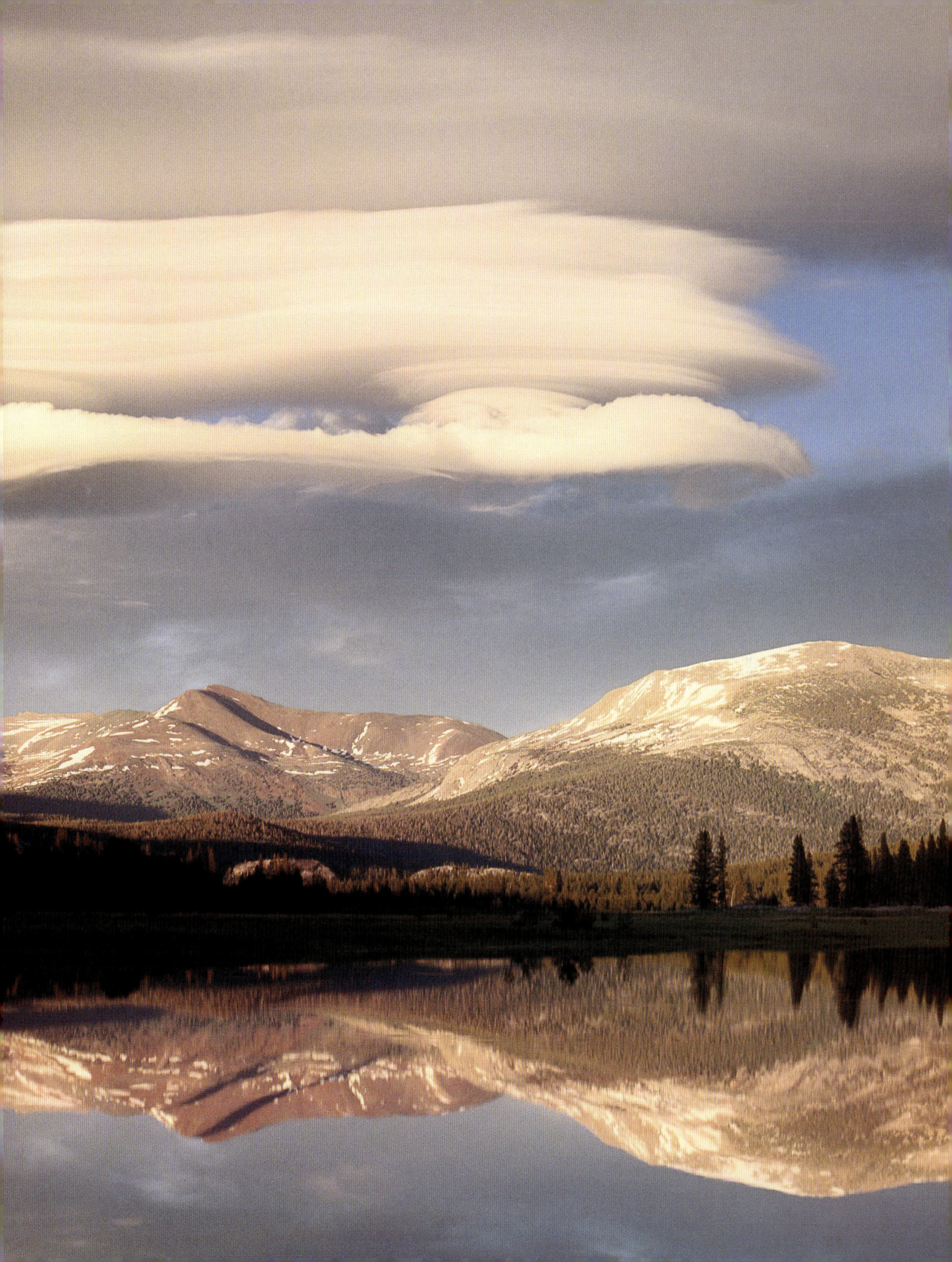

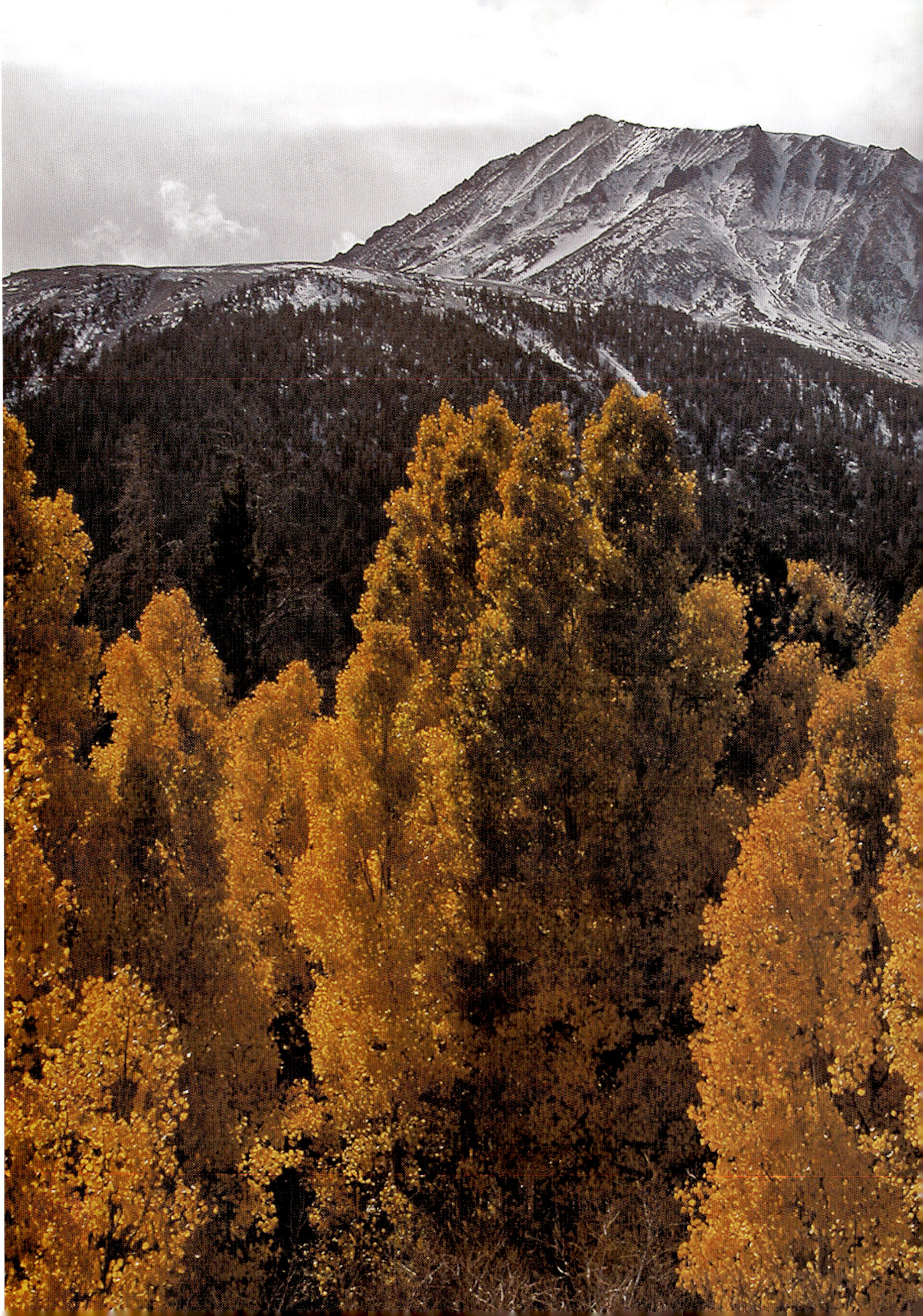

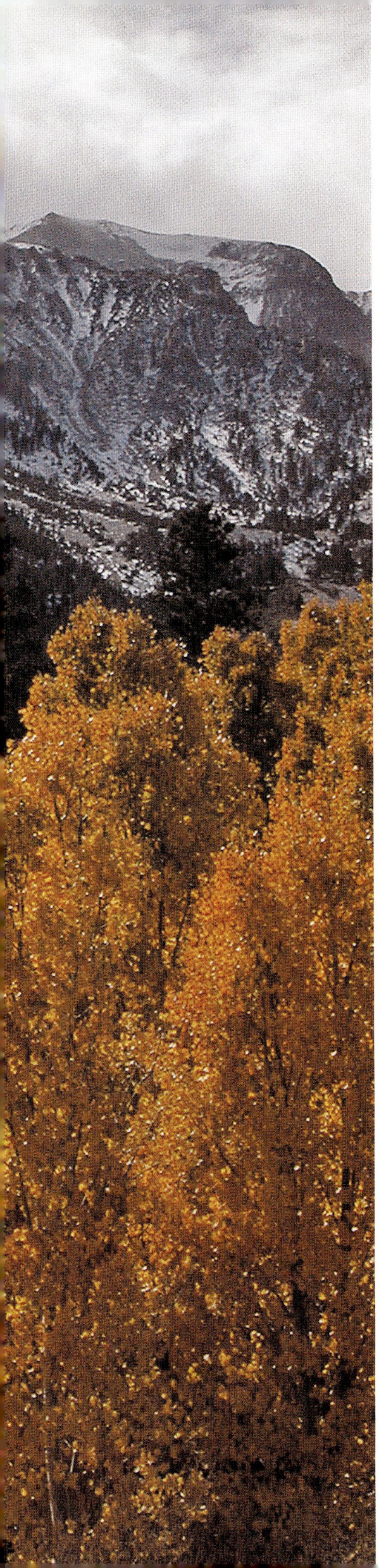

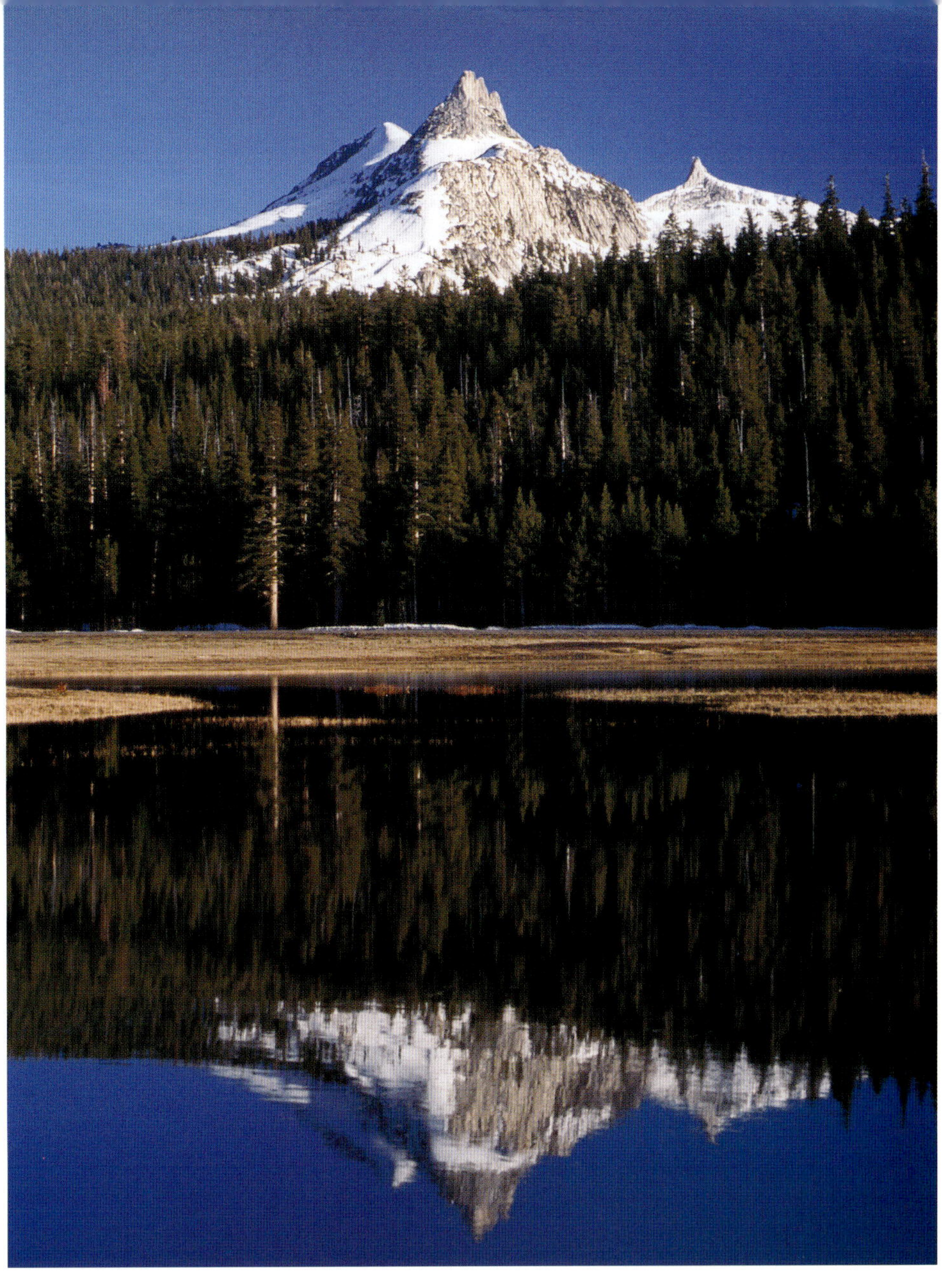

Above

UNICORN PEAK

Unicorn Peak, with Cockscomb Peak on the right in the background, are two well-known landmarks in the Yosemite high country. The peaks are viewed here from Tuolumne Meadows, near Pothole Dome. The base of the mountain can be reached by hiking up the Elizabeth Lake trail, which begins just south of the sprawling Tuolumne Meadows campground, about 2.5 miles. The ascent of the Unicorn's spire itself requires climbing experience.

Left

LEE VINING CANYON

Lee Vining Canyon connects Yosemite National Park with the western edge of the Great Basin Desert. Crowned by the majestic peaks of the High Sierra, the flat base of the canyon shelters meadows, pines, and groves of aspens.

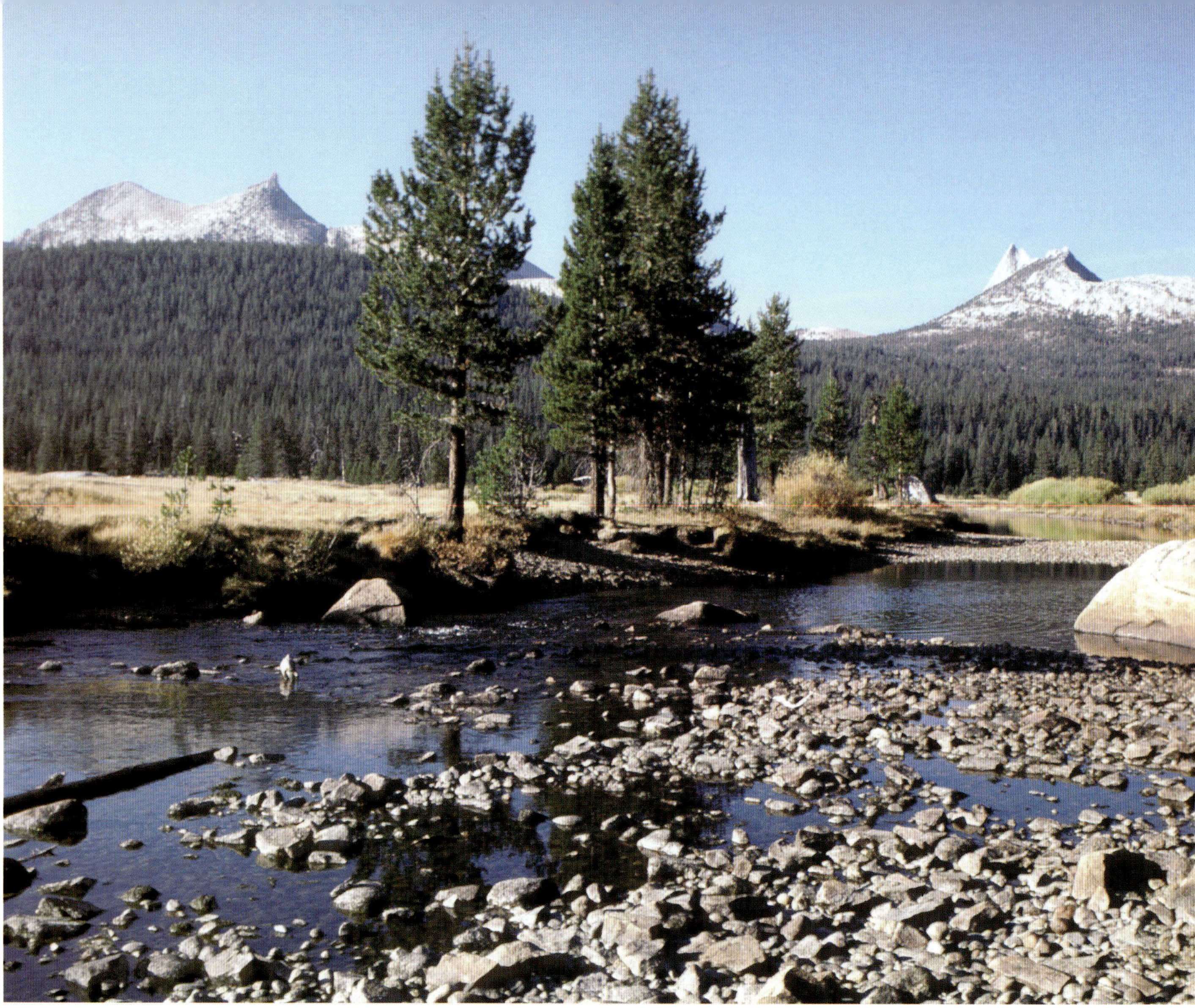

Above
TUOLUMNE RIVER
Longer than the Merced River, the Tuolumne River runs east to west, draining the western slopes of the Sierra Nevada mountains. The river gathers its strength while meandering through Tuolumne Meadows, beyond which it pours through the Grand Canyon of the Tuolumne, to find itself in the Hetch Hetchy Resevoir.

Right
TUOLUMNE MEADOWS
At an elevation of 8,600 feet above sea level, Tuolumne Meadows is a cool summer alternative to Yosemite Valley. The meadow is surrounded by alpine peaks and domes, and is bisected by the meandering Tuolumne River. The combination of a Park Service visitor center, campground, store, café, and gas station, as well as the nearby Tuolumne Lodge, and rock climbing routes and trails leading into the back country, make Tuolumne Meadows a focal point in the park.

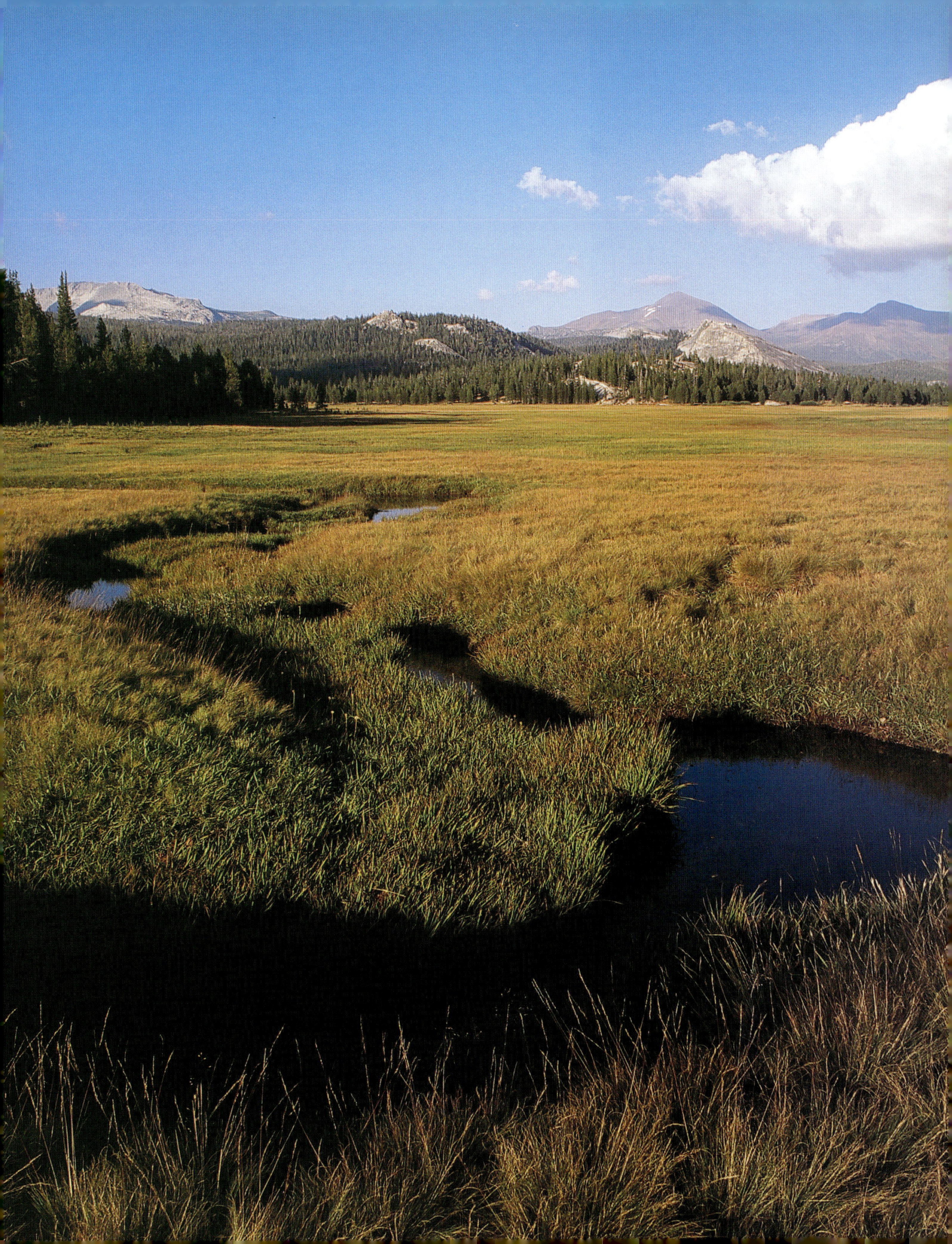

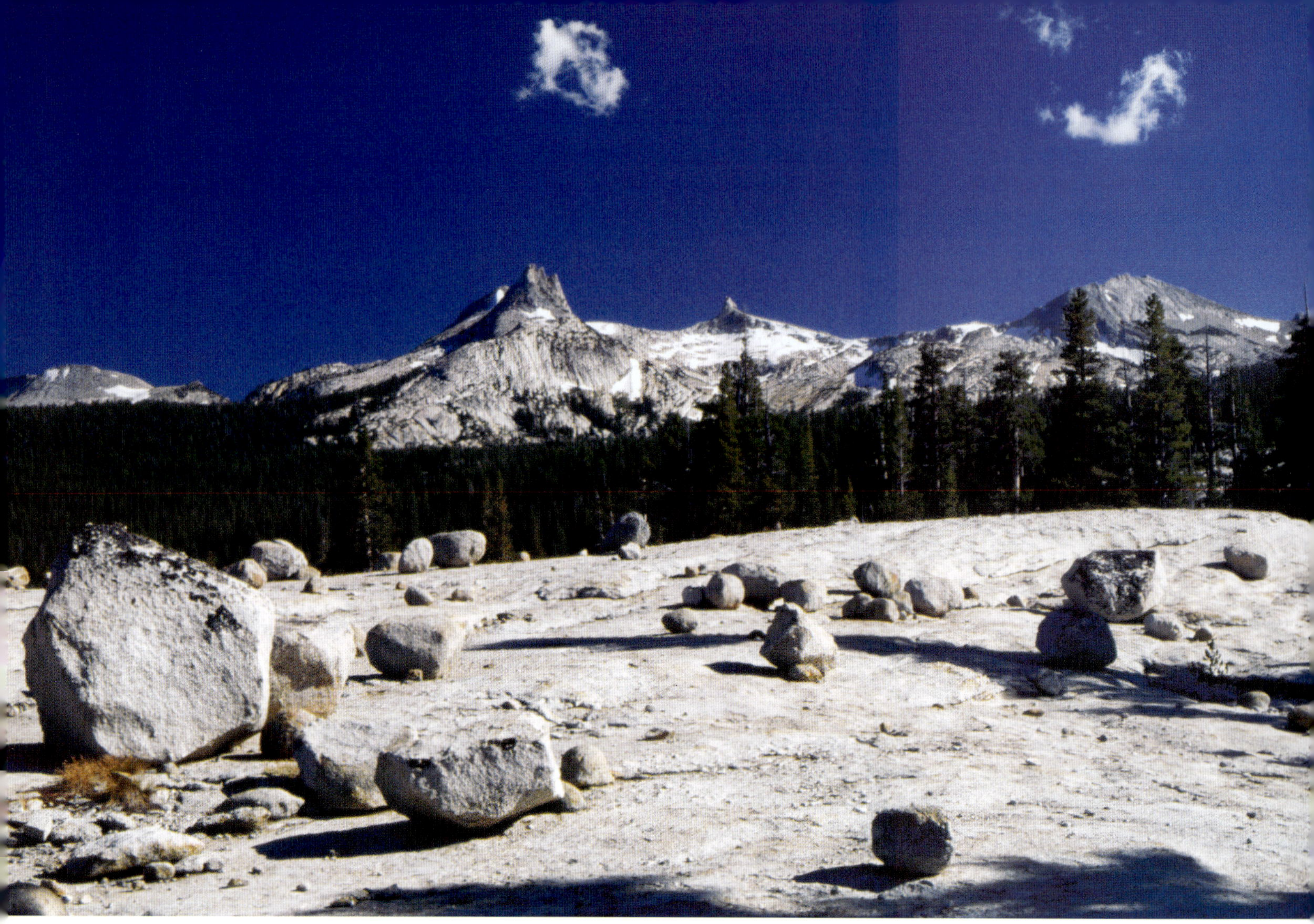

Above

POTHOLE DOME

Pothole Dome sits at the western edge of Tuolumne Meadows. The summit provides splendid views of the meadows and surrounding highlands. Rock climbers enjoy ascending the west side of the dome, while the low-angled route up is on the east side.

Right

LEMBERT DOME

Lembert Dome was named for homesteader John Baptist Lembert, who settled in the meadows around 1882. The dome, which anchors the eastern end of Tuolumne Meadows, can be easily ascended from the east, via a forested trail and then a short scramble to the treeless top. From the summit the 360-degree panoramic view includes Mount Hoffman, Lyell Glacier, Unicorn and Cathedral Peaks, and Tuolumne Meadows, spread out 850 feet below.

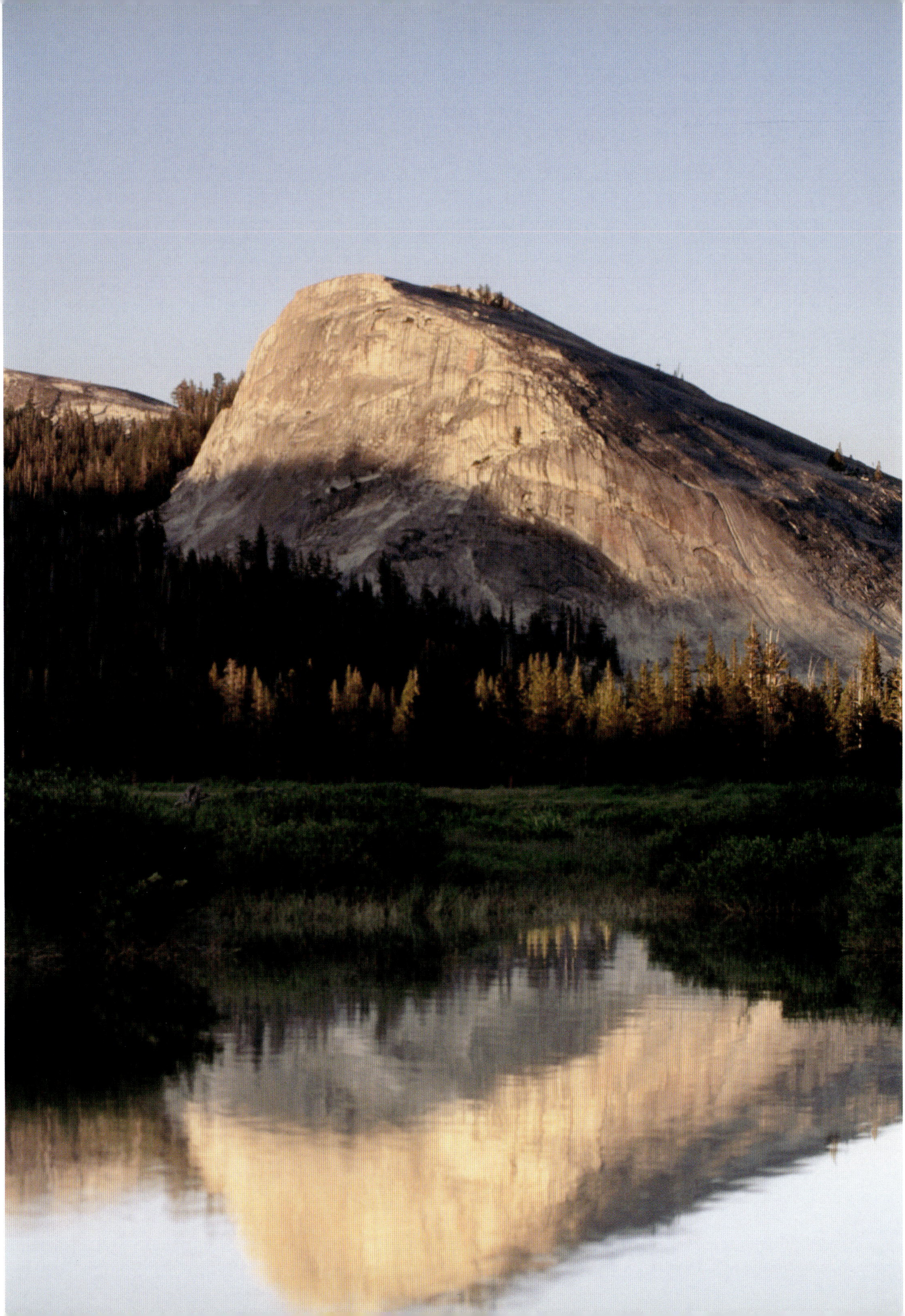

Below

TUOLUMNE MEADOWS SODA SPRINGS

On the north side of Tuolumne Meadows, carbonated water bubbles to the surface, pooling in little puddles in the red-tinged earth. The remains of a log cabin, built by poineer homesteader John Baptist Lembert, protect a portion of the Springs.

Right

DEER

Mule deer like to forage at dawn and dusk. They often appear near Curry Village, particularly in Stoneman Meadow, and browse in Cooks Meadow, just east of Yosemite Lodge. They are usually shy but can be dangerous if approached.

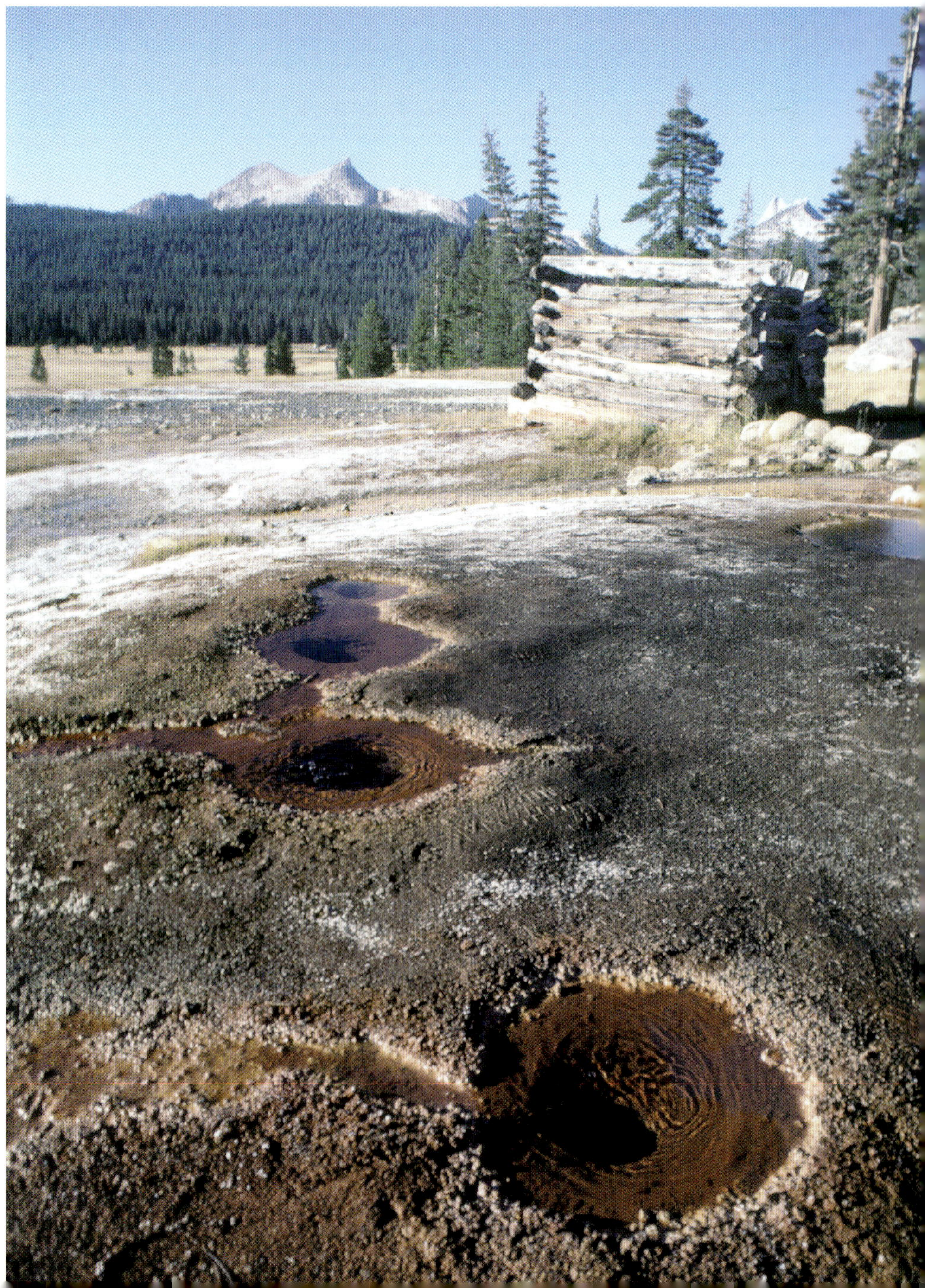

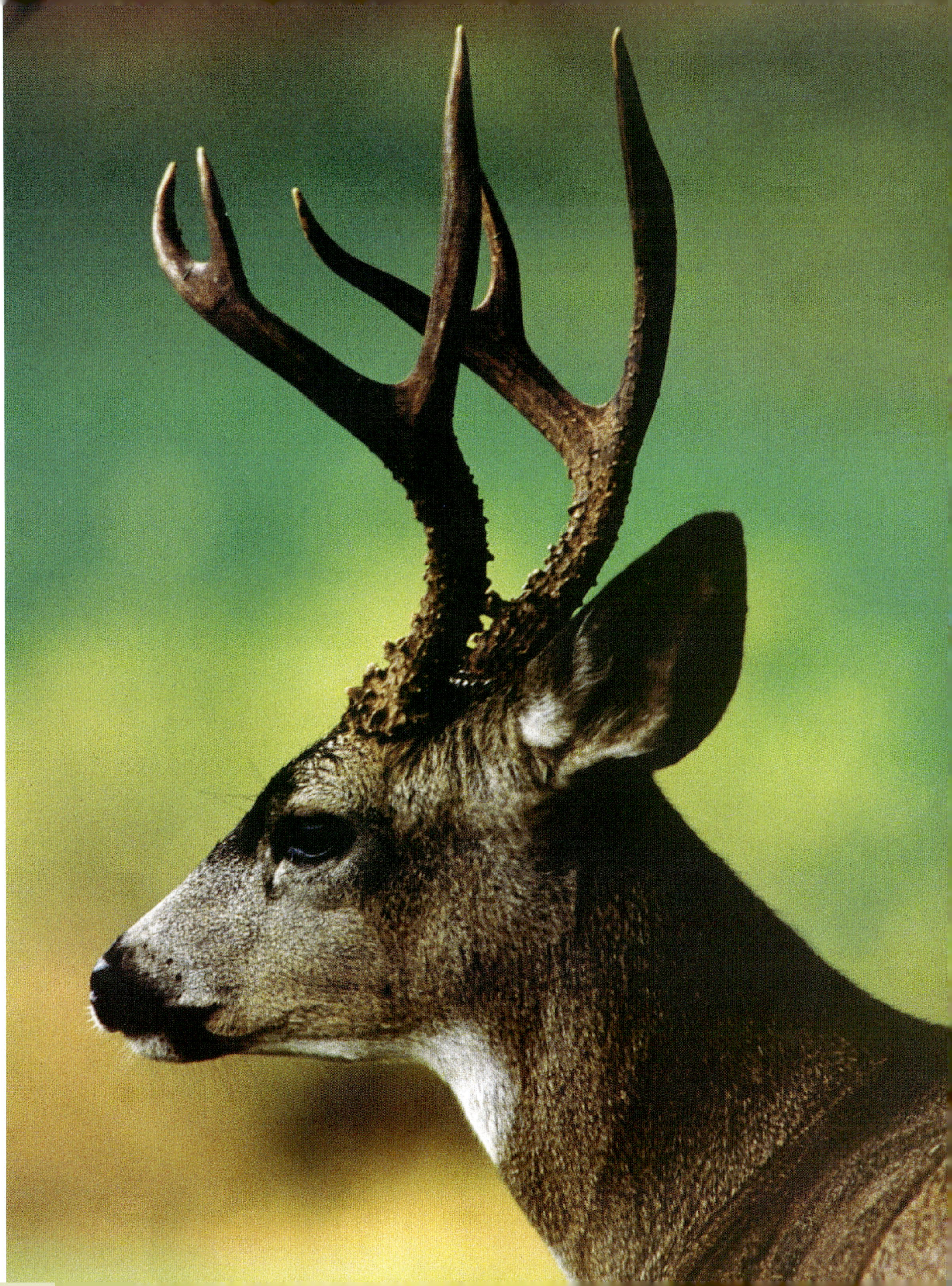

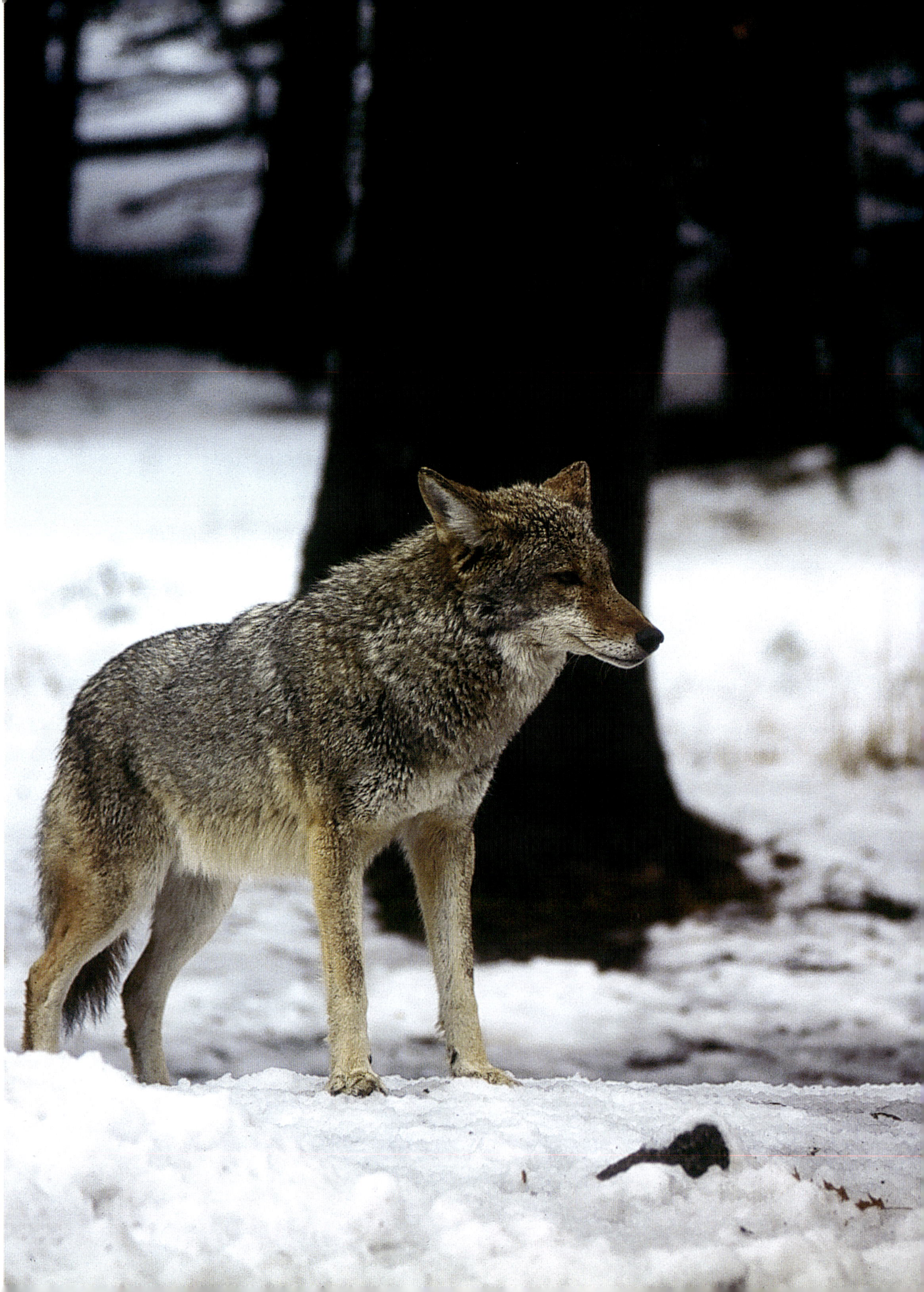

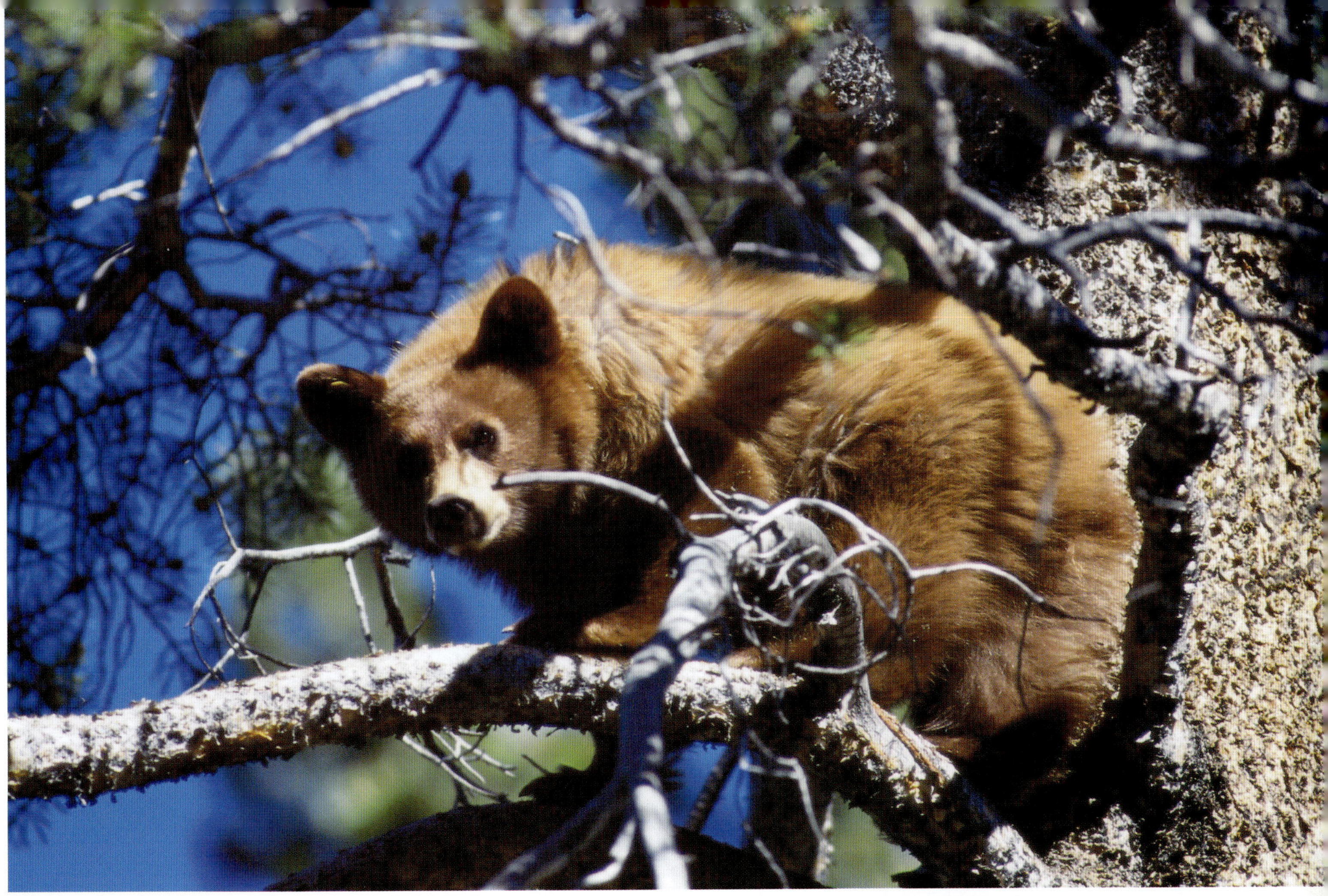

Above
BEAR

There are between 300 and 500 Black bears in Yosemite. They like to eat berries, acorns, insect larvae, grasses, clover, and other wild flora and fauna. Not always black, they are more often brown or cinnamon in color.

Left
COYOTE

Coyotes thrive over much of North America and are emblematic of the American West. Coyotes are excellent hunters and are chiefly responsible for keeping the rodent population in check. They often perform a chorus of eerie, high-pitched yips, barks, and howls.

Right
INDIAN PAINTBRUSH

This vivid wildflower can appear alongside a road or at the edge of a meadow, usually by early summer. A close-up look at this one growing near Mirror Lake reveals a number of tiny insects perching on the bright red petals.

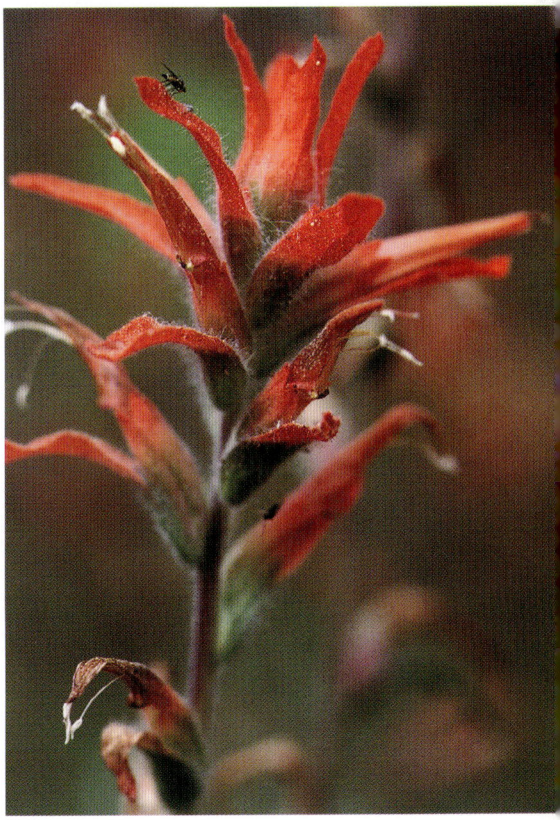

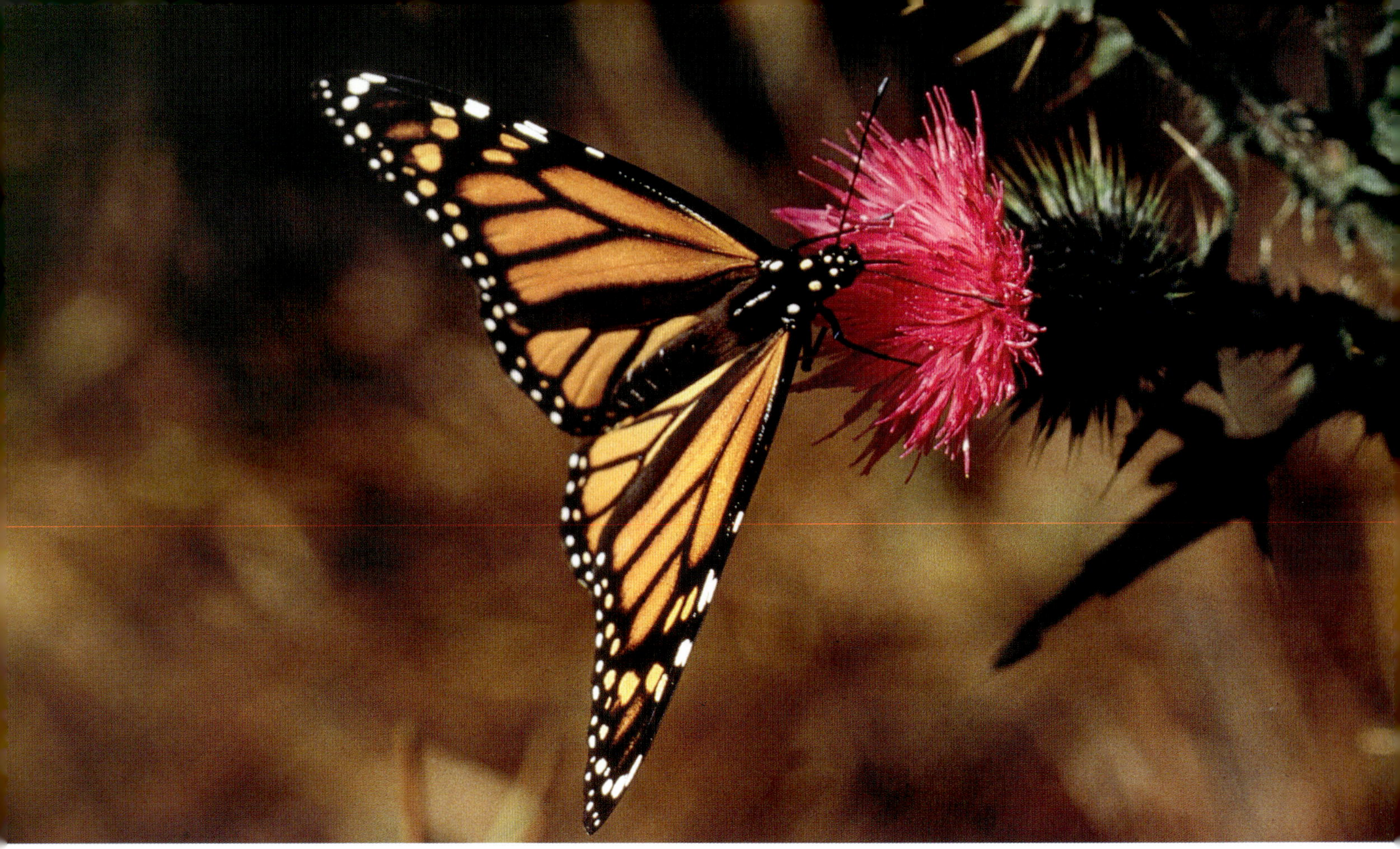

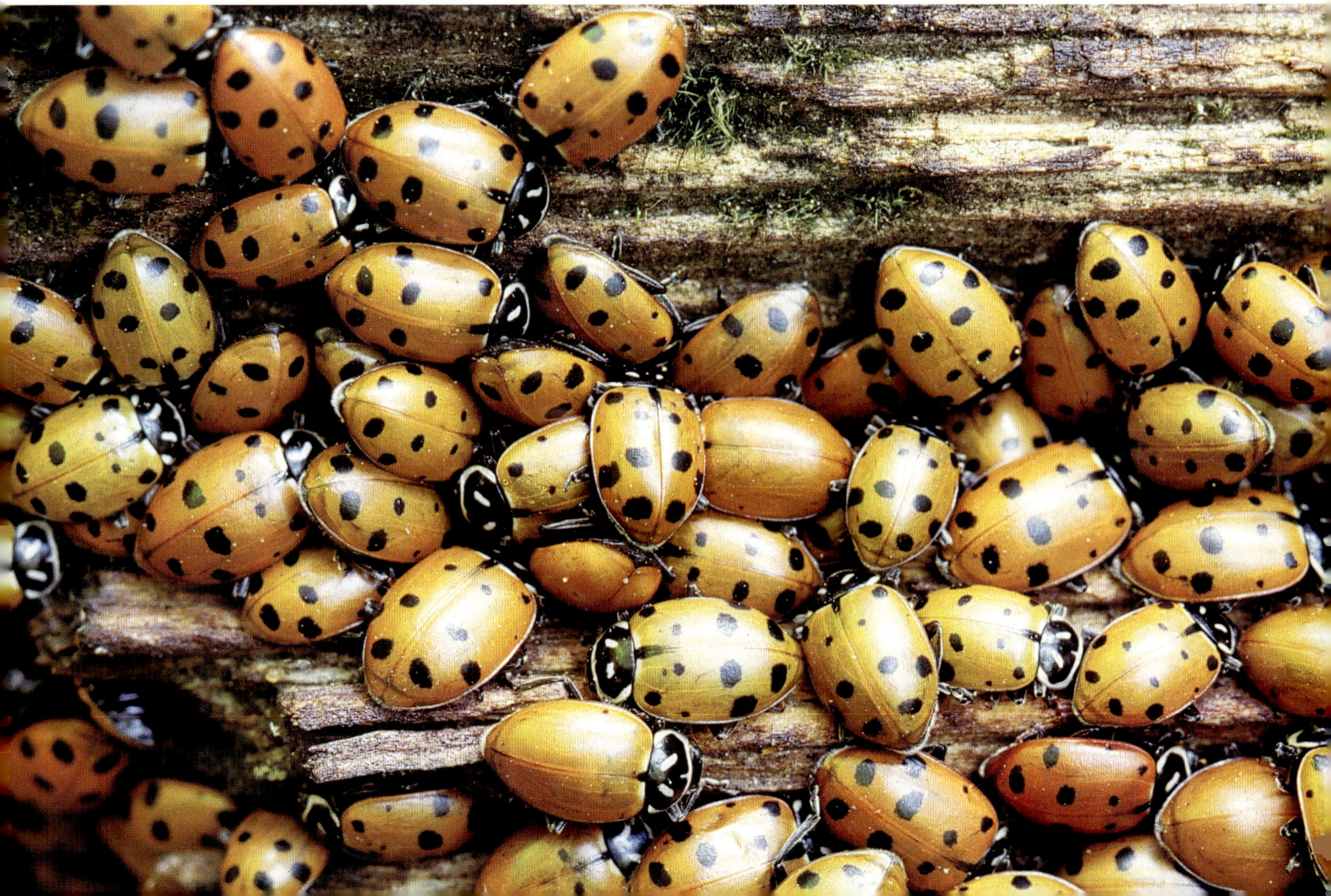

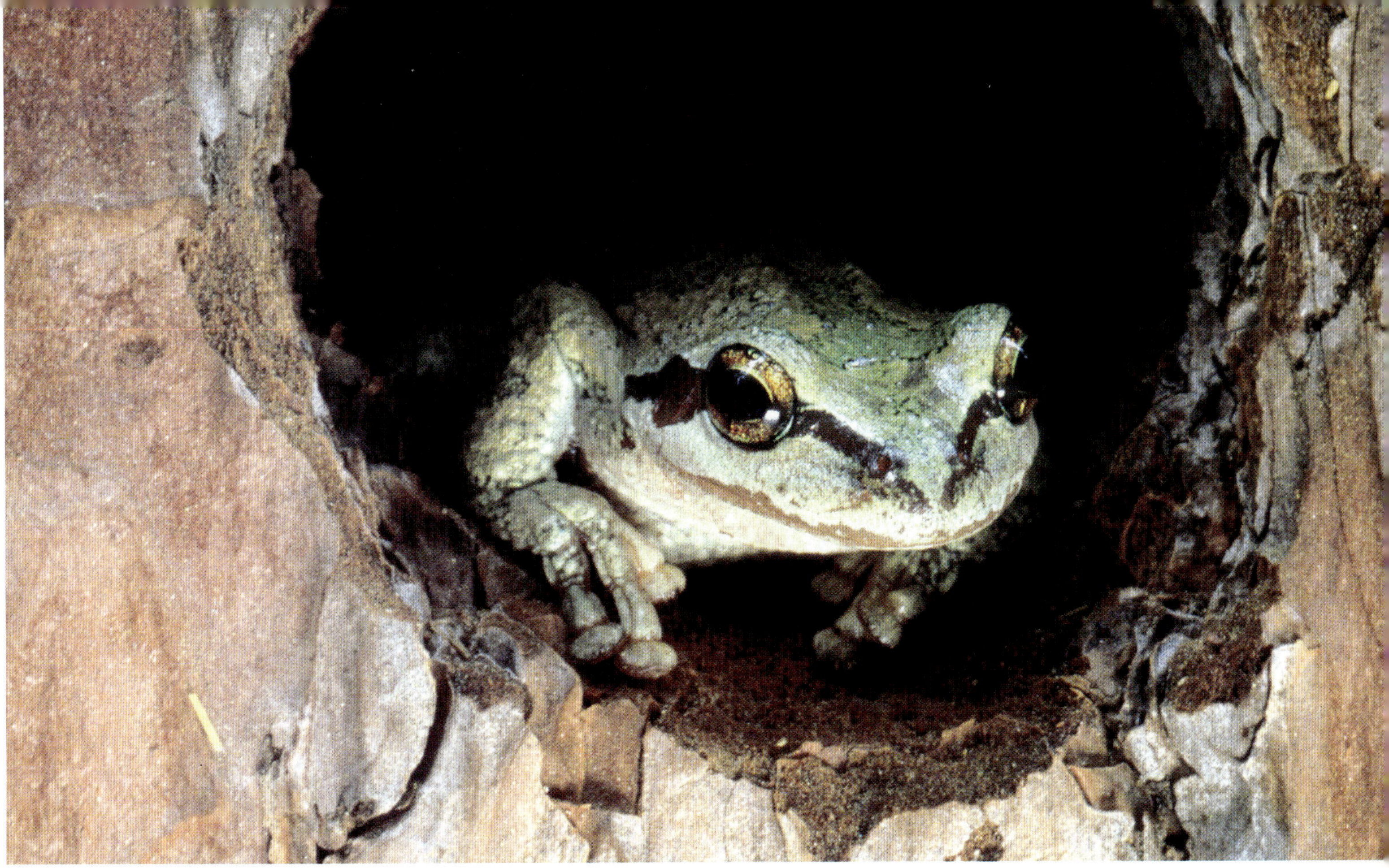

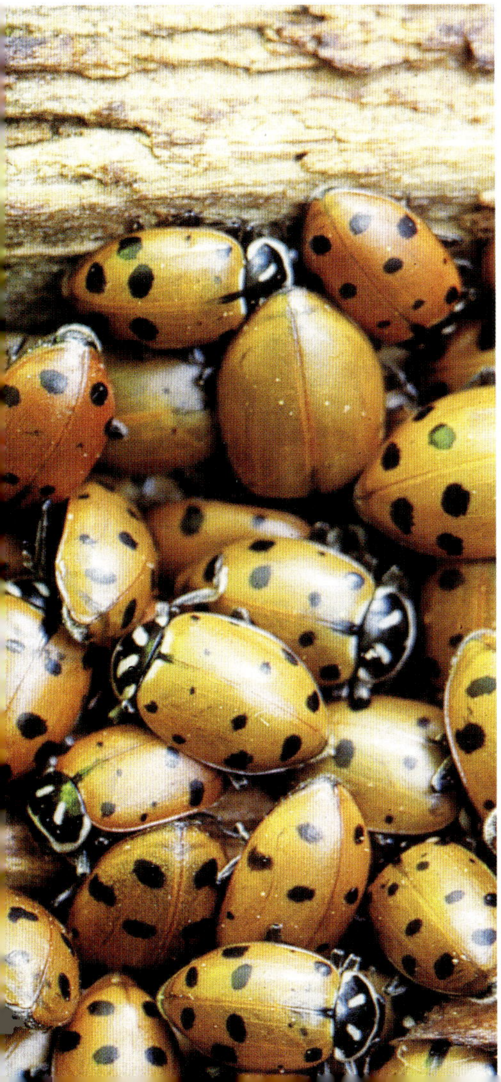

Left top

MONARCH BUTTERFLY

In its caterpillar stage, the monarch butterfly happily and safely munches on the milkweed, a plant that is poisonous to most other creatures. By the time they metamorphose into butterflies, the monarchs are loaded with toxins. They would themselves be consumed by any number of birds, but the consequences of dining on a monarch can be severe, and so predators leave these colorful insects alone.

Above

TREE FROG

The tiny Pacific tree frog prefers to take up residence in marshy places or in vegetation growing alongside streams and rivers. A good place to look for them in Yosemite is at Summit Meadow, on the Glacier Point Road.

Left

LADYBUGS

Ladybugs will sometimes swarm in Yosemite. The colorful insects, 1/4-1/2-inches long, will hibernate in winter and like to congregate in huge masses. In spring or early summer they can still be found swarming in shady places, usually under vegetation, a downed tree, or rocks.

INDEX